VISUAL QUICKSTART GUIDE

PageMill 2

FOR MACINTOSH

Maria Langer

 **Peachpit Press**

Visual QuickStart Guide
PageMill 2 for Macintosh
Maria Langer

Peachpit Press
2414 Sixth Street
Berkeley, CA 94710
510/548-4393
510/548-5991 (fax)

Find us on the World Wide Web at: http://www.peachpit.com

Peachpit Press is a division of Addison Wesley Longman

Editor: Nancy Davis
Copy Editor: Terry Wilson
Technical Editor: John Pirone
Proofreader: Terry Wilson
Indexer: Maria Langer
Cover Design: The Visual Group
Production: Maria Langer, John Horn

Colophon
This book was produced with QuarkXPress 3.31 on a Power Macintosh 7100/66. The fonts used were Charlotte, Charlotte Sans, and Corinthian Bold from Letraset.

Notice of Rights

Notice of Liability

ISBN 0-201-69402-6

9 8 7 6 5 4 3 2

Printed and bound in the United States of America.

♻ Printed on recycled paper

Dedication

To Nice Guy Tom

Thanks for being there for us.

Happy 60th Birthday!

Thanks!

To Nancy Davis for being kind, gentle, and, above all, *patient*.

To the rest of the folks at Peachpit Press for letting me revise and expand my first PageMill book.

To Terry Wilson and John Pirone, for applying their copy editing, technical editing, and proofreading skills.

To the folks at Adobe Systems, including Robert Seidl, Kelly Davis, Sean McKenna, and Meg Ross, for helping me get the materials and information I needed to write this book. And a big thanks to the PageMill 2 development staff for putting together a great program.

And to Mike, for putting up with me while I churned out another one.

http://www.intac.com/~gilesrd/

TABLE OF CONTENTS

Table of Contents

Table of Contents

INTRODUCTION TO WEB PUBLISHING

Before You Begin...

If buying PageMill was your first big step into the realm of World Wide Web publishing, stop right here. There may be gaps in your understanding of the Web and how it works. It's a good idea to fill those gaps with basic background information before you go any further.

This introductory chapter was written for people who are brand new to the Internet and the World Wide Web. It explains what the Internet and World Wide Web are. It tells you about HTML and how it is interpreted by a special kind of software called a Web browser. It explains what PageMill does for you so you know exactly why you should be glad you use it. Finally, it provides a list of things to keep in mind when planning your Web site. All along the way, it defines important terms that will be used throughout this book.

You won't find many pictures in this introduction, but you will find lots of good, useful information. If you're new to the Internet or Web publishing, don't skip this introduction. The few minutes you spend here could save you hours in the future.

About the Internet

The Internet is a global network of computers. It's a lot like the network you might find in an office environment—but instead of the networked computers being separated by walls or cubicle partitions, they may be separated by miles, mountains, and oceans.

The Internet has been around since the 1960s, so it isn't new. What is new, however, is the boom in Internet interest and access. More people access the Internet today than ever before. And with access getting cheaper and easier all the time, it looks like the Internet will continue to grow long into the future.

The Internet offers access to many features. Here are just a few that interest most Internet users:

- **E-mail.** Electronic mail makes it possible to exchange written messages with other people all over the world, quickly and cost effectively.

- **Software.** FTP (file transfer protocol) sites offer the latest and greatest shareware and freeware files.

- **Discussion groups.** Newsgroups and mailing lists let participants join in topical discussions with people who share their interests.

- **"Published" Information.** Gopher, WAIS, and World Wide Web servers make it possible to publish and retrieve information from a wide variety of sources.

✔ Tip

- A lot of people think the phrase *World Wide Web* is the same as *Internet*. This isn't true. The World Wide Web is only part of the Internet. The Internet is far more than just the World Wide Web.

Figure 1. *The home page for American Express,...*

Figure 2. *...Peachpit Press,...*

About the World Wide Web

The World Wide Web is the fastest growing part of the Internet. Often the first part of the Internet that new users explore, its popularity is due primarily to its graphic user interface and ease of use.

Each week, thousands of new Web *pages* appear on the World Wide Web. Web *publishers* include:

- Major corporations interested in global exposure (see **Figure 1**).

- Small, medium, and large businesses interested in advertising (and selling) products and services (see **Figure 2**).

- Individuals interested in sharing information about themselves (see **Figure 3**).

The truth is, *anyone* can publish on the World Wide Web. If you've got something to say, the Web is a good place to say it—especially if you're ready for millions of people to get your message.

Figure 3. *...and yours truly.*

About Web Pages

A Web *page* may include any combination of the following elements:

- **Formatted text.** Headings, bold and italic styles, indented lists, and other kinds of formatting can make text easier and more interesting to read.

- **Graphics and Multimedia.** Whether images, colorful lines, background patterns, QuickTime movies, or Java applets, graphics and multimedia can make pages visually appealing or share information that cannot be expressed in words.

- **Hypertext links.** Clicking a text or graphic link can display another page, download a file, or open a mail form.

- **Forms.** Edit boxes, radio buttons, check boxes, and pop-up menus are some of the form elements that can collect information from a Web page viewer.

- **Tables.** Displaying text and graphics in table layout keeps page appearance neat.

- **Frames.** By splitting a browser window into frames, more than one Web page can be displayed at a time.

Figure 4 shows an example of a Web page with many of these elements.

✔ Tip

- Don't let the word *page* confuse you. In Web lingo, page is the same as *document* or *file*. A Web page can be any length—it has nothing to do with the size of a printed piece of paper.

Figure 4. *Here's an example of a Web page with many commonly used elements.*

Figure 5. *Underlying every Web page is raw HTML code. Here's what the code for the page in* **Figure 4** *looks like in PageMill's HTML view.*

About HTML

One of the benefits of publishing on the World Wide Web is that Web pages can be read by any kind of computer using any kind of Web browser. (I tell you more about browsers on the next page.) This is possible through the use of a programming language called HyperText Markup Language (HTML). Plain text documents written with HTML codes can be interpreted by Web browsers, which display the codes as formatted text and graphics.

Figure 5 shows an example of what the HTML document for the Web page in **Figure 4** looks like. If you look closely, you can find and read the text that appears on the page. Everything else is an HTML markup code or tag that tells a Web browser how to format text, where to find graphics, and how to make form elements.

Fortunately, you don't need to deal with HTML codes. PageMill writes the codes for you automatically as you enter and format text, graphics, links, and form elements. It doesn't even show the codes to you.

✔ Tips

- ■ PageMill supports HTML version 3.2 codes, along with some Netscape Navigator and Microsoft Internet Explorer extensions. Appendix D lists the codes PageMill supports.

- ■ If you know HTML, you can enter raw HTML codes in the HTML Source view of a PageMill document. If entered correctly, these codes will be read and understood by browsers that support them. If PageMill does not support them, it will ignore them.

About HTML

About Web Browsers

Web browser software is what makes HTML code work. Programs like Netscape Navigator, Microsoft Internet Explorer, and NCSA Mosaic read HTML code, interpret it, and display it the way the Web page designer intended.

Well, not always. Unfortunately, not all Web browsers interpret HTML codes the same way. And not all Web browsers support all HTML codes. The only way to see exactly how your Web page will look when viewed with a specific browser is to open the page with that browser.

The good news is that the most commonly used browsers—Netscape Navigator and Microsoft Internet Explorer, which account for more than 90% of the browsers in use today—can interpret all the HTML codes that PageMill supports.

✔ Tips

- ■ Each major computer platform—Macintosh, Windows, and UNIX—has its own collection of Web browsers. Because of this, your Web pages can look very similar from one platform to the next. This makes the Web a perfect cross-platform environment for sharing information—even if that information is accessible only within an organization's intranet and not the Internet.

- ■ Throughout this book, the term Web browser refers to a *graphic* browser—one that is capable of displaying formatted text and graphics on Web pages. A *text* browser is another kind of browser that displays Web pages as unformatted text documents. Although text browser users will not see the graphics and formatting of your pages, they will see the textual content.

About Your Web Site

If you're creating a Web site from the ground up, you can create an effective site and save yourself a lot of aggravation by planning ahead. Here are a few things to consider:

- **What do you want your pages to look like?** If you plan on having multiple pages, you may want to use consistent formatting, colors, background patterns, logos, or other elements to give your site its own identity and set it apart from the others.

- **Will your pages be long or short?** Long pages make it possible to provide more information with fewer hits to the site. Short pages load more quickly. Each approach has its pros and cons.

- **Will your pages rely heavily on graphics?** Remember that not all people who browse the World Wide Web do so with graphic browsers. These people won't be able to see your pictures.

- **How do you want to organize your pages?** Create an outline showing the relationship between pages so you know how the pages will link to each other.

- **How do you want to store your pages and other files on disk?** Take advantage of the hierarchical file system to organize files in folders and subfolders.

These are just a few things to think about before you even launch PageMill. Browse the World Wide Web to see what other Web publishers are doing. Examine the sites that appeal to you and figure out what makes you like them more than others. Anyone can create Web pages, but it takes creativity and planning to put together *effective* Web pages—the ones people visit regularly and share with their friends.

About Your Web Site

GETTING STARTED WITH PAGEMILL 1

Introduction

PageMill is an Internet authoring tool that makes it easy to create Web pages. You can use PageMill's word processor-like interface and drag-and-drop editing techniques to enter, edit, and format Web pages, add graphics and links to other pages, use complex formatting like tables and frames, and even create forms for gathering information from the Internet "surfers" who browse your pages. With PageMill, there's no need to struggle with complex HyperText Markup Language (HTML) codes. PageMill does all the HTML coding work for you, behind the scenes.

This Visual QuickStart Guide will help you master PageMill 2 by providing step-by-step instructions, plenty of illustrations, and a generous helping of tips. On these pages you'll find everything you need to know about PageMill—and more!

This book is designed for page-flipping. Use the thumb tabs, index, or table of contents to find the topics for which you need help. If you're brand new to PageMill, however, I recommend that you begin by reading at least this first chapter. In it, you'll find important introductory information about PageMill's interface.

The World Wide Web has opened the world of publishing to anyone with something to say. PageMill is one of the best tools around to get your message out on the Web with the least amount of effort.

About Running PageMill

The PageMill Installer places a number of files on your hard disk in a folder called Adobe® PageMill™ 2.0 (see **Figure 1**). One of these files is the PageMill application.

To launch PageMill

1. Locate and open the Adobe® PageMill™ 2.0 folder (see **Figure 1**) on your hard disk.
2. Double-click the Adobe® PageMill™ 2.0 application icon.

or

Double-click a PageMill document icon (see **Figure 2**).

✔ Tips

■ The first time you launch PageMill, a registration screen appears. Enter your name, organization, and PageMill registration number in the appropriate edit boxes and click OK to proceed.

■ If you launched PageMill by double-clicking its application icon, an empty document window appears (see **Figure 3**).

■ If you launched PageMill by double-clicking a document icon, a document window containing that document appears (see **Figure 5**).

To quit PageMill

Choose Quit from the File Menu (see **Figure 4**) or press ⌘⌘Q.

✔ Tip

■ Closing all document windows is not the same as quitting the program. PageMill continues to run and take up RAM until you use its Quit command.

Figure 1.
Inside the Adobe® PageMill™ 2.0 folder.

Figure 2.
A PageMill document icon.

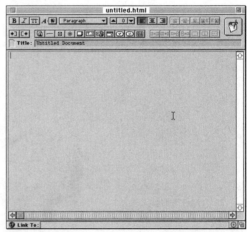

Figure 3. *When you launch PageMill by double-clicking its application icon, an empty document window appears.*

Figure 4.
To quit PageMill, choose Quit from the File menu.

Figure 5. *Edit mode lets you create and edit Web pages.*

Figure 6. *Preview mode lets you see what your page will look like on the World Wide Web and test your local links.*

Figure 7a. *In Edit mode, the Toggle Preview Mode button looks like this…*

Figure 7b. *…and in Preview mode, the Toggle Preview Mode button looks like this.*

About PageMill's Modes

PageMill offers two modes for working with the Web documents you create:

■ Edit mode (see **Figure 5**) lets you create and edit Web pages. You'll work in Edit mode throughout this book.

■ Preview mode (see **Figure 6**) lets you see what your Web pages will look like on the World Wide Web and test any internal links you may have included on them. I tell you about previewing and testing pages in **Chapter 11**.

✔ Tips

■ By default, when you open an existing PageMill document, it opens in Preview mode. You can use the General Preferences dialog box to change the default mode to Edit mode. I tell you about changing preferences in **Chapter 12**.

■ At first glance, Edit and Preview modes appear very similar. You can tell the difference between them by the toolbar that appears in Edit view (see **Figure 5**) and by the appearance of the Toggle Preview Mode button (see **Figures 7a** and **7b**).

■ In addition to Edit and Preview modes, PageMill also offers an Image window for specifying the way an image appears on a page and an HTML Source view for editing the HTML code underlying a page. I tell you about the Image window in **Chapters 5** and **7** and about HTML Source view in **Chapter 11**.

To toggle between Edit & Preview modes

Click the Toggle Preview Mode button in the upper right corner of the document window (see **Figures 7a** and **7b**). The mode and button icon change.

About the Button Bar

In Edit mode, a button bar beneath the window's title bar (see **Figure 8**) offers easy access to a wide varity of options and commands. I tell you about using button bar buttons throughout this book.

Character Styles Text Color Paragraph Format Font Size Text Alignment Object Alignment Toggle Preview Mode

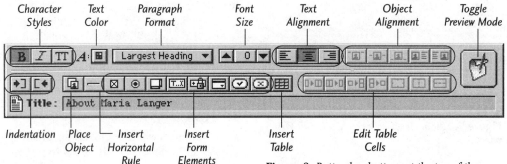

Indentation Place Object Insert Horizontal Rule Insert Form Elements Insert Table Edit Table Cells

Figure 8. *Button bar buttons at the top of the PageMill window give you easy access to commands and other options.*

✔ Tips

- ■ Buttons will be active or inactive (gray) depending on what is selected in the document window.

- ■ To learn what a button does, point to it with your mouse. The button name or description appears immediately to the left of the Toggle Preview Mode button (see **Figure 9**).

- ■ When you double-click an image, the client-side image map buttons appear on the right end of the button bar (see **Figure 10**).

- ■ In Preview mode, the button bar changes to offer several navigation buttons (see **Figure 11**).

Figure 9. *Point to a button to learn what it does.*

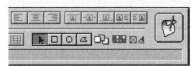

Figure 10. *When you double-click an image, the image map buttons appear on the button bar.*

Figure 11. *In Preview mode, the button bar looks like this.*

Figure 12.
PageMill's
Edit menu.

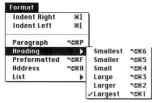

Edit	
Undo Copy	⌘Z
Cut	⌘H
Copy	⌘C
Paste	⌘U
Clear	
Select All	⌘A
Remove Link	⌘R
△ Insert Placeholder	
Insert Invisible	▶
Hide Invisibles	⌘,
HTML Source	⌘H
⊟ Split Horizontally	⌥⌘H
⊟ Split Vertically	⌥⌘U
No Frames Message	⌘M
Download Statistics...	⌘U
Preferences...	⌥⌘P

Figure 13.
PageMill's
Format
menu and
its Heading
submenu.

Format			
Indent Right	⌘]		
Indent Left	⌘[		
Paragraph	⌥⌘P		
Heading	▶	Smallest	⌥⌘6
Preformatted	⌥⌘F	Smaller	⌥⌘5
Address	⌥⌘A	Small	⌥⌘4
List	▶	Large	⌥⌘3
		Larger	⌥⌘2
		✓Largest	⌥⌘1

About PageMill's Menus

Most of PageMill's commands are accessible through its menus. **Figures 12** and **13** illustrate two of PageMill's menus.

■ A menu command that appears in gray cannot currently be selected.

■ A menu command followed by an ellipsis (…) displays a dialog box.

■ A menu command followed by a triangle has a submenu. The submenu displays additional commands when the main command is highlighted.

■ A menu command followed by the ⌘ (Command key) symbol and one or more other symbols or letters can be chosen with a shortcut key. **Table 1** on the next page lists the symbols that appear on menus and their keyboard equivalents.

■ A menu command preceded by a check mark has been "turned on."

To use a menu

1. Point to the menu from which you want to choose a command.

2. Press the mouse button and hold it down to display the menu.

3. Drag the mouse pointer down until the command you want is highlighted.

4. Release the mouse button. The command may blink before the menu disappears, confirming that it has been successfully selected.

✔ Tip

■ If the command is on a submenu, display the submenu (see **Figure 13**), then drag the mouse pointer to the right and down until the submenu command is highlighted and release the mouse button.

To use a shortcut key

1. Hold down the modifier key(s) (normally (⌘), but sometimes also (Shift), (Option), and/or (Control)).

2. Press the letter, number, or punctuation key for the equivalent.

For example, as the Format menu indicates (see **Figure 13**), the shortcut key for the Address command is ⌥⌘A. To use this shortcut, hold down the (Option) and (⌘) keys and press (A).

✔ Tips

■ If a menu command is not available, its shortcut key won't work either.

■ Shortcut keys for menu commands and button bar buttons are discussed with their corresponding commands or buttons throughout this book.

■ **Appendix A** at the end of this book includes a complete listing of all shortcut keys, including shortcut keys for button bar buttons and commands that do not appear on the menu.

Menu Symbol	Keyboard Key
⌘	(⌘)
⌥	(Option)
⇧	(Shift)
⌃	(Control)

Table 1. *Shortcut key menu symbols and corresponding keyboard keys.*

Figure 14.
Choose Show Pasteboard from the Window menu to display the Pasteboard while you work.

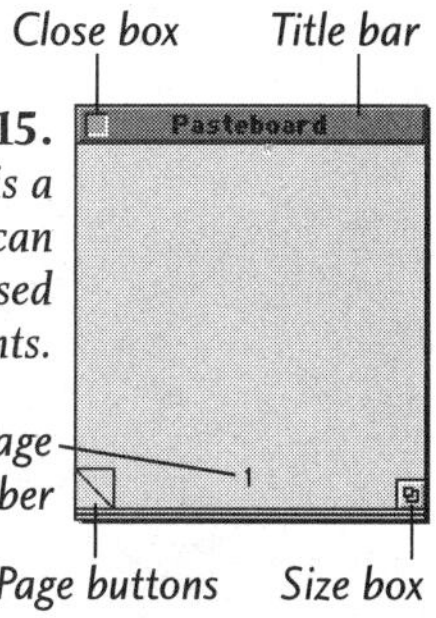

About the Pasteboard

The Pasteboard (see **Figure 15**) is a place within PageMill where you can store frequently used Web page elements like text and graphics.

For example, say you include your company logo on every Web page you create. If you store it on the Pasteboard, it will be within mouse pointer reach each time you create a new page.

Close box   *Title bar*

Figure 15.
The Pasteboard is a place where you can store frequently used page elements.

Page number

Page buttons   *Size box*

✔ Tips

- To change Pasteboard pages, click one of the page button triangles. Clicking the top triangle switches to the next page; clicking the bottom triangle switches to the previous page.

- You can store more than one item on each Pasteboard page.

- To move the Pasteboard, drag it by its title bar.

- To resize the Pasteboard, drag its size box. When you release the mouse button, the Pasteboard is resized.

- I provide details on adding items to the Pasteboard, using items stored on the Pasteboard, and removing items from the Pasteboard in **Chapters 2** and **5**.

To show the Pasteboard

Choose Show Pasteboard from the Window menu (see **Figure 14**) or press ⌘ /.

To hide the Pasteboard

Choose Hide Pasteboard from the Window menu or press ⌘ /.

or

Click the Pasteboard's close box (see **Figure 15**).

About the Pasteboard

About the Inspector

The Inspector (see **Figure 17**) is a floating palette to set attributes for Web page elements. Click a tab near the top of the Inspector to view the corresponding panel:

- Use the *Frame* panel to set attributes for frames. I tell you about working with frames in **Chapter 8**.

- Use the *Page* panel (see **Figure 17**) to set attributes for an entire page. I tell you about setting page attributes in **Chapter 10**.

- Use the *Form* panel to set attributes for CGI scripts used with forms. I tell you about creating forms in **Chapter 9**.

- Use the *Object* panel to set attributes for selected objects, including images, form elements, and table cells. I tell you about working with these things in **Chapters 5**, **9**, and **6** respectively.

✔ Tips

- The Inspector will only offer options when a page is in Edit mode. When no page is open or when the open page is in Preview mode, the Inspector window is empty.

- I tell you how to use the Inspector's options throughout this book.

- To move the Inspector, drag it by its title bar.

To show the Inspector

Choose Show Inspector from the Window menu (see **Figure 16**) or press ⌘⌘;.

To hide the Inspector

Choose Hide Inspector from the Window menu or press ⌘⌘;.

or

Click the Inspector's close box (see **Figure 17**).

Figure 16.
Choose Show Inspector from the Window menu.

Figure 17.
The Page panel of the Inspector.

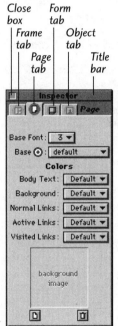

Figure 18.
Choose Show Color Panel from the Window menu to display a palette of 16 colors you can apply to text, link, and backgrounds.

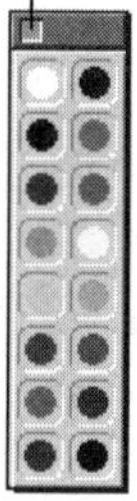

About the Color Panel

The Color panel (see **Figure 19**) is a floating palette of 16 color swatches you can use to change text, link, and background colors.

✔ Tips

■ The colors on the Color panel can be customized. Simply double-click a color to display a color wheel, then select a new color and click OK.

■ I tell you how to use the Color panel in **Chapters 3**, **6**, and **10**.

Close box

Figure 19.
The Color panel.

To show the Color panel

Choose Show Color Panel from the Window menu (see **Figure 18**).

✔ Tip

■ To move the Color panel, drag it by its title bar.

To hide the Color panel

Choose Hide Color Panel from the Window menu.

or

Click the Color panel's close box (see **Figure 19**).

About the Color Panel

About Invisibles

PageMill offers commands to insert four different kinds of hidden HTML codes, which PageMill calls *invisibles*, in your Web documents:

■ *Anchors* let you create links to specific positions within a page. I tell you about anchors and links in **Chapter 7**.

■ *Margin breaks* insert blank space between a positioned object and the margin at the bottom of the object. I tell you about positioned objects in **Chapter 5**.

■ *Comments* let you insert notations within a Web page that do not appear anywhere on the page. I tell you about inserting comments in **Chapter 2**.

■ *Hidden fields* are special form fields for passing default information to form CGIs. I tell you about forms and CGIs in **Chapter 9**.

Figure 20 shows an example of a Web page in Edit mode with all four kinds of invisibles.

✔ Tip

■ By default, invisibles are displayed in Edit mode.

To hide invisibles

Choose Hide Invisibles from the Edit menu (see **Figure 21**).

or

Press ⌘,.

Figure 22 shows the same page as **Figure 20**, but with the invisibles hidden.

To show invisibles

Choose Show Invisibles from the Edit menu.

or

Press ⌘,.

Comment   Margin break   Hidden field

Anchor

Figure 20. *Here's a Web page with all four kinds of invisibles.*

Figure 21. *To hide invisibles, choose Hide Invisibles from the Edit menu.*

Figure 22. *Here's the page from* **Figure 20** *with the invisibles hidden.*

Figure 23.
The File menu offers commands to create, open, and perform other tasks with files.

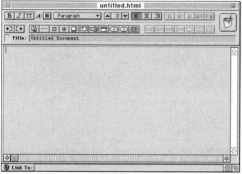

Figure 24. *When you use the New Page command, an "untitled" window appears.*

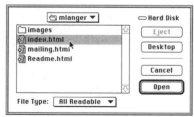

Figure 25. *Use the Open dialog box to open existing files.*

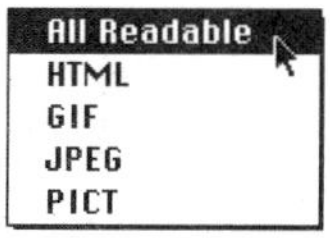

Figure 26.
Use the File Type pop-up menu to display only certain types of files in the Open dialog box.

About Page Files

Each document you create with PageMill is a *page*. Don't let this familiar term fool you—a Web page can be as long or short as you like.

To create a new page

Choose New Page from the File menu (see **Figure 23**).

or

Press ⌘N.

An empty document window named *untitled.html* (or *untitled1.html*, etc.) appears (see **Figure 24**).

To open an existing page

1. Choose Open from the File menu (see **Figure 23**).

   or

   Press ⌘O.

   A standard Open dialog box appears (see **Figure 25**).

2. Locate and select the Web page document you want to open.

3. Click OK or press Return or Enter.

or

In the Finder, double-click the icon for the PageMill document you want to open. If PageMill isn't already running, double-clicking the document icon will launch it, too.

or

In the Finder, drag a Web page document icon onto the PageMill application icon. This is a good way to use PageMill to open a Web page created by another program.

✔ Tip

■ You can use the File Type pop-up menu (see **Figure 26**) to display only certain types of files in the Open dialog box.

About Saving Pages

When you save a page, you place a copy of it on disk. The finished version of the page will eventually wind up on your Web server, where other people on the Internet can access it.

✔ Tip

■ Until you save a page file, it (or any change to it) exists only in your computer's random access memory (RAM). If your computer loses power or crashes, all work you've done since the last time you saved is lost. If you've never saved a page, the entire page is lost. This is why it's important to save frequently while you work.

To save a page for the first time

1. Choose Save Page (see **Figure 27**) or Save Page As from the File menu.

   or

   Press ⌃⌘S.

2. Use the standard Save As dialog box that appears (see **Figure 28**) to open the folder in which you want to save the file.

3. Enter a name for the file in the Save File As edit box.

4. Click Save or press Return or Enter.

The file is saved in the folder you specified with the name you entered. The name you gave the file appears in the file's title bar (see **Figure 29**).

✔ Tips

■ The first time you save a file, the Save Page and Save Page As commands do the same thing.

■ Be sure to follow any file naming guidelines required by your server. If you're not sure what they are, ask the Webmaster or System Administrator.

Figure 27. *PageMill offers three different commands to save a page file.*

Figure 28. *Use the Save As dialog box to select a disk location and name a file.*

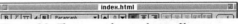

Figure 29. *The name of a saved page file appears in its title bar.*

Saving Pages

Figure 30.
*Use the Save
Page As
command to
save a page with
a different name
or in a different
location.*

To save changes to a saved page

Choose Save Page from the File menu (see **Figure 27**).

or

Press ⌘S.

✔ Tips

■ When you use the Save Page command to save a page that has already been saved, PageMill updates the file on disk to add your changes since the last save. It does not display a dialog box.

■ Save frequently as you work to prevent data loss in the event of a power outage or computer crash.

To save a page with a different name or in a different location

1. Choose Save Page As from the File menu (see **Figure 30**).

2. Use the standard Save As dialog box that appears (see **Figure 28**) to select a new folder and/or enter a new name.

3. Click Save or press Return or Enter.

✔ Tip

■ When you use the Save Page As command, the page is saved with the information you specified. If you changed the name of the file, its new name appears in the title bar. Subsequently using the Save command to save changes to the page will save changes to this new version, not the original.

Saving Pages

Saving Pages

To save a copy of a page

1. Choose Save A Copy As from the File menu (see **Figure 31**).

2. Use the Save As dialog box that appears (see **Figure 28**) to select a folder and/or enter a name for the copy.

3. Click Save or press Return or Enter.

✔ Tip

■ When you use the Save A Copy As command, a copy of the page is saved with the information you specified. Subsequent saves using the Save command will save changes to the *original* version of the page, not the copy.

To save all open documents

1. Choose Save Everything from the File menu (see **Figure 32**).

   or

   Press ⌂⌘E.

2. A standard Save As dialog box (see **Figure 28**) appears for each file that has not yet been saved. Use it to select a folder and/or enter a name. Then click Save or press Return or Enter. Repeat this step as necessary until all files have been saved.

Figure 31.
Use the Save A Copy As command to save a copy of the page. Subsequent saves will save to the original file.

Figure 32.
Use the Save Everything command to save all open documents.

Figure 33.
*Choose Page
Setup from the
File menu to
specify page
setup options
before printing.*

About Printing

Even though Web pages are normally
viewed on screen and are seldom printed,
you can use the Page Setup and Print Page
commands to prepare pages for printing
and print them.

To specify Page Setup options

1. Choose Page Setup from the File menu
   (see **Figure 33**).

2. In the Page Setup dialog box that
   appears (see **Figure 34**), change settings for paper size, orientation, and
   other options as desired.

3. If the dialog box includes an Options
   button, click it to view and change
   other options if desired. When you're
   finished with the options dialog box,
   click OK or press [Return] or [Enter] to
   save your settings.

4. Click OK or press [Return] or [Enter] in
   the Page Setup dialog box to save your
   settings.

✔ Tip

■ The way the Page Setup dialog box
   appears (see **Figure 34**) depends on
   your printer and the printer driver you
   selected in Apple's Chooser. Consult
   the documentation that came with
   your printer or Macintosh for more
   information about printer options or
   the Chooser.

Figure 34. *The appearance of the Page Setup
dialog box varies depending on your selected printer
driver. Here's what it looks like with the LaserWriter
8 driver selected.*

Setting Page Setup Options

To print a page

1. Choose Print Page from the File menu (see **Figure 35**).

   or

   Press ⌘⌘P.

2. In the Print dialog box that appears (see **Figure 36**), set the number of copies, page range, and paper source.

3. To print the page's background (which I tell you about in **Chapter 10**), be sure to turn on the Print Page Background check box.

4. If the dialog box includes an Options button, click it to view and change other options if desired. When you're finished with the options dialog box, click OK or press Return or Enter to save your settings.

5. Click Print or press Return or Enter to print.

✔ Tips

■ The way the Print dialog box appears depends on your printer and the printer driver you selected in Apple's Chooser. Consult the documentation that came with your printer or Macintosh for more information about printer options or the Chooser.

■ PageMill automatically paginates documents when it prints them. You cannot override its page breaks. It will not, however, break a page in the middle of a graphic object.

Figure 35. *When you're ready to print, choose Print Page from the File menu.*

Figure 36. *The selected printer driver also changes the way the Print dialog box looks. Here's a Print dialog box with the LaserWriter 8 driver selected.*

Figure 37.
*The Window
menu offers
commands for
working with
windows.*

About Windows

Like most other Macintosh applications, PageMill enables you to have more than one document window open at a time.

✔ Tips

- The active window is the one with the striped title bar.

- You can resize a window by clicking its zoom box (in the top right corner) or dragging its size box (in the bottom right corner).

- You can move a window by dragging its title bar.

To switch windows

Click any exposed portion of the window with which you want to work.

or

Choose the name of the window with which you want to work from the list at the bottom of the Window menu (see **Figure 37**).

The window you clicked or chose comes to the front and becomes the active window.

✔ Tip

- Each window has a shortcut key consisting of ⌘ and a number (see **Figure 37**). You can press a window's shortcut key to switch to that window.

To arrange windows

- To stack windows, choose Stack from the Window menu (see **Figure 37**). The windows are neatly stacked, with the active window on top (see **Figure 38**).

- To tile windows, choose Tile from the Window menu (see **Figure 37**). The windows are resized and tiled across the entire screen (see **Figure 39**), with the active window on top.

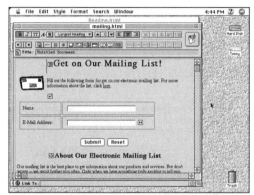

Figure 38. *Stacking windows shows the title bar for each window.*

Figure 39. *Tiling windows resizes them and places them side by side so they fill the screen. This makes it possible to view the contents of more than one window at a time.*

Switching & Arranging Windows

To close a window

1. If necessary, switch to the window you want to close.

2. Choose Close from the File menu (see **Figure 40**).

   or

   Press ⌃⌘W.

   or

   Click the window's close box.

3. If you have made changes to the contents of the window since the last time you saved it, a dialog box like the one in **Figure 41** appears.

   ▲ Click Save or press Return or Enter to save the changes. If you have never saved the file at all, a Save As dialog box (see **Figure 28**) appears so you can choose a folder, enter a name, and save the file.

   ▲ Click Don't Save to close the window without saving changes.

   ▲ Click Cancel to dismiss the dialog box without closing the window or saving its contents.

To close all windows

Choose Close All from the Window menu (see **Figure 42**).

A dialog box like the one in **Figure 41** appears for every window whose contents you have changed since you last saved. Follow the instructions in step 3 above to dismiss this dialog box each time it appears.

Figure 40.
Choose Close from the File menu to close the active window.

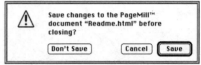

Figure 41. *If you try to close a window with unsaved changes, a dialog box like this one appears.*

Figure 42.
To close all windows at once, choose Close All from the Window menu.

TEXT ENTRY & EDITING BASICS

2

About Entering & Editing Text with PageMill

One of the best features of PageMill is its word processor-like interface. As you work with PageMill, you'll use the same techniques you use with your word processor. Here are some examples:

■ Enter text by typing at an insertion point.

■ Edit text by selecting and typing to replace or pressing [Delete] to delete.

■ Cut, copy, and paste text to duplicate or move it.

■ Use the Undo command to reverse your last action.

In addition to these standard techniques, PageMill offers additional features and techniques that make it easy to enter and edit text in documents, including:

■ Drag and drop text editing to move or copy text quickly.

■ The Pasteboard to store items you use repeatedly.

■ The Revert command to throw away all changes to an open document.

Best of all, at any time during the Web page creation process, you can click the Toggle Preview button to see how your page will look and work on the World Wide Web.

✔ Tip

■ To enter or edit the contents of a PageMill document, you must be in Edit mode. To go to Edit mode, click the Toggle Preview Mode button which, in Preview mode, looks like the button in **Figure 1**.

Figure 1. *If you're in Preview mode, you must click the Toggle Preview Mode button before you can enter or edit a page file.*

About Entering Text

In most cases, text will form the basis of your Web page. Entering text in a PageMill document is as easy as entering it in any word processing document.

To enter text by typing

1. Position the blinking insertion point where you want the text to appear (**see Figure 2**) by clicking or using the arrow keys on your keyboard.

2. Type the text you want to enter.

The text you type appears at the insertion point (see **Figure 3**).

✔ Tips

■ Text automatically wraps when it reaches the right side of the window (see **Figure 3**).

■ Word wrap is determined by the width of the window.

■ When you press Return, a new paragraph is created with an empty line between it and the previous paragraph (see **Figure 3**).

■ To start a new line without starting a new paragraph, press Shift Return.

To enter a special character

Type the character you want.

Table 1 provides a list of some of the characters PageMill supports, along with the keys you press to type them.

✔ Tip

■ "Special" characters are either not among the standard keyboard characters or reserved for use within HTML. PageMill automatically converts these characters to HTML codes so they can be used in Web pages and interpreted properly by Web browsers.

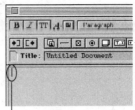

Figure 2.
The blinking insertion point indicates where the text you type will appear.

Insertion point

PageMill puts a blank line between paragraphs.

Text automatically wraps to the next line as you type.

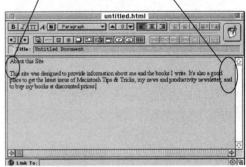

Figure 3. *The PageMill document window works very much like a word processing document window.*

Character	Keystroke
<	Shift ,
>	Shift .
&	Shift 7
®	Option R
©	Option G
ß	Option S
¢	Option 4
£	Option 3

Table 1. *Some commonly used special characters supported by PageMill.*

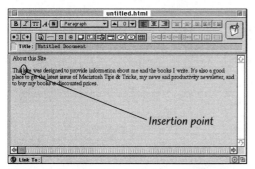

Figure 4. *To insert text, begin by positioning the insertion point...*

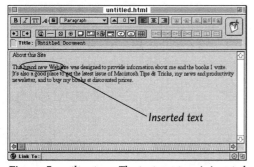

Figure 5. *...then type. The text you type is inserted and the text to the right of it moves to the right or down to make room for it.*

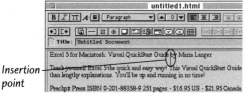

Figure 6. *To break a line, position the insertion point...*

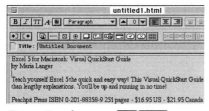

Figure 7. *...then press* Shift Return.

About Editing Text

Once text has been entered, it's easy to edit. As you might imagine, standard word processing techniques apply.

To insert text

1. Position the blinking insertion point where you want the text to appear (see **Figure 4**). You can do this by clicking or using the arrow keys.

2. Type the text you want to insert.

Because PageMill uses an insertion cursor, text you type is inserted at the blinking insertion point (see **Figure 5**). Text to the right of or below the insertion point is pushed aside or down to make room for the new text.

To insert a line break character

1. Position the insertion point before the character you want to appear on the next line (see **Figure 6**).

2. Press Shift Return to break the line (see **Figure 7**).

✔ Tip

■ Pressing Shift Return ends the line without beginning a new paragraph. Pressing Return ends the line and begins a new paragraph (see **Figure 3**).

To delete text

1. Position the blinking insertion point to the right of the character(s) you want to delete.

2. Press (Delete) to delete the character to the left of the insertion point. To delete multiple characters, just keep pressing (Delete) until they're all gone.

   or

1. Position the blinking insertion point to the left of the character(s) you want to delete.

2. Press ⌦ to delete the character to the right of the insertion point. To delete multiple characters, just keep pressing ⌦ until they're all gone.

or

1. Select the text you want to delete. (I tell you how to select text on the next page.)

2. Press (Delete).

   or

   Choose Clear from the Edit menu (see **Figure 8**).

To remove a line break

1. Position the insertion point at the beginning of the second line (see **Figure 7**). This is immediately after the line break you want to remove.

2. Press (Delete) to delete the invisible line break character at the end of the previous line.

Figure 8.
One way to delete text is to select it and then choose the Clear command from the Edit menu.

I-beam pointer —

> This brand new Web site was d
> It's also a good place to get the l
> newsletter, and to buy my book

Figure 9. *Position the I-beam pointer at the beginning of the text you want to select...*

Drag to select —

> This brand new Web site was d
> It's also a good place to get the l
> newsletter, and to buy my book

Figure 10. *...then drag to select the text.*

Insertion point   Mouse pointer

> This brand new Web site was d
> It's also a good place to get the l
> newsletter, and to buy my book

Figure 11. *Hold down* ⌊Shift⌋ *and click to select all text between the blinking insertion point and the mouse pointer.*

Mouse pointer

Figure 12. *Position the mouse pointer on the word...*

> This brand new Web
> It's also a good place
> newsletter, and to buy

Figure 13. *...then double-click to select it.*

> This brand new Web
> It's also a good place
> newsletter, and to buy

Figure 14. *To select everything on the page, choose Select All from the Edit menu.*

Edit	
Undo Typing	⌘Z
Cut	⌘H
Copy	⌘C
Paste	⌘U
Clear	
Select All	⌘A
Remove Link	⌘R
⚠ Insert Placeholder	
Insert Invisible	▸
Hide Invisibles	⌘,
HTML Source	⌘H
⊟ Split Horizontally	⌄⌘H
⊡ Split Vertically	⌄⌘U
No Frames Message	⌘M
Download Statistics...	⌘U
Preferences...	⌄⌘P

To select text characters

1. Position the mouse pointer, which must look like an I-beam pointer (see **Figure 9**), at the beginning of the text you want to select.

2. Press the mouse button down and drag to the end of the text you want to select (see **Figure 10**). As you drag, text is selected.

or

1. Click at the beginning of the text you want to select to position the insertion point there (see **Figure 11**).

2. Hold down ⌊Shift⌋ and click at the end of the text you want to select (see **Figure 11**). The text between the first and second click is selected.

✔ Tip

- If the mouse pointer looks like an arrow pointer when you drag to select text using the first technique above, you probably already have text selected and will move it when you drag. Click once on any other text in the document window to clear the selection and try again.

To select a word

1. Position the mouse pointer, which must look like an I-beam pointer (see **Figure 12**), in the middle of a word you want to select.

2. Double-click. The entire word is selected and the mouse pointer turns into an arrow pointer (see **Figure 13**).

To select all document contents

Choose Select All from the Edit menu (see **Figure 14**).

or

Press ⌊⌃⌘A⌋.

Selecting Text

To replace text

1. Select the text you want to replace (see **Figure 15**).

2. Type the replacement text.

The text you type replaces whatever text was selected when you began typing (see **Figure 16**).

✔ Tips

■ Pressing [Delete] or choosing Clear from the Edit menu (see **Figure 8**) while text is selected deletes the text and replaces it with nothing.

■ You can also replace text by using the Paste command when text is selected. I tell you about the Paste command on the next few pages.

■ If you accidentally replace text instead of inserting it, immediately use the Undo command, which I tell you about later in this chapter, to get back the original text.

To deselect text

Click once on any other text in the document window. The selection clears.

✔ Tip

■ It's vital that no text is selected when you type if you want to insert (not replace) text. Make sure you know exactly where the insertion point is before typing. If text is selected, there won't be an insertion point. Remember, when text is selected, anything you type will overwrite the selected text.

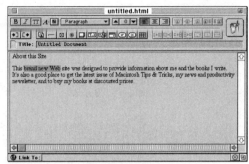

Figure 15. *To replace text, begin by selecting the text you want to replace...*

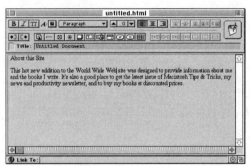

Figure 16. *...then just type. The new text replaces the selected text.*

Replacing & Deselecting Text

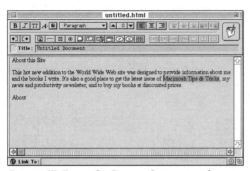

Figure 17. *To use the Copy or Cut commands, you must begin by selecting something.*

Figure 18.
To put a copy of the selection on the Clipboard without removing it from the document, choose Copy from the Edit menu.

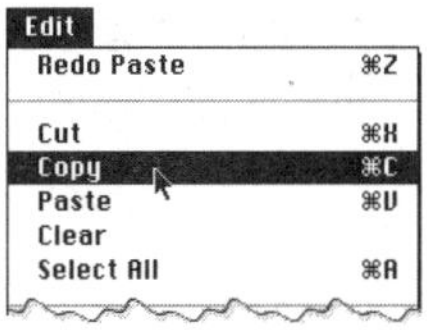

Figure 19. *Position the insertion point where you want the Clipboard contents to appear.*

Figure 20.
Once something is on the Clipboard, you can use the Paste command to paste a copy of it at the insertion point.

Figure 21. *The Paste command puts a copy of the Clipboard contents into the document.*

About Copying & Moving Text

PageMill offers a variety of ways to copy and move text:

- The Copy and Paste commands let you copy text from one place and paste it in another.

- The Cut and Paste commands let you cut text from one place and paste it in another, thus moving the original text.

- Drag and drop text editing lets you move or copy selected text by simply dragging it.

- The Pasteboard lets you store text that you can drag into a document window.

To copy text with Copy & Paste

1. Select the text you want to copy (see **Figure 17**).

2. Choose Copy from the Edit menu (see **Figure 18**).

   or

   Press ⌘ C.

   The text is copied to the Clipboard. It remains selected in the document.

3. Position the insertion point where you want the copied text to be inserted (see **Figure 19**).

4. Choose Paste from the Edit menu (see **Figure 20**).

   or

   Press ⌘ V.

   A copy of the text on the Clipboard is pasted into the document at the insertion point (see **Figure 21**).

Using the Copy & Paste Commands

To move text with Cut & Paste

1. Select the text you want to move (see **Figure 22**).

2. Choose Cut from the Edit menu (see **Figure 23**).

   or

   Press ⌃⌘X.

   The text is removed from the document and placed on the Clipboard.

3. Position the insertion point where you want the cut text to be moved (see **Figure 24**).

4. Choose Paste from the Edit menu (see **Figure 20**).

   or

   Press ⌃⌘V.

   A copy of the text on the Clipboard is pasted into the document at the insertion point (see **Figure 25**).

✔ Copy, Cut, & Paste Tips

■ The Clipboard is a temporary holding place for information. Information is put on the Clipboard when you use the Copy or Cut command. It stays there until you use the Copy or Cut command again or shut off your Macintosh.

■ You can use the Paste command to paste the contents of the Clipboard again and again in the same document or in other documents.

■ You can use the Paste command to put a copy of the Clipboard contents into another PageMill document (see **Figures 24** and **25**) or any other document.

■ You can also use Copy and Paste or Cut and Paste to take text from other documents and paste it into PageMill documents.

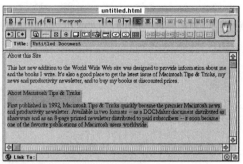

Figure 22. *To move text, begin by selecting it.*

Figure 23. *Choose Cut from the Edit menu to remove the selection from the document and put it on the Clipboard.*

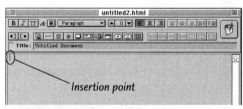

Figure 24. *Position the insertion point where you want the text to be moved. In this example, I've created a new PageMill document.*

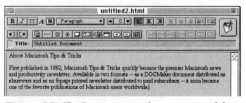

Figure 25. *The Paste command puts a copy of the Clipboard contents into the document.*

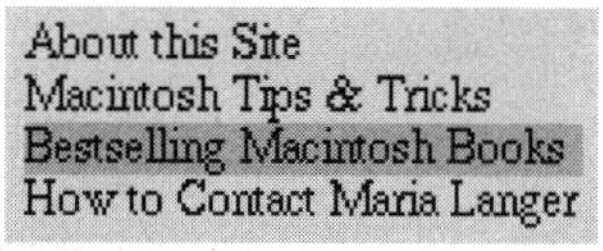

Figure 26.
Begin by selecting the text you want to move...

> About this Site
> Macintosh Tips & Tricks
> Bestselling Macintosh Books
> How to Contact Maria Langer

Figure 27.
...point to the selection...

> About this Site
> Macintosh Tips & Tricks
> Bestselling Macintosh Books
> How to Contact Maria Langer

Figure 28.
... and drag to the new position.

> About this Site
> Macintosh Tips & Tricks
> Bestselling Macintosh Books
> How to Contact Maria Langer

Figure 29.
When you release the mouse button, the selection moves.

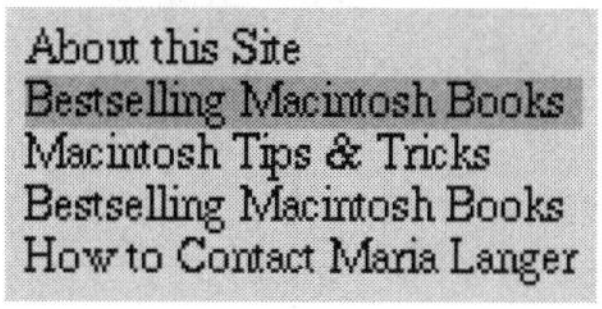

> About this Site
> Bestselling Macintosh Books
> Macintosh Tips & Tricks
> How to Contact Maria Langer

Figure 30.
If you hold down (Option) *while dragging, the selection is copied.*

> About this Site
> Bestselling Macintosh Books
> Macintosh Tips & Tricks
> Bestselling Macintosh Books
> How to Contact Maria Langer

To move text with drag & drop

1. Select the text you want to move (see **Figure 26**).

2. Position the mouse pointer within the selected text. It turns into an arrow pointer (see **Figure 27**).

3. Press the mouse button down and drag. As you drag, a dotted line box the same size as the selection moves along with the mouse pointer. A blinking insertion point indicates where the text will go when you let go of the mouse button. You can see all this in **Figure 28**.

4. When the blinking insertion point is in the proper position, release the mouse button. The selected text moves (see **Figure 29**).

To copy text with drag & drop

1. Select the text you want to copy (see **Figure 26**).

2. Position the mouse pointer in the middle of the selected text. It turns into an arrow pointer (see **Figure 27**).

3. Hold down (Option) as you press the mouse button down and drag (see **Figure 28**).

4. When the blinking insertion point is in the proper position, release the mouse button. The selected text is copied (see **Figure 30**).

✔ Tip

■ You can drag and drop text to copy it from one document window to another—even between documents of different applications! This works with any application that supports Macintosh drag and drop, including SimpleText and the Scrapbook.

Moving & Copying with Drag & Drop

To copy text to the Pasteboard

1. If the Pasteboard is not showing, choose Show Pasteboard from the Window menu (see **Figure 31**) or press ⌘ ⌘ /.

2. Select the text you want to put on the Pasteboard (see **Figure 17**).

3. Use the drag and drop techniques discussed on the previous page to drag the text from the PageMill document window to the Pasteboard window (see **Figure 32**).

4. When a selection border appears around the inside of the Pasteboard window (see **Figure 32**), release the mouse button. A copy of the selected text is placed on the Pasteboard (see **Figure 33**).

✔ Tips

◼ Although the Pasteboard has only five pages, you can copy more than one item to each page (see **Figure 34**).

◼ You can add an item to the Pasteboard by dragging it from the window of any application that supports Macintosh drag and drop, including the Finder.

◼ I tell you more about working with the Pasteboard in **Chapters 1** and **5**.

To use Pasteboard contents

1. Position the mouse pointer on the Pasteboard item you want to use (see **Figure 34**).

2. To move the Pasteboard item, drag the item into position in a PageMill document.

   or

   To copy the Pasteboard item, hold down (Option) while dragging the item into position in a PageMill document.

Figure 31
To show the Pasteboard, choose Show Pasteboard from the Window menu.

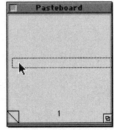 

Figure 32. *To put text on the Pasteboard, simply drag it on.*

Figure 33. *When you release the mouse button, the text appears.*

Figure 34.
To use an item on the Pasteboard, "grab it" with your mouse pointer and drag it into a PageMill document.

✔ Tip

◼ Dragging an item off the Pasteboard and into a PageMill window is the only way to remove it from the Pasteboard.

Figure 35. *The Undo command, which is the first command on the Edit menu, reverses your last action.*

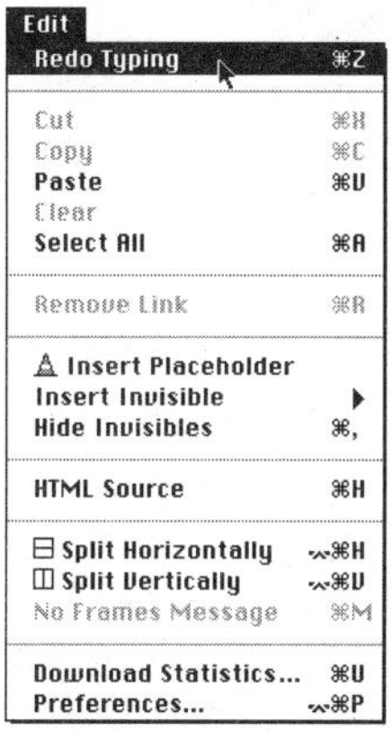

Figure 36. *If the last command you chose was Undo, the Undo command turns into a Redo command.*

Figure 37.
The Revert to Saved command throws out all the changes you made to a page since the last time you saved it.

Figure 38. *When you choose the Revert to Saved command, PageMill confirms that you want to throw out changes to the file.*

About Undoing Actions

PageMill offers two commands to help you correct errors by undoing or reversing them:

■ Undo reverses your last action.

■ Revert to Saved throws away all changes you made to a document since the last time you saved it.

To undo the last action

Choose Undo from the Edit menu.

or

Press ⌃⌘Z.

The last action you performed is reversed.

✔ Tips

■ The exact wording of this command depends on the last action you performed. For example, if the last thing you did was type text, the command will be Undo Typing (see **Figure 35**).

■ If the Undo command is unavailable, the first command under the edit menu will be Cannot Undo, which will be gray.

■ If the last action you performed was to use the Undo command, the first command under the Edit menu will be the Redo command (see **Figure 36**). This "undoes" the Undo command, restoring the document to the way it was before you chose Undo.

To revert to the saved page

1. Choose Revert to Saved from the File menu (see **Figure 37**).

2. A dialog box appears, asking you to confirm that you want to revert to the last saved version of the file (see **Figure 38**). Click Revert.

All changes you made to the file since the last time it was saved are reversed.

About Finding & Replacing Text

PageMill's find and replace features make it easy to locate and/or change text, URLs, and objects throughout a Web page document. You use the Find dialog box (see **Figure 40**) to specify your find and, if applicable, replacement text. Then use buttons within the Find dialog box or on the Search menu to locate and/or replace text as specified.

✔ Tips

■ When you use the find and replace features, the search begins at the insertion point and goes forward to the end of the document.

■ Until you specify find and/or replacement text, the only find and replace command you can select from the Search menu is Find (see **Figure 39**); all others will be gray.

■ I tell you about URLs in **Chapter 7** and about objects in **Chapter 5**.

■ The find and replace features can also be used in HTML Source view. I tell you about working with HTML source in **Chapter 11**.

Figure 39.
To begin a search, choose Find from the Search menu.

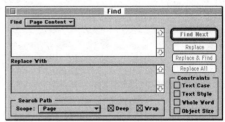

Figure 40. *Use the Find dialog box to enter search criteria.*

Figure 41.
Once you've specified
Find text, other options
on the Search menu
become available.

Found text

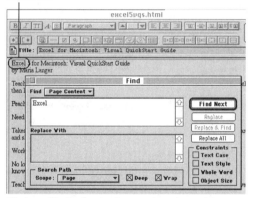

Figure 42. *A selection box appears around text in the document as it is found.*

To find text

1. Make the document you want to search the active document window.

2. Choose Find from the Search menu (see **Figure 39**) or press ⌘F.

3. In the Find dialog box that appears (see **Figure 40**), select Page Content from the Find pop-up menu.

4. Enter the text you want to find in the Find scrolling window.

5. Turn on check boxes for find constraints as desired:

   ▲ *Text Case* finds text only if its capitalization exactly matches the search text.

   ▲ *Text Style* finds text only if its style matches the search text. You can use Style and Format menu commands to change the appearance of selected text in the Find dialog box. I tell you about styles in **Chapter 3**.

   ▲ *Whole Word* finds text only if it is not part of another word.

   ▲ *Object Size* is for searching for objects. I tell you about objects in **Chapter 5**.

6. To search the entire document, including text within tables and forms, turn the Deep check box on.

7. To search the entire document, no matter where the insertion point is, turn the Wrap check box on.

8. Click the Find Next button or choose Find Next from the Search menu (see **Figure 41**) or press ⌘G. If the text exists in the document, a selection box appears around it (see **Figure 42**).

9. To find the next occurrence of the text, repeat step 8.

10. To close the Find dialog box, click its close box.

Finding Text

To replace text

1. Follow steps 1 through 7 on the previous page to specify criteria for the text you want to replace.

2. In the Replace With scrolling window, enter the replacement text (see **Figure 43**).

3. To replace text one occurrence at a time, click the Find Next button, choose Find Next from the Search menu (see **Figure 41**), or press ⌘G to locate the first occurrence of the Find text (see **Figure 45**). Then:

   ▲ Click the Replace button, choose Replace from the Search menu (see **Figure 44**), or press ⌘L to replace that occurrence. Repeat step 3 until all desired occurrences are replaced.

   or

   ▲ Click the Replace & Find button, choose Replace & Find Again from the Search menu (see **Figure 44**), or press ⌘= to replace that occurrence and find the next one. Repeat this step until all desired occurrences are replaced.

4. When you are finished, click the close box in the Find dialog box to close it.

✔ Tips

■ To replace all occurrences of the text, follow steps 1 and 2 above, then click the Replace All button or choose Replace All from the Search menu (see **Figure 44**).

■ To delete text, follow the steps above to enter the text you want to delete in the Find scrolling window. Leave the Replace With scrolling window empty. When you follow step 3 to replace some or all of the occurrences of the Find text with nothing, it is deleted.

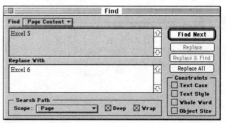

Figure 43. *To replace text, enter the replacement text in the Replace With scrolling window.*

Figure 44. *Once you enter replacement text and have found one occurrence of the find text, all find and replace commands become available.*

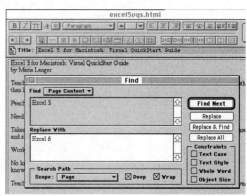

Figure 45. *Once text has been found, you can click the Replace, Replace & Find, or Replace All buttons to replace it.*

About Checking Spelling

PageMill includes a spelling check feature that you can use to check your Web page documents for spelling, typographical, and possible capitalization errors before publishing them on the Web. This feature works with three dictionaries:

- The language dictionary (named *US English*, *UK English*, etc.) contains thousands of words that PageMill refers to first when checking spelling.

- The *Internet Dictionary* contains words commonly found on the Internet, like *cyberspace*, *Netscape*, *WWW*, and *Yahoo*. PageMill refers to this dictionary when it can't find a word in the language dictionary.

- The *User Dictionary* contains the words you add while performing a spelling check. This would include uncommon words like your name or company name. PageMill refers to this dictionary when it can't find a word in the language or Internet dictionaries.

✔ Tip

- A spelling check always begins at the insertion point and moves forward through the document.

To check spelling

1. Make the document you want to check the active document window.

   or

   Select the words you want to check within the document window.

2. Choose Check Spelling from the Search menu (see **Figure 46**) or press ⌘⌘〜.

3. The spelling checker goes to work. When it finds an unknown word, it displays the Spell Checker dialog box (see **Figure 47**). You have several options:

   ▲ To ignore the word, click the Ignore button (to ignore just one occurrence) or the Ignore All button (to ignore all occurrences).

   ▲ To change the word to one of the words in the Suggestions scrolling window, select the word you want to use and click the Change button (to change just one occurrence) or the Change All button (to change all occurrences).

   ▲ To change the word to a word that is not in the Suggestions scrolling window, click in the Change to edit box and enter the word you want to use (see **Figure 48**). Then click the Change button (to change just one occurrence) or the Change All button (to change all occurrences).

   ▲ To add the word to the User Dictionary, click the Add button.

4. Each time you act on an unknown word, PageMill continues the check. Repeat step 3 as necessary until the spelling check is complete.

5. When the spelling check is complete, the phrase "no unknown words" appears above the Start button (see **Figure 49**). Click the close box to dismiss the Spell Checker dialog box.

Figure 46.
To begin a spelling check, choose Check Spelling from the Search menu.

Figure 47. *The Spell Checker dialog box displays unknown words so you can act on them.*

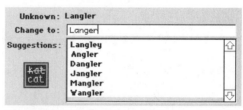

Figure 48. *If the word is spelled incorrectly but the correct spelling is not in the Suggestions scrolling window, simply enter the correct spelling in the Change to edit box.*

Figure 49.
The spelling check is complete when the phrase "no unknown words" appears above the Start button.

✔ Tip

■ Do not click the Add button unless the unknown word is spelled correctly! If you add an incorrectly spelled word to the User Dictionary, PageMill will never identify it as unknown again!

Checking Spelling

To set spelling check options

1. Choose Check Spelling from the Search menu (see **Figure 46**) or press ⌃⌘~.

2. In the Spell Checker dialog box that appears (see **Figure 47**), set any of the following options as desired:

   ▲ To limit the spelling check to a selected table or form, choose Object from the Scope pop-up menu (see **Figure 50**).

   ▲ To prevent PageMill from checking words within tables or forms on the page, make sure the Deep check box is turned off.

   ▲ To prevent PageMill from continuing a spell check at the top of the page if it began somewhere other than the top of the page, turn off the Wrap check box.

3. Continue the spelling check as discussed on the previous page.

   or

   Click the close box to dismiss the Spell Checker dialog box. Your settings will be saved for the next spelling check you perform.

✔ Tip

■ I tell you about tables in **Chapter 6** and about forms in **Chapter 9**.

Figure 50.
The Scope pop-up menu can limit the words checked.

●Page
Object

Setting Spelling Check Options

To replace the User Dictionary

1. If PageMill is running, choose Quit from the File menu to quit it.

2. In the Finder, locate the Adobe® PageMill™ 2.0 folder and double-click it to open it.

3. Double-click the Plug-ins folder to open it.

4. Double-click the Spelling folder to open it (see **Figure 51**).

5. Drag the User Dictionary icon out of the Spelling window.

6. To use a different User Dictionary file, drag its icon into the Spelling window.

   or

   To create a brand new User Dictionary file, do nothing. A new User Dictionary will be created automatically when you perform your first spelling check.

✔ Tips

■ You can get a replacement User Dictionary file from another PageMill 2.0 user. For example, if another user in your workplace has been collecting company-related words in his User Dictionary for a while, you can use his User Dictionary file with your copy of PageMill to speed up spelling checks.

■ You can only have one language dictionary file.

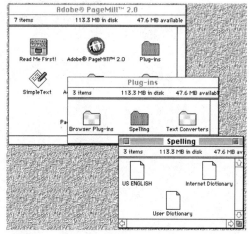

Figure 51. *The User Dictionary file is inside the Spelling folder inside the Plug-ins folder inside the Adobe® PageMill™ 2.0 folder.*

APPLYING CHARACTER STYLES

About Character Styles

In HTML, the underlying language of the World Wide Web, there are two kinds of text formatting:

- *Physical Styles* use tags to specify how text should look, regardless of its use within the document. A physical style like bold, for example, will always look bold, no matter how it is used in the document or which Web browser is used to view it.

- *Logical Styles* use tags to specify how text should look based on its use within a document. A logical style like strong, for example, may appear bold when viewed with some browsers and underlined when viewed with others. The point is, strong-formatted characters are formatted differently from unformatted characters, making them stand out.

The main problem with using logical styles is that you can't always predict how logical style-formatted characters will appear when viewed with various Web browsers. For that reason, you may prefer to use physical styles.

Of course, no matter what kind of character formatting you apply, PageMill takes care of inserting the proper tags for you. You simply select the text you want to format and choose the style you want.

✔ Tip

- Formatting individual text characters is occasionally referred to as *highlighting* since formatted characters stand out from unformatted characters.

About Physical Styles

PageMill supports four physical styles:

- *Plain* is plain text, without formatting.
- *Bold* is bold text.
- *Italic* is italicized text.
- *Teletype* is monospaced text.

Figure 1 shows an example of each of these physical styles.

PhysicalStyles.html
Back
Forward
Home
Title: Physical Styles Examples
This is an example of characters formatted with the Plain physical style.
This is an example of characters formatted with the Bold physical style.
This is an example of characters formatted with the Italic physical style.
This is an example of characters formatted with the Teletype physical style.
Link To:

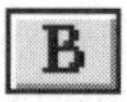

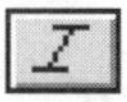

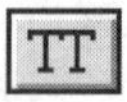

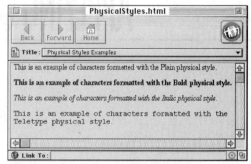

Figure 1. *PageMill's four physical styles.*

To apply a physical style

1. Select the text you want to format (see **Figure 2**).
2. Choose a physical style command from the Style menu (see **Figure 3**):
   - ▲ For plain text, choose Plain.
   - ▲ For bold style, choose Bold.
   - ▲ For italic style, choose Italic.
   - ▲ For monospaced type, choose Teletype.

   or

   Press a physical style shortcut key:
   - ▲ For plain text, press Shift ⌘ P.
   - ▲ For bold style, press ⌘ B.
   - ▲ For italic style, press ⌘ I.
   - ▲ For monospaced type, press Shift ⌘ T.

   or

   Click a physical style button on the button bar:
   - ▲ For bold style, click the Bold button.
   - ▲ For italic style, click the Italic button.
   - ▲ For monospaced type, click the Teletype button.

The selected text changes to the style you specified (see **Figure 4**).

plunge.html
Title: Taking the Plunge
Taking the Plunge -- My First Bungee Jumping Experience
It was at MacWorld Expo in Boston in August 1996 that I first took the plunge. Power Computing Corporation, Macintosh clone-maker extraordinaire, had set up a 225-foot bungee jumping tower on the pier beside the World Trade Center. Bungee jumping passes were free for the asking at the Power Computing booth.
As soon as I heard about the tower, I wanted to take the plunge. But I never seemed to remember to get the required pass. (Perhaps my subconscious was sending a message?) Finally, just before lunchtime on Friday, I remember to stop by and sign up. Too late! All the passes for the day were
Link To:

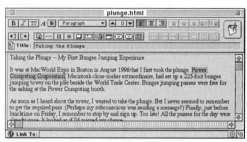

Figure 2. *Begin by selecting the text you want to format…*

Style
✓Plain ⇧⌘P
Bold ⌘B
Italic ⌘I
Teletype ⇧⌘T
Strong ⇧⌘S
Emphasis ⇧⌘E
Citation ⇧⌘C
Sample ⇧⌘A
Keyboard ⇧⌘K
Code ⇧⌘O
Variable ⇧⌘V
Increase Font Size ⇧⌘>
Decrease Font Size ⇧⌘<

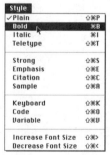

Figure 3. *…then choose the physical style you want to apply from the Style menu.*

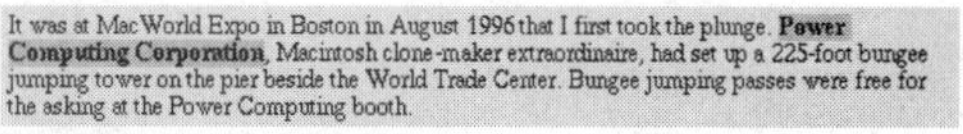

It was at MacWorld Expo in Boston in August 1996 that I first took the plunge. Power Computing Corporation, Macintosh clone-maker extraordinaire, had set up a 225-foot bungee jumping tower on the pier beside the World Trade Center. Bungee jumping passes were free for the asking at the Power Computing booth.

Figure 4. *The style you chose—in this case Bold—is applied immediately.*

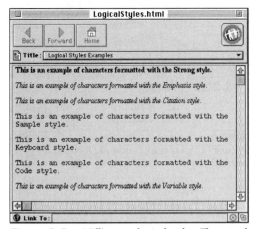

Figure 5. *PageMill's seven logical styles. The actual appearance of these styles may vary from browser to browser.*

Figure 6.
Choose the logical style you want from the Style menu.

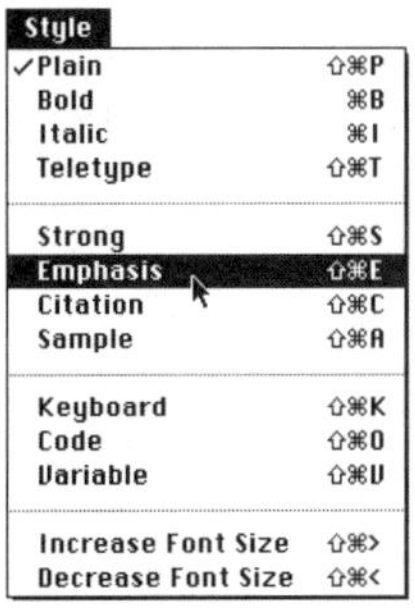

Style	
✓ Plain	⇧⌘P
Bold	⌘B
Italic	⌘I
Teletype	⇧⌘T
Strong	⇧⌘S
Emphasis	⇧⌘E
Citation	⇧⌘C
Sample	⇧⌘A
Keyboard	⇧⌘K
Code	⇧⌘0
Variable	⇧⌘U
Increase Font Size	⇧⌘>
Decrease Font Size	⇧⌘<

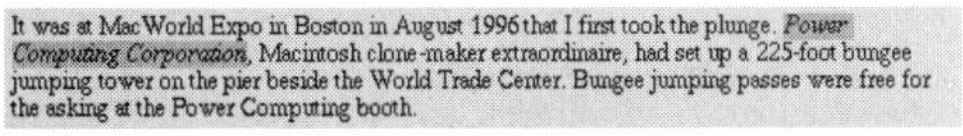

It was at MacWorld Expo in Boston in August 1996 that I first took the plunge. *Power Computing Corporation*, Macintosh clone-maker extraordinaire, had set up a 225-foot bungee jumping tower on the pier beside the World Trade Center. Bungee jumping passes were free for the asking at the Power Computing booth.

Figure 7. *The selected text changes to the style you chose—in this case, Emphasis.*

About Logical Styles

PageMill supports seven logical styles:

- ■ *Strong* is for strong emphasis.
- ■ *Emphasis* is for emphasis.
- ■ *Citation* is for the titles of books and other references.
- ■ *Sample* is for computer status messages.
- ■ *Keyboard* is for user keyboard entry.
- ■ *Code* is for computer programming code.
- ■ *Variable* is for variables which must be replaced by the user.

Figure 5 shows samples of logical styles.

✔ Tips

- ■ The appearance of logical styles may vary from one Web browser to another.
- ■ In some instances, two or more logical styles—like Sample, Keyboard, and Code—may look exactly the same.

To apply a logical style

1. Select the text you want to format (see **Figure 2**).

2. Choose a logical style command—Strong, Emphasis, Citation, Sample, Keyboard, Code, or Variable—from the Style menu (see **Figure 6**).

   or

   Press a logical style shortcut key:

   - ▲ For Strong style, press (Shift)(⌃)(⌘)(S).
   - ▲ For Emphasis style, press (Shift)(⌃)(⌘)(E).
   - ▲ For Citation style, press (Shift)(⌃)(⌘)(C).
   - ▲ For Sample style, press (Shift)(⌃)(⌘)(A).
   - ▲ For Keyboard style, press (Shift)(⌃)(⌘)(K).
   - ▲ For Code style, press (Shift)(⌃)(⌘)(O).
   - ▲ For Variable style, press (Shift)(⌃)(⌘)(V).

The selected text changes to the style you specified (see **Figure 7**).

Applying Logical Styles

✔ Tips

■ You can apply more than one style to text. Simply apply each style, one at a time, as discussed on the previous two pages. **Figure 8** shows an example of text with bold and italic style applied.

■ You can combine physical and logical styles if desired. For example, you can apply Bold and Emphasis styles to get bold, italic-looking text. Just remember that the appearance of logical styles varies from one Web browser to another, so you may not get the results you expect on all browsers.

■ If you're not sure what style is applied to characters, select the characters and pull down the Style menu. As illustrated in **Figures 3**, **6**, **9**, and **12**, a check mark appears beside the name of each style applied to selected text. (This technique does not work when different styles are applied to characters within a selection.)

■ You can apply character styles to text already formatted with paragraph formatting. I tell you about paragraph formatting in **Chapter 4**.

■ Character styles do not change the way PageMill or Web browsers treat multiple spaces, tabs, or returns in a page document. These characters are stripped out as discussed in **Chapter 2**. In order to include additional spaces or empty lines, use Preformatted paragraph formatting. I discuss paragraph formatting in **Chapter 4**.

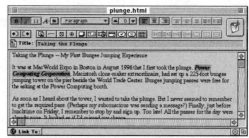

Figure 8. *You can apply more than one style to selected text.*

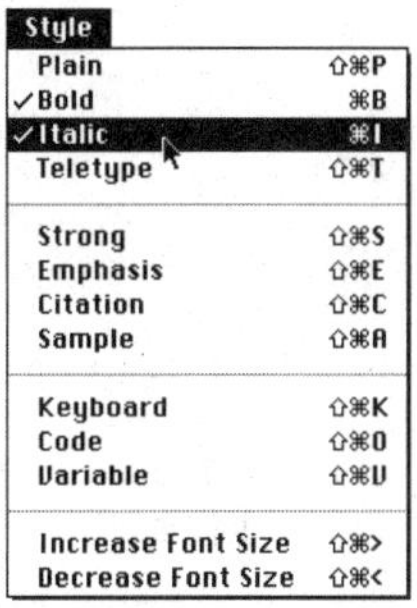

Figure 9.
To remove an applied style, simply choose it from the Style menu…

About Removing Styles

When you apply a style you, in effect, "turn it on" for selected text. To remove a style, simply "turn it off."

To remove a style

1. Select the text from which you want to remove the style (see **Figure 8**).

2. Choose the name of the style you want to remove from the Style menu (see **Figure 9**).

   or

   Press the shortcut key for the style you want to remove.

   or

   Click the button bar button for the style you want to remove (see **Figure 10**).

The style you chose is removed from the selected text (see **Figure 11**).

Figure 10.
…or click its button bar button.

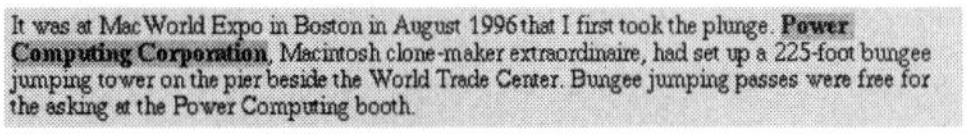

It was at MacWorld Expo in Boston in August 1996 that I first took the plunge. **Power Computing Corporation**, Macintosh clone-maker extraordinaire, had set up a 225-foot bungee jumping tower on the pier beside the World Trade Center. Bungee jumping passes were free for the asking at the Power Computing booth.

Figure 11. *By removing or "turning off" the Italic style, the text in* **Figure 8** *retains only its Bold style.*

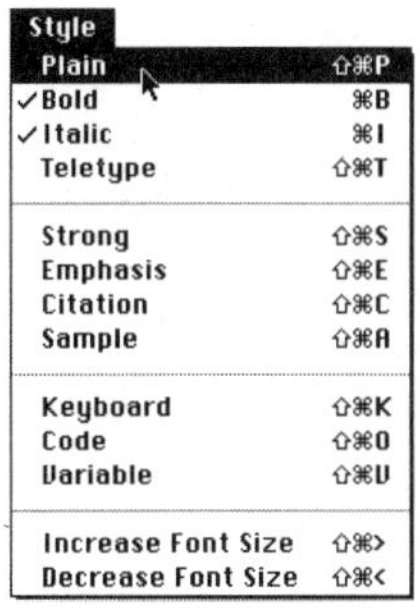

To remove all styles

1. Select the text from which you want to remove all styles (see **Figure 8**).

2. Choose Plain from the Style menu (see **Figure 12**).

   or

   Press [Shift][⌃][⌘][P].

All styles are removed from the selected text.

Figure 12.
To remove all styles, choose Plain from the Style menu.

✔ Tip

■ If the above techniques do not remove a physical style, some kind of paragraph formatting is probably applied to the text. You must remove the paragraph formatting to change the appearance of the text. I tell you about paragraph formatting in **Chapter 4**.

Removing Styles

About Font Size

Default font size is determined by font preferences set within the browser used to view the page, as well as any Base Font settings specified for the page.

You can increase or decrease the size of selected text characters relative to the size of the default font. **Figure 13** shows some examples.

✔ Tips

- The Relative Font Size button indicates the font size for selected characters relative to the default font size. If the button displays +2 as shown here, for example, the selected characters are two sizes larger than the plain paragraph font size.

- Unless you set Base Font settings, you have no control over the default font size for the page. I tell you how to set a page's base font size in **Chapter 10**.

- Another way to change the size of text characters is to use heading formats. Heading formats change the size of all the text within a paragraph. I tell you about heading formats in **Chapter 4**.

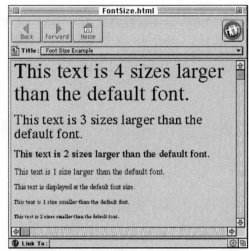

Figure 13. *Font characters can be resized relative to the default font size.*

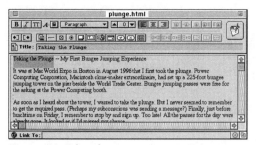

Figure 14. *Select the text you want to resize.*

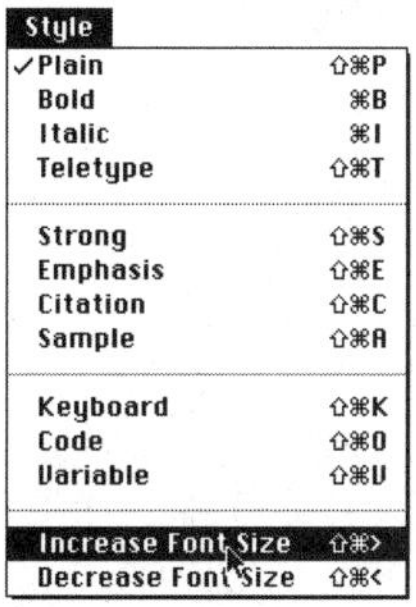

Figure 15.
Choose a font size command from the Style menu to increase or decrease the size of selected characters.

Figure 16.
To select a specific increase or decrease, use the Relative Font Size button's menu.

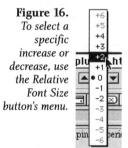

Taking the Plunge -- My Fir

It was at MacWorld Expo in Boston i

Figure 17. *The changes you make to the selected characters' size appear immediately.*

To change font size

1. Select the text you want to resize (see **Figure 14**).

2. Choose a font size command from the Style menu (see **Figure 15**):

   ▲ To make selected text larger, choose Increase Font Size.

   ▲ To make selected text smaller, choose Decrease Font Size.

   or

   Press a font size shortcut key:

   ▲ To make selected text larger, press [Shift] [⌃] [⌘] [>].

   ▲ To make selected text smaller, press [Shift] [⌃] [⌘] [<].

   or

   Click a Relative Font Size button on the button bar:

   ▲ To make selected text larger, click the Increase Relative Font Size button.

   ▲ To make selected text smaller, click the Decrease Relative Font Size button.

   ▲ To select a specific relative increase or decrease, click the Relative Font Size button and choose an option from the pop-up menu (see **Figure 16**).

3. Repeat step 2 until the characters are the desired size (see **Figure 17**).

To restore font size

1. Select the text you want to restore to the default font size.

2. Click the Relative Font Size button (see **Figure 16**) and choose 0 from the pop-up menu.

Changing & Restoring Font Size

About Font Color

Default font color is determined by color preferences set within the browser used to view the page, as well as any Colors settings specified for the page.

You can change the color of selected text characters a variety of ways.

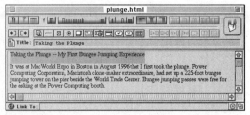

Figure 18. *Select the text you want to recolor.*

✔ Tips

■ You can change the default text colors for an entire page by setting Colors options for the page. I tell you how in **Chapter 10**.

■ You cannot change the color of a text link using any of the methods in this section. I tell you about changing the color of links in **Chapter 10**.

Figure 19. *Choose Custom from the Text Color pop-up menu.*

To change font color with the Color Wheel

1. Select the text you want to recolor (see **Figure 18**).

2. Click the Text Color button and choose Custom from the pop-up menu (see **Figure 19**).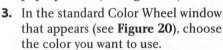

3. In the standard Color Wheel window that appears (see **Figure 20**), choose the color you want to use.

4. Click OK or press [Return] or [Enter] to dismiss the Color Wheel and apply the color (see **Figure 21**).

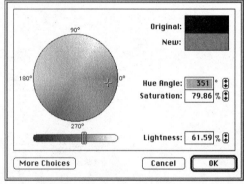

Figure 20. *Choose a color from the Color Wheel and click OK to apply it.*

✔ Tip

■ The actual appearance of the Color Wheel may vary depending on the version of the System software installed on your Macintosh.

Figure 21. *The color you selected is applied immediately.*

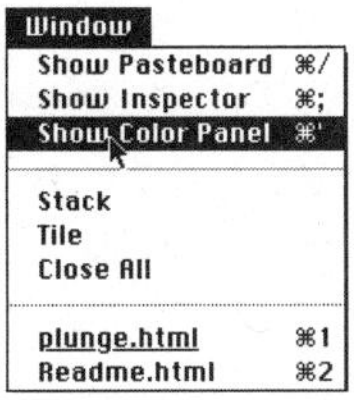

Figure 22.
*If necessary,
choose Show
Color Panel from
the Window menu.*

To change font color with the Color Panel

1. Select the text you want to recolor (see **Figure 18**).

2. If the Color Panel is not already displayed, choose Show Color Panel from the Window menu (see **Figure 22**) to display it (see **Figure 23**).

3. Drag one of the color swatches on the Color Panel to the selected text. When you release the mouse button, the color is applied.

Figure 23.
*The Color Panel
includes swatches
for commonly-used
colors you can
apply to selected
text by dragging.*

To restore font color

1. Select the text you want to restore to the default color (see **Figure 24**).

2. Click the Text Color button and choose Default from the pop-up menu (see **Figure 25**). The color of the selected text characters returns to the default color for the page.

Figure 24. *Select the text you want to restore to the default color.*

Figure 25.
*Choose Default
from the Text
Color pop-up menu to restore
colored text to the default color.*

Changing & Restoring Font Color

APPLYING PARAGRAPH FORMATS

About Paragraph Formats

Unlike character styles, which I discuss in **Chapter 3**, paragraph formats are used to format entire paragraphs of information.

PageMill supports a wide range of HTML paragraph formatting options:

- *Alignment* options specify the way text is positioned between the left and right sides of the window.

- *Indentation* options specify the amount of space between the left side of the window and the text.

- *Heading* options specify the size of headings.

- *List* options specify the way lists of information appear.

- *Preformatted* formatting enables you to create tables of information.

- *Address* formatting applies special formatting to addresses.

No matter what kind of paragraph formatting you apply, PageMill takes care of inserting HTML tags for you. You simply select the paragraph(s) you want to format, then choose the format option you want.

✔ Tips

- In PageMill (as in most other programs), a paragraph is defined by return characters. Each time you press (Return), you end the current paragraph and begin a new one.

- When applying paragraph formatting to only one paragraph, just position the insertion point in the paragraph before choosing the formatting option. Formatting is applied to the entire paragraph.

About Alignment

PageMill's alignment options specify the way text is positioned between the left and right sides of the browser window. PageMill offers three options:

■ *Left Align* aligns text with the left side of the window.

■ *Center Align* centers text between the left and right sides of the window.

■ *Right Align* aligns text with the right side of the window.

Figure 1 shows an example of each alignment option.

✔ Tip

■ By default, text is left aligned.

To set paragraph alignment

1. Select all or part of the paragraph(s) whose alignment you want to change (see **Figure 2**).

2. Click an alignment button on the button bar:

   ▲ For left alignment, click the Left Align Text button.

   ▲ For center alignment, click the Center Align Text button.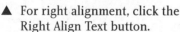

   ▲ For right alignment, click the Right Align Text button.

   or

   Press an alignment shortcut key:

   ▲ To shift alignment to the right, press ⌘ Control →.

   ▲ To shift alignment to the left, press ⌘ Control ←.

The selected paragraph(s) change accordingly (see **Figure 3**).

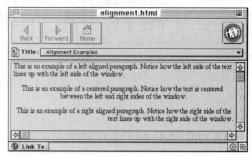

Figure 1. *PageMill's text alignment options.*

Figure 2. *Select the paragraph(s) you want to format.*

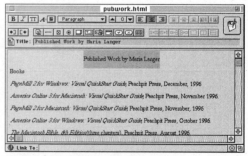

Figure 3. *Here's the selection from* **Figure 2** *after clicking the Center Align Text button.*

Aligning Paragraphs

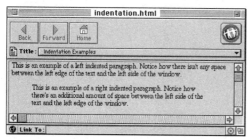

Figure 4. *PageMill's indentation options.*

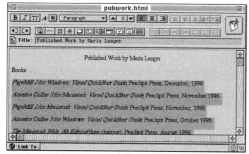

Figure 5. *Select the paragraph(s) you want to format.*

Figure 6.
Choose the indentation option you want from the Format menu.

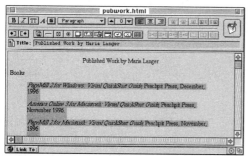

Figure 7. *Here's the selection from* **Figure 5** *after choosing Indent Right from the Format menu.*

About Indentation

PageMill's indentation options specify the amount of space between the left side of the browser window and the text.

- *Indent Left* removes space between the text and the left side of the window.

- *Indent Right* adds space between the text and the left side of the window.

Figure 4 shows an example of each indentation option.

✔ Tip

- By default, text is left indented.

To set paragraph indentation

1. Select all or part of the paragraph(s) whose indentation you want to change (see **Figure 5**).

2. Choose the indentation option you want—Indent Left or Indent Right— from the Format menu (see **Figure 6**).

   or

   Click an indentation button on the button bar:

   - ▲ To shift text to the right, click the Indent Right button.

   - ▲ To shift text to the left, click the Indent Left button.

   or

   Press an alignment shortcut key:

   - ▲ To shift text to the right, press ⌘].

   - ▲ To shift text to the left, press ⌘[.

   The selected paragraph(s) change accordingly (see **Figure 7**).

✔ Tip

- You can apply indentation more than once to increase or reduce the amount of indentation.

Indenting Paragraphs

About Headings

PageMill's heading options let you choose from among six heading levels, each of which applies a different text size:

- *Large*, *Larger*, and *Largest* set headings larger than the standard text size.
- *Small*, *Smaller*, and *Smallest* set headings at the same size or smaller than the standard text size.

Paragraphs formatted as headings also have bold style applied. **Figure 8** illustrates each heading option.

✔ Tip

- By default, no heading is applied.

To apply a heading format

1. Select all or part of the paragraph(s) you want to format as a heading (see **Figure 2**).

2. Choose the heading option you want from the Heading submenu under the Format menu (see **Figure 9**).

    or

    Choose the heading option you want from the Change Format pop-up menu on the button bar (see **Figure 10**).

    or

    Press the shortcut key for the heading format you want:

    ▲ For Largest, press Option ⌃⌘ 1.
    ▲ For Larger, press Option ⌃⌘ 2.
    ▲ For Large, press Option ⌃⌘ 3.
    ▲ For Small, press Option ⌃⌘ 4.
    ▲ For Smaller, press Option ⌃⌘ 5.
    ▲ For Smallest, press Option ⌃⌘ 6.

The selected paragraph(s) change accordingly (see **Figure 11**).

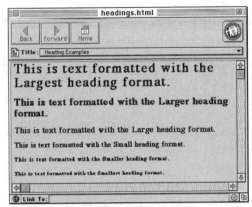

Figure 8. *PageMill's heading formats.*

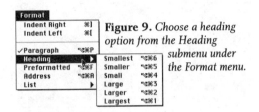

Figure 9. *Choose a heading option from the Heading submenu under the Format menu.*

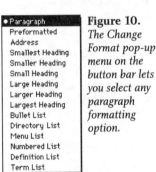

Figure 10. *The Change Format pop-up menu on the button bar lets you select any paragraph formatting option.*

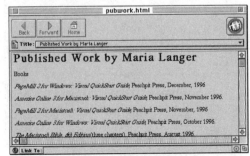

Figure 11. *Here's the paragraph that's selected in Figure 2 with the Largest heading applied.*

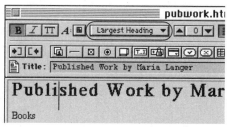

Figure 12. *When you position the insertion point within a paragraph, you can see what format is applied by looking at the Change Format pop-up menu in the button bar.*

Figure 13. *This example has several headings applied, one of which has italic style applied, too.*

Figure 14. *Choose Paragraph from the Format menu to remove applied formats from selected paragraphs.*

✔ Tips

■ The shortcut keys for the heading formats correspond to the heading HTML tags. For example, the HTML tag for the largest heading format is <H1>; the shortcut key for the same heading format in PageMill is ⟨Option⟩ ⌃ ⌘ 1. This makes it easy for PageMill users with HTML knowledge to remember the shortcut keys.

■ You can see which heading format is applied to a paragraph by clicking in the paragraph and looking at the Change Format pop-up menu on the button bar (see **Figure 12**).

■ You cannot remove the bold style from a heading.

■ You can combine heading formats with other formatting and style options to achieve the effects you want. **Figure 13** shows an example with three different headings applied, one of which has italic style applied. I discuss character styles in **Chapter 3**.

To remove a heading format

1. Select the paragraph(s) with the heading format applied.

2. Choose Paragraph from the Format menu (see **Figure 14**).

   or

   Choose Paragraph from the Change Format pop-up menu on the button bar (see **Figure 10**).

   or

   Press ⟨Option⟩ ⌃ ⌘ P.

The heading format is removed.

About List Formats

PageMill's six list format options let you create a variety of nicely formatted lists:

- *Bullet List*, *Directory List*, and *Menu List* create bulleted lists. The bullets are inserted automatically.

- *Numbered List* creates a numbered list. The numbers are inserted automatically.

- *Definition List* indents the paragraph. It is designed to be used with Term List.

- *Term List*, when used with Definition List, lets you create glossary-style lists.

Figure 15 illustrates the list formats. (Directory List and Menu List formats, which are not illustrated, are identical in appearance to Bullet List format.)

✔ Tips

- By default, no list formatting is applied.

- Consecutive paragraphs with the same list formatting applied do not have additional space between them. You can see this in **Figure 15**; each list item is a separate paragraph.

- When you create a numbered list, PageMill displays pound signs (#) where the numbers should go (see **Figure 15**). Don't worry—when your page is viewed with a Web browser, the numbers will appear.

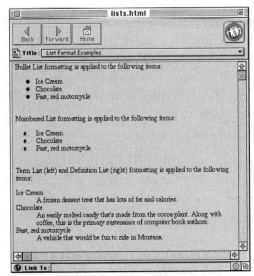

Figure 15. *PageMill's list formats.*

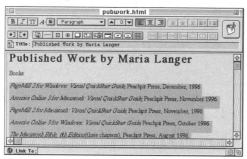

Figure 16. *Select the paragraphs you want to include in the list.*

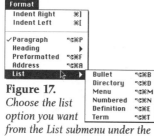

Figure 17.
Choose the list option you want from the List submenu under the Format menu.

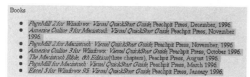

Figure 18. *Here's the selection from Figure 16 formatted as a bulleted list.*

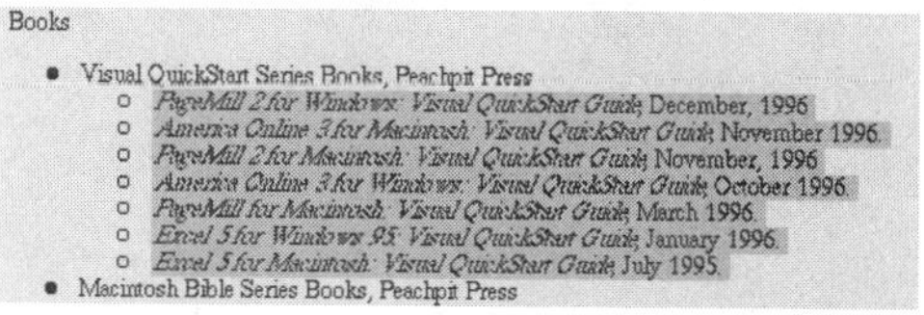

Figure 19. *To create a nested list, select the items you want to indent and choose Indent Right from the Format menu.*

To create a list

1. Select all or part of the paragraphs you want to include in your list (see **Figure 16**).

2. Choose the list option you want from the List submenu under the Format menu (see **Figure 17**).

   or

   Choose the list option you want from the Change Format pop-up menu on the button bar.

   or

   Press the Command key equivalent for the list option you want:

   ▲ For Bullet, press Option ⌃⌘ B.

   ▲ For Directory, press Option ⌃⌘ D.

   ▲ For Menu, press Option ⌃⌘ M.

   ▲ For Numbered, press Option ⌃⌘ N.

   ▲ For Definition, press Option ⌃⌘ E.

   ▲ For Term, press Option ⌃⌘ T.

The selected paragraphs change to become part of a list (see **Figure 18**).

To create a nested list

1. Follow the steps above to create a list.

2. Select the list items you want to indent.

3. Choose Indent Right from the Format menu (see **Figure 6**), click the Indent Right button on the button bar, or press ⌃⌘].

The items are indented and the bullet or numbering scheme changes (see **Figure 19**).

✔ Tip

■ To remove a nested list, select the nested items and choose Indent Left from the Format menu (see **Figure 6**), click the Indent Left button on the button bar, or press ⌃⌘ [.

Creating Lists

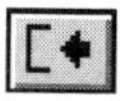

To create a definition list

1. Enter the text for the list by alternating between terms and definitions (see **Figure 20**).

2. Select a term in the list (see **Figure 21**).

3. Choose Term from the List submenu under the Format menu (see **Figure 17**), choose Term List from the Change Format pop-up menu on the button bar (see **Figure 10**), or press Option ⌃⌘ T.

4. Select the definition immediately following the term you just formatted (see **Figure 22**).

5. Choose Definition from the List submenu under the Format menu (see **Figure 17**), choose Definition List from the Change Format pop-up menu on the button bar (see **Figure 10**), or press Option ⌃⌘ E.

   The definition indents and moves up under the term (see **Figure 23**).

6. Repeat steps 2 through 5 for each term and definition in the list.

When you're finished, your list might look something like the one in **Figure 24**.

To remove list formats

1. Select the paragraph(s) from which you want to remove the list format.

2. Choose Paragraph from the Format menu (see **Figure 14**).

   or

   Choose Paragraph from the Change Format pop-up menu on the button bar (see **Figure 10**).

   or

   Press Option ⌃⌘ P.

   The list format is removed from the selection.

-I-
In Print
A book that is still in production. Opposite: out of print.

Index
A listing of key terms used throughout a book with corresponding page reference numbers. An index is usually at the end of a book and is a real nuisance to prepare. (Try it sometime.)

ISBN
A reference number for a book consisting of a publisher-specific prefix and additional unique digits.

Figure 20. *Begin by entering the terms and definitions you want to include in the definition list.*

In Print
A book that is still in production. Opposite: out of print.

Figure 21. *Select a term in the list.*

In Print
A book that is still in production. Opposite: out of print.
Index

Figure 22. *Select the definition beneath the formatted term.*

In Print   A book that is still in production. Opposite: out of print.
Index

Figure 23. *When you apply Definition formatting, the definition moves up and becomes indented.*

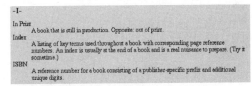

-I-
In Print   A book that is still in production. Opposite: out of print.
Index   A listing of key terms used throughout a book with corresponding page reference numbers. An index is usually at the end of a book and is a real nuisance to prepare. (Try it sometime.)
ISBN   A reference number for a book consisting of a publisher-specific prefix and additional unique digits.

Figure 24. *A completed term/definition list.*

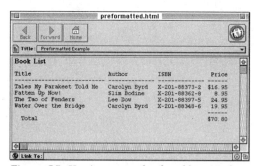

Figure 25. *Here's an example of a table created in PageMill with the Preformatted format.*

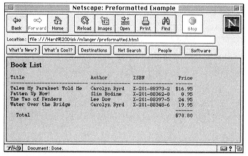

Figure 26. *Here's the table from* **Figure 25** *when viewed with Netscape.*

About Preformatted Paragraphs

The characters you'd normally use to format documents in your favorite word processor or page layout application aren't always interpreted properly by Web browsers. Here are some examples:

- Multiple consecutive space characters are usually treated as a single space.

- Multiple consecutive return or line break characters are usually treated as a single return or line break character.

- Tab characters are often ignored or treated as a single space.

As you might imagine, this makes it a bit tougher to create spreadsheet-like tables in your Web page documents.

That's where the Preformatted format comes in. By combining the ability to include multiple consecutive spaces and return characters with a monospaced (or fixed-width) font like Courier, you can create simple tables—without creating HTML tables—and be confident that they'll look the same when viewed on any browser.

Figures 25 and **26** show examples of a table created with the Preformatted format.

✔ Tips

- PageMill does not allow you to enter multiple consecutive space characters in a paragraph unless that paragraph has the Preformatted format applied.

- You can enter multiple consecutive *nonbreaking space* characters regardless of how a paragraph is formatted. To type one of these characters, press Option Spacebar. Since these characters are interpreted differently by different Web browsers, you should not use them as an alternative to regular spaces in Preformatted format paragraphs.

- You can drag or paste in text containing multiple consecutive spaces that was created in another application.

- Using a monospaced style like Code or Sample is not the same as using the Preformatted format. Styles will not retain the extra spaces. I tell you about styles in **Chapter 3**.

- Another way to create a table is with HTML tables. I tell you how to use PageMill's table feature in **Chapter 6**.

To apply the Preformatted format to existing text

1. Type, drag in, or paste in text you want to format with the Preformatted format (see **Figure 27**).

2. Select all or part of the paragraph(s) you want to format (see **Figure 28**).

3. Choose Preformatted from the Format menu (see **Figure 29**).

   or

   Choose Preformatted from the Change Format pop-up menu on the button bar (see **Figure 10**).

   or

   Press (Option)(⌘)(F).

The selected paragraph(s) change accordingly (see **Figure 25**).

✔ Tips

- I tell you how to enter text by pasting or dragging it into a PageMill document in **Chapter 2**.

- Text you drag or paste in can contain multiple consecutive spaces.

- Once you apply the Preformatted format to text, you can adjust the spacing between words with space characters as necessary.

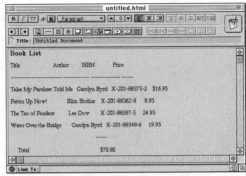

Figure 27. *Here's an example of tabular text prepared in another program and pasted into a PageMill document.*

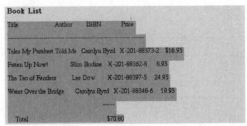

Figure 28. *Select the text you want to format.*

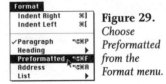

Figure 29. *Choose Preformatted from the Format menu.*

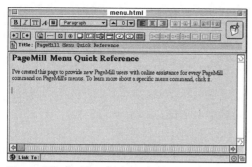

Figure 30. *Position the insertion point on an empty line where you want to begin typing preformatted text.*

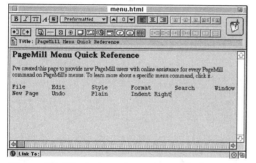

Figure 31. *The text you type appears in the Preformatted format.*

To use the Preformatted format as you enter text

1. Position the insertion point on an empty line where you want the preformatted text to begin (see **Figure 30**).

2. Choose Preformatted from the Format menu (see **Figure 29**).

   or

   Choose Preformatted from the Change Format pop-up menu on the button bar (see **Figure 10**).

   or

   Press Option ⌘ F.

   This "turns on" preformatted formatting.

3. Type the text you want preformatted. It is entered in monospaced type (see **Figure 31**).

4. Press Return after the last line of preformatted text.

5. Choose Paragraph from the Format menu (see **Figure 14**).

   or

   Choose Paragraph from the Change Format pop-up menu on the button bar (see **Figure 10**).

   or

   Press Option ⌘ P.

   This "turns off" preformatted formatting.

To remove the Preformatted format

1. Select the paragraph(s) from which you want to remove the Preformatted format.

2. Choose Paragraph from the Format menu (see **Figure 14**), or choose Paragraph from the Change Format pop-up menu on the button bar (see **Figure 10**), or press Option ⌘ P.

   The Preformatted format is removed from the selection.

About the Address Format

Often, one of the last lines in a Web page is the page author's name, e-mail address, page revision date, and/or copyright notice. Traditionally, the Address format is used to format this kind of information.

To apply the Address format

1. Select all or part of the paragraph(s) to which you want to apply the Address format (see **Figure 32**).

2. Choose Address from the Format menu (see **Figure 33**).

   or

   Choose Address from the Change Format pop-up menu on the button bar (see **Figure 10**).

   or

   Press (Option) ⌃ ⌘ (A).

The selected paragraph(s) change accordingly. As you can see in **Figure 34**, Address format includes italic style.

✔ Tip

■ You cannot remove italic style from the Address format. I tell you about character styles in **Chapter 3**.

To remove the Address format

1. Select all or part of the paragraph(s) from which you want to remove the Address format.

2. Choose Paragraph from the Format menu (see **Figure 14**).

   or

   Choose Paragraph from the Change Format pop-up menu on the button bar (see **Figure 10**).

   or

   Press (Option) ⌃ ⌘ (P).

Address formatting is removed.

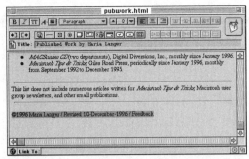

Figure 32. *Select the text you want to format.*

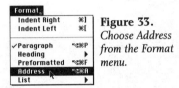

Figure 33.
Choose Address from the Format menu.

Figure 34. *As you can see here, Address format applies an italic style to text when viewed in PageMill and many Web browsers.*

ADDING MULTIMEDIA OBJECTS

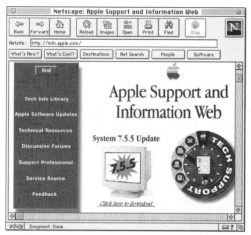

Figure 1. *The Apple Support and Information Web home page uses many graphic elements to add visual appeal.*

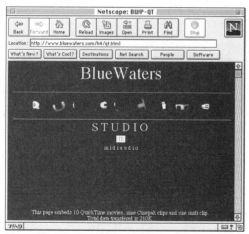

Figure 2. *Blue Waters has a number of pages that use QuickTime movies and sounds. This page combines ten QuickTime movies to scramble the letters in the word* QuickTime *and play a MIDI sound track.*

About Multimedia

One of the best features of the World Wide Web is its ability to support graphic images, animations, movies, and sounds. These multimedia elements or objects can be viewed by Web browsers on all major computer platforms. When used properly, they can help communicate information and make your Web pages stand out from the rest.

Figures 1 and **2** show examples of Web pages that include multimedia objects.

✔ Tips

■ When using multimedia objects in your Web pages, be sure to keep file size in mind. Many Web "surfers" access the Internet via 14.4k and 28.8k bps modems. Large graphics, movies, and sounds are time-consuming to download through modem connections. If your pages contain many large multimedia elements, you'll discourage visits from modem users—and even many impatient users with direct connections.

■ Multimedia elements can be used as simple page enhancements as well as links to other pages and form submission buttons. I tell you about links in **Chapter 7** and about forms in **Chapter 9**.

About Multimedia File Formats

PageMill directly supports the following types of multimedia:

- *Images* in GIF, Interlaced GIF, JPEG, Progressive JPEG, and Adobe Acrobat Portable Document File (PDF) formats.
- *Animations* in Animated GIF, Shockwave Director, and Java Applet formats.
- *Movies* in QuickTime, Windows AVI, and MPEG formats.
- *Sounds* in AU, Audio Interchange File Format (AIFF), and Windows WAVE formats.

✔ Tips

- GIF and JPEG are the standard image formats for the World Wide Web. GIF is an 8-bit (256 colors) format good for simple graphic images. JPEG is a 24-bit (16 million colors) format good for high quality graphics and photographic images.

- PageMill can also import PICT files, which it automatically converts to GIF file format.

- Animated GIF files contain multiple GIF images that, when displayed in sequence, make an animation. They offer a great way to include animation in your Web pages without inserting movie files, which tend to be large. You can create animated GIF files with shareware utilities like GIFBuilder and GraphicConverter.

- If you do not use the correct file extension when including multimedia objects in your Web pages, the objects will not display properly when viewed with a Web browser. A file *extension* is a series of characters at the end of a file name that is used by browsers and some operating systems to identify file format. **Table 1** lists the file formats PageMill supports and their extensions.

Format Name	Extension
GIF	.gif
Interlaced GIF	.gif
JPEG	.jpeg or .jpg
Progressive JPEG	.jpeg or .jpg
Acrobat PDF	.pdf
Animated GIF	.gif
Shockwave Director	.dcr
Java Applet	.class
QuickTime	.mov
AVI	.avi
MPEG	.mpeg or .mpg
AU	.au
AIFF	.aiff or aifc
WAVE	.wav

Table 1. *List of supported multimedia object formats with corresponding file name extensions.*

Plug-in & URL
Acrobat (and Reader)   http://www.adobe.com/acrobat/
Shockwave   http://www.macromedia.com/shockwave/
QuickTime   http://quicktime.apple.com/
Maczilla (for all movies)   http://maczilla.com/
Navigator Plug-ins   http://home.netscape.com/
Internet Explorer Plug-ins   http://www.microsoft.com/ie/

Table 2. *Here's a list of plug-in sources. The Netscape site is a great source for dozens of plug-ins that work with Navigator and Internet Explorer.*

Figure 3. *Open your browser's folder. The browser in this example is Netscape Navigator 3.0.*

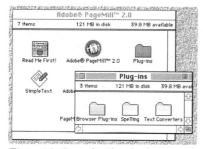

Figure 4. *Open the Plug-ins folder inside PageMill's folder.*

Figure 5.
After duplicating, moving, and renaming Netscape's Plug-ins folder, PageMill's Plug-ins folder looks like this.

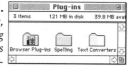

About Browser Plug-ins

In order to include certain types of multi-media objects in your PageMill documents, you must have the appropriate browser plug-in file installed. Multimedia objects that require plug-ins include Acrobat PDF files, Shockwave Director files, and movie files.

✔ Tip

- **Table 2** lists the plug-ins you might want to get, along with Web sites where you can find them.

To install browser plug-ins

1. If PageMill is running, choose Quit from the File menu to quit it.
2. Open your Web browser folder (see **Figure 3**).
3. Click the Plug-ins folder once to select it.
4. Choose Duplicate from the Finder's File menu or press ⌃⌘D.

   or

   Choose Make Alias from the Finder's File menu or press ⌃⌘M.
5. Open the Adobe® PageMill™ 2.0 folder.
6. Open the Plug-ins folder (see **Figure 4**).
7. Drag any existing Browser Plug-ins folder icon to the Trash and empty the trash.
8. Drag the duplicate or alias you created in step 4 from the Web browser's folder window to PageMill's Plug-in folder window.
9. Rename the duplicate or alias *Browser Plug-ins*.

When you're finished, PageMill's Plug-ins folder contents might look like **Figure 5**.

About Inserting Multimedia Objects

PageMill offers several ways to insert object files into PageMill Web documents:

- Use the Place command, Place Object button, or the corresponding shortcut key. This method will work with any type of multimedia object you want to insert in a PageMill Web document.

- Use the Copy and Paste commands. This method is handy when inserting objects from other windows.

- Drag it from another document window, the Pasteboard, or a Finder window. This method is also handy when inserting objects from other windows. In order for this method to work, however, the application in which the object resides must support Macintosh drag and drop.

✔ Tips

- Not all methods work with all types of multimedia objects. When in doubt, use the Place command since it recognizes all types of objects.

- When you insert an object into a PageMill document, PageMill automatically writes HTML code to indicate the image size. This can speed up the loading of the page when viewed with a Web browser.

- Before adding multimedia files to your Web page documents, *it is vital* that you properly set Resources preferences (see **Figure 6**). Neglecting this simple step can cause errors in the pathnames to object files written in the PageMill Web page document. I tell you about preferences in **Chapter 12**.

Figure 6. *By default, PageMill saves resources it creates to a folder it creates on your startup disk. You must properly set the Resource Folder path before adding objects to your pages. I tell you how in* **Chapter 12.**

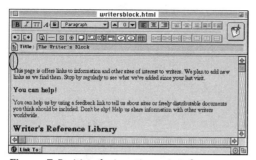

Figure 7. *Position the insertion point where you want the object to appear.*

Figure 8. *Choose Place from the File menu.*

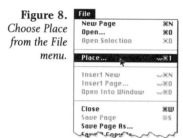

Figure 9. *Use a standard Open dialog box to locate and place an object.*

Figure 10. *Here's an example of a GIF file placed at the top of a Web page document.*

Figure 11. *You can use the Object Type pop-up menu to select the type of objects you want to appear in the Open dialog box.*

To place an object

1. Position the insertion point where you want the object to appear (see **Figure 7**).

2. Choose Place from the File menu (see **Figure 8**).

   or

   Click the Place Object button on the button bar.

   or

   Press [Control] [⌘] [1].

   A standard Open dialog box appears (see **Figure 9**).

3. Locate and select the file containing the object you want to insert.

4. Click the Place button.

The object in the file you selected appears in the PageMill window (see **Figure 10**).

✔ Tips

- Only the file formats recognized by PageMill will appear in the Open dialog box (see **Figure 9**).

- To narrow down the list of files that appear in the Open dialog box (see **Figure 9**), choose a specific file type from the Object Type pop-up menu (see **Figure 11**).

- If the file you insert is a PICT file, PageMill automatically converts it to GIF format and saves it in the folder you specified in Resources preferences (see **Figure 6**). Converted files have the name *Imagen.gif*, where n is a number.

Placing Objects

To insert an object that resides on another Web server

1. Position the insertion point where you want the object to appear (see **Figure 12**).

2. Choose Place from the File menu (see **Figure 8**).

   or

   Click the Place Object button on the button bar.

   or

   Press [Control][⌃][⌘][1].

   A standard Open dialog box appears (see **Figure 9**).

3. Turn on the Remote URL check box at the bottom of the dialog box.

4. Enter the complete URL for the object you want to insert in the Remote URL edit box (see **Figure 13**).

5. Click the Place button.

✔ Tips

■ The object you inserted appears as an icon in the PageMill document window (see **Figure 14**). If the URL was entered correctly, however, the actual object will appear when viewed with a Web browser.

■ By using a reference to an object on a remote server, it's possible to include objects in your Web pages without maintaining them on your own server. This can save disk space—especially when the objects are large.

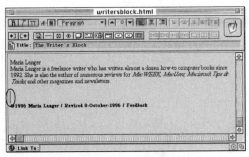

Figure 12. *Position the insertion point where you want the remote object to appear.*

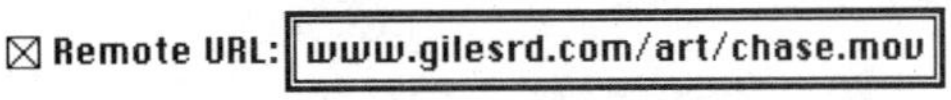

Figure 13. *Use the Remote URL edit box to enter the URL for an object on a remote server.*

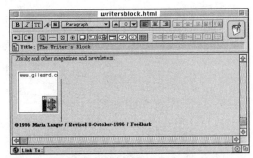

Figure 14. *Here's what the page looks like in PageMill's edit mode with a QuickTime movie on a remote server inserted.*

Figure 15. *Select the object you want to copy. In this example, a Photoshop graphic is selected.*

Figure 16.
Choose Copy from the Edit menu. Since the image is in Photoshop, the Copy command is on Photoshop's Edit menu.

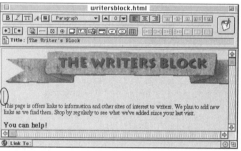

Figure 17. *Position the insertion point where you want the object to appear in the PageMill document.*

Figure 18.
Choose Paste from the Edit menu. Since the object is being pasted into PageMill, the Paste command is on PageMill's Edit menu.

To insert an object with the Copy & Paste commands

1. Open the document containing the object you want to use.

2. Select the object you want to copy (see **Figure 15**).

3. Choose Copy from the Edit menu (see **Figure 16**) or press ⌃⌘C to copy the object to the Clipboard.

4. Open or activate the PageMill document in which you want to insert the object.

5. Position the insertion point where you want the copied object to appear (see **Figure 17**).

6. Choose Paste from the Edit menu (see **Figure 18**) or press ⌃⌘V to paste a copy of the object on the Clipboard into the PageMill document (see **Figure 19**).

✔ Tips

- You can use this method to copy and paste objects between PageMill windows or, as the figures on this page illustrate, between PageMill and another application's windows.

- To select an object in another application's window, consult the documentation that came with that application. I tell you how to select objects in a PageMill window later in this chapter.

Figure 19. *The image appears at the insertion point.*

To insert an object by dragging

1. Open the document containing the object you want to use.

2. Open the PageMill document in which you plan to use the object.

3. Arrange the two document windows so that you can see both of their contents (see **Figure 20**).

4. Activate the window containing the object you want to use.

5. Select the object you want to copy (see **Figure 21**).

6. Position the mouse pointer within the selected image. (If the image has selection handles, don't position the mouse pointer on one of them.)

7. Press the mouse button down and drag the object from its window to the PageMill document window. As you drag, a dotted line box the same size as the object moves along with the mouse pointer. A blinking insertion point indicates where the object will go when you release the mouse button. You can see all this in **Figure 22**.

8. When the blinking insertion point is in the proper position, release the mouse button. The object is copied from its source window to the PageMill document window (see **Figure 23**).

✔ Tips

■ For this to work, the application in which the object resides must support drag and drop editing.

■ You can use this method to drag and drop objects between PageMill windows or, as the figures on this page illustrate, between PageMill and another application's windows.

■ You can also use this method to drag object icons from Finder windows to PageMill document windows.

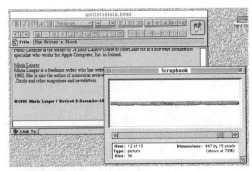

Figure 20. *Arrange the windows so you can see the contents of both of them.*

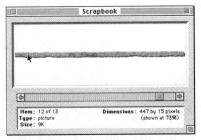

Figure 21. *Select the object you want to copy. Since the object in this example is in the Scrapbook, displaying it selects it.*

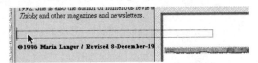

Figure 22. *As you drag, the object's outline appears at the mouse pointer and insertion point.*

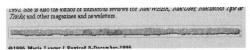

Figure 23. *When you release the mouse button, the object appears in the document.*

Figure 24. *Choose Show Pasteboard from the Window menu.*

To copy an object to the Pasteboard

1. If the Pasteboard is not showing, choose Show Pasteboard from the Window menu (see **Figure 24**) or press ⌃⌘/.

2. Use the drag and drop techniques discussed on the previous page to drag an object from a PageMill document window to the Pasteboard window.

3. When a selection border appears around the inside of the Pasteboard window (see **Figure 25**), release the mouse button.

A copy of the object is placed on the Pasteboard (see **Figure 26**).

✔ Tips

■ Although the Pasteboard has only five pages, you can copy more than one item to each page (see **Figure 27**).

■ I tell you more about working with the Pasteboard in **Chapters 1** and **2**.

Figure 25. *The object outline moves with the mouse pointer to the Pasteboard as you drag it.*

Figure 26. *When you release the mouse button, the object appears on the Pasteboard.*

To insert an object from the Pasteboard

1. Position the mouse pointer on the Pasteboard item you want to use (see **Figure 27**).

2. Use the drag and drop techniques discussed on the previous page to move (just drag) or copy (hold down Option while dragging) the item from the Pasteboard into position in a PageMill document.

✔ Tip

■ Dragging an item off the Pasteboard is the only way to remove it from the Pasteboard.

Figure 27. *You can place as many items as you like on each Pasteboard page. When using an item, be sure to position the mouse pointer right on it.*

About the Missing-Image Icon

If PageMill cannot locate the file for an object on a page, it displays a missing-image icon (see **Figure 28**). This can occur if you rename, move, or delete an image referred to by a PageMill document.

✔ Tips

■ One way to avoid seeing missing-image icons is to make sure all objects you insert in a PageMill document are within the Resources folder you specified in the Preferences dialog box (see **Figure 6**). I tell you about setting preferences in **Chapter 12**.

■ If you insert an image that resides on another server (as discussed earlier in this chapter), a missing-image icon will appear instead of the image when the page is viewed within PageMill. If the image does not appear when you test the page, you'll need to resolve the missing object problem before you can publish the page. I tell you about testing in **Chapter 11**.

■ Similar icons appear for missing objects. **Figure 14** shows an example of a missing object icon for a QuickTime movie.

To find a missing object

1. Double-click the missing-image icon.
2. Use the Open dialog box that appears (see **Figure 9**) to locate and select the image that's missing.
3. Click the Place button to reinsert the image in the document.

To delete a missing-image icon

1. Click the missing-image icon once to select the image placeholder.
2. Press (Delete) to remove the icon and its placeholder.

Figure 28. *The missing-image icon appears in a box the same size as the missing image. The pathname to the missing image also appears.*

Figure 29.
When you select an image, a selection box and handles appear around it.

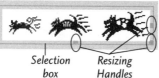

Selection box   Resizing Handles

About Selecting Objects

To modify, copy, move, or delete an object in a PageMill document, you need to begin by selecting it.

To select an object

Click once on the object you want to select.

A selection box appears around the object and three resizing handles appear (see **Figure 29**).

✔ Tip

■ You can only select one object at a time.

To deselect an object

Click inside the document window anywhere other than on the selected object.

The selection box and handles disappear.

Selecting & Deselecting Objects

About Copying, Moving, & Deleting Objects

Like text, once an object is in a PageMill document, it can be moved or copied a number of different ways:

■ The Copy and Paste commands let you copy an object from one place and paste it in another.

■ The Cut and Paste commands let you cut an object from one place and paste it in another, thus moving the original object.

■ Drag and drop editing lets you move or copy a selected object simply by dragging it.

■ The Pasteboard lets you store objects that you can drag into a document window.

I discuss the first three techniques for text in **Chapter 2**. They work the same way for objects. I discuss using the Pasteboard for objects earlier in this chapter.

To delete an object

1. Select the object you want to delete.

2. Press [Delete].

   or

   Choose Clear from the Edit menu (see **Figure 30**).

The object disappears.

✔ Tip

■ When you delete an object, its file remains on disk, even if it is an image file that was saved into the Resources folder by PageMill. I tell you about the Resources folder earlier in this chapter and in **Chapter 12**.

Figure 30.
Choosing Clear from the Edit menu deletes whatever is selected, including objects.

Figure 31. *This example shows how the Find dialog box can be used to replace one image with another throughout a document.*

About Finding & Replacing Objects

PageMill's find and replace features can be used to locate and/or change objects throughout a Web page document. You use the Find dialog box (see **Figure 31**) to specify your find and, if applicable, replacement objects. Then use buttons within the Find dialog box or on the Search menu to locate and/or replace objects as specified.

I discuss the find and replace features in detail in **Chapter 2**. They work the same way for objects, with the following exceptions:

■ To enter a search object in the Find or Replace With scrolling windows (see **Figure 31**):

▲ Use the Copy and Paste commands to copy the image to the Clipboard and then paste it into the appropriate scrolling window.

▲ Drag the object from a document window into the appropriate scrolling window.

■ To find only those objects that match the size of the object in the Find scrolling window, turn on the Object Size check box in the lower right corner of the Find window (see **Figure 31**).

✔ Tips

■ I provide step-by-step instructions for using the find and replace features in **Chapter 2**.

■ To delete an object throughout a document, leave the Replace With scrolling window empty. Then replace every occurrence of the object with nothing, thus deleting it.

About Resizing Objects

Once an object has been inserted in a PageMill document, it can be resized as needed by either dragging its resizing handles or using the Inspector.

✔ Tip

■ Although you can make an object larger or smaller, you may find that images lose their clarity when enlarged.

To resize an object by dragging

1. Select the object you want to resize.

2. Position the mouse pointer over one of its resizing handles (see **Figure 32**):

   ▲ To change its width, position the mouse pointer over the handle on the right side of the object.

   ▲ To change its height, position the mouse pointer over the handle on the bottom of the object.

   ▲ To change its width and height, position the mouse pointer over the handle in the bottom right corner of the object.

3. Press the mouse button down and drag. As you drag, an outline indicates the size of the object when you release the mouse button (see **Figure 33**).

4. Release the mouse button. The object resizes (see **Figure 34**).

✔ Tip

■ To change both the width and height of an object without changing its proportions, press (Shift) and hold it down while you press down the mouse button and drag the bottom right handle as instructed above. Release the mouse button first, then release (Shift).

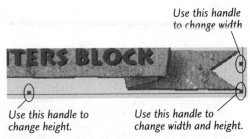

Use this handle to change width

Use this handle to change height.

Use this handle to change width and height.

Figure 32. *Choose a resizing handle based on the way you want to resize the object.*

Figure 33. *As you drag, an outline indicates the final size of the object.*

Figure 34. *When you release the mouse button, the object resizes.*

Figure 35.
If the Inspector is not already showing, choose Show Inspector from the Window menu.

To resize an object with the Inspector

1. If the Inspector is not displayed, choose Show Inspector from the Window menu (see **Figure 35**) or press ⌃⌘;.

2. In the page document window, select the object you want to resize.

3. If necessary, click the Object tab to display the Inspector's Object panel (see **Figure 36**).

4. To change the width or height to an exact pixel measurement or percentage of the window's size, make sure the Scale to Height and Scale to Width check boxes are turned off. Then choose Pixels or Percent from the Width and Height pop-up menus (see **Figure 37**) and enter values in the Width and Height edit boxes.

   or

   To resize an object proportionally, turn on either the Scale to Height or Scale to Width check box. Then choose Pixels or Percent from the opposite pop-up menu (see **Figure 37**) and enter a value in the edit box near it (see **Figure 38**).

5. Press Return or Enter to accept your settings.

Figure 36.
With an object selected, click the Object tab to display the Object panel's options.

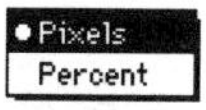

Figure 37.
You can resize an object based on a pixel measurement or percent of the original image.

✔ Tips

■ To reset an object to its original size, turn on both the Scale to Height and Scale to Width check boxes in the Object panel of the Inspector (see **Figure 36**).

■ Make sure the Behavior radio button is set to Picture unless the object will be used as a button or an image map. I tell you about buttons in **Chapter 9** and about image maps in **Chapter 7**.

Figure 38.
This example shows how an object can be resized proportionally by turning on only the Scale to Width check box and entering a new value in the Width edit box.

Resizing an Object with the Inspector

About Object Alignment

Objects can be aligned two ways:

■ Align an object vertically to adjust its position in relation to the top or baseline of the text around it. This is effective when the image is in the same line as text (see **Figures 39**, **40**, and **41**).

■ Align an object horizontally to adjust its position in relation to the edges of the Web page. This is effective when wrapping text around an object (see **Figures 43** and **44**).

✔ Tip

■ By default, object alignment is set to bottom aligned.

To align an object vertically

1. Select the object you want to align (see **Figure 39**).

2. Click the appropriate vertical object alignment button on the button bar:

   ▲ Click the Top Align Object button to align the top of the object with the top of the text (see **Figure 40**).

   ▲ Click the Middle Align Object button to align the middle of the object with the middle of the text (see **Figure 41**).

   ▲ Click the Bottom Align Object button to align the bottom of the object with the baseline of the text (see **Figure 39**).

   or

   Press the shortcut keys to shift the alignment up or down:

   ▲ To shift alignment up, press Control ⌃ ⌘ ↑.

   ▲ To shift alignment down, press Control ⌃ ⌘ ↓.

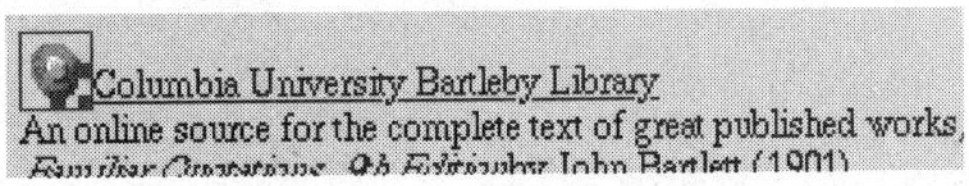

Figure 39. *Begin by selecting the object you want to align. By default, objects are bottom aligned as shown here.*

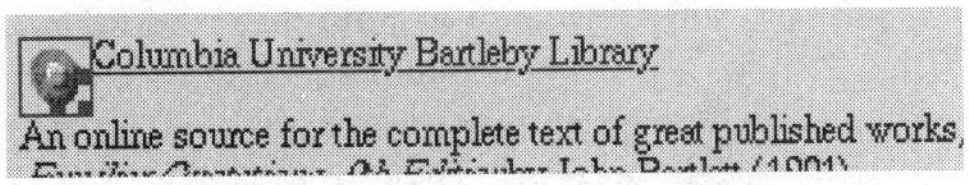

Figure 40. *Click the Top Align Object button to align the top of the object with the top of the text.*

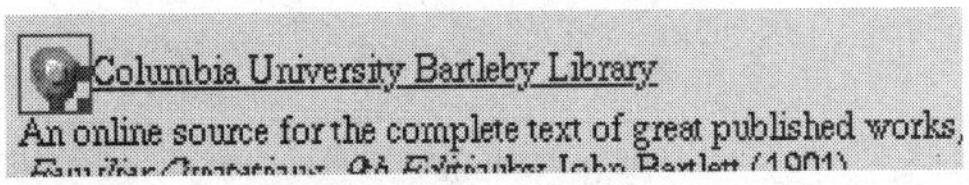

Figure 41. *Click the Middle Align Object button to align the middle of the object with the middle of the text.*

Aligning Objects Vertically

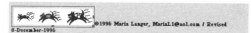

Figure 42. *Select the object you want to align.*

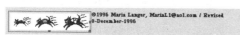

Figure 43. *Click the Left Align Object button to shift the object to the left side of the page.*

Figure 44. *Click the Right Align Object button to shift the object to the right side of the page.*

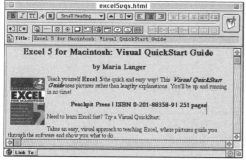

Figure 45. *To stop word wrap, begin by positioning the insertion point where you want word wrap to end.*

Figure 46. *Choose Margin Break from the Insert Invisible submenu under the Edit menu.*

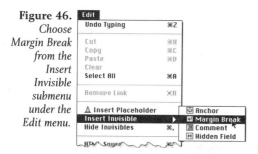

Figure 47. *Word wrap ends at the margin break.*

To align an object horizontally

1. Select the object you want to align (see **Figure 42**).

2. Click the appropriate horizontal object alignment button on the button bar:

   ▲ Click the Left Align Object button to shift the object to the left and wrap the text beside the object around the object's right side (see **Figure 43**).

   ▲ Click the Right Align Object button to shift the object to the right and wrap the text beside the object around the object's left side (see **Figure 44**).

   or

   Press the shortcut keys to shift the alignment left or right:

   ▲ To shift alignment to the left, press [Control] [⌃ ⌘] [↑].

   ▲ To shift alignment to the right, press [Control] [⌃ ⌘] [↓].

To end word wrap around a horizontally aligned object

1. Position the insertion point where you want the word wrap to end (see **Figure 45**).

2. Choose Margin Break from the Insert Invisible submenu under the Edit menu (see **Figure 46**).

A margin break character is inserted and the word wrap ends (see **Figure 47**).

✔ Tip

■ A margin break character can be deleted like any other character or object—by selecting it and pressing [Delete].

About the Image Window

The Image window (see **Figure 50**) gives you access to several image-related features:

- Make a certain color within the image transparent so the background shows through it.

- Create an image map so that clicking "hot spots" in the image displays another page. I tell you more about image maps in **Chapter 7**.

- Save an image as an interlaced GIF, which loads into a Web browser quickly as a blurred image, then progressively clears. This is especially useful for large images that could take more than a few seconds to load.

To open an image in the Image window

Click once on the image you want to open to select it, then choose Open Selection from the File menu (see **Figure 48**) or press ⌘D.

or

Hold down ⌘ while double-clicking the image you want to open.

or

Choose Open from the File menu (see **Figure 48**) or press ⌘O. Use the Open dialog box that appears (see **Figure 49**) to locate and open the image you want.

The image opens in an Image window (see **Figure 50**).

✔ Tip

- The image you want to open must be visible in a PageMill document window before you can open it in an Image window using one of the first two techniques above.

Figure 48.
Use the Open Selection or Open command to open an image in the Image window.

Figure 49. *Use the Open dialog box to locate and open an image file on disk.*

Figure 50.
The Image window contains tools you can use to work with images.

Opening an Image in the Image Window

Mouse pointer

Figure 51.
*When you click
the Transparency
tool, the mouse
pointer turns into
a transparency
tool icon.*

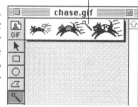

Figure 52.
*Click the background
color to make it
transparent.*

Figure 53.
*Choose Save
Image from the
File menu to save
your changes to
the image.*

Figure 54. *This example shows two images with
their backgrounds colors (white) turned transparent.
Set against a background pattern, the images have a
polished look.*

To make an image color transparent

1. In the Image window, click the Transparency tool. The mouse pointer, when moved atop the image, changes to the Transparency tool icon (see **Figure 51**).

2. Click any color you want to make transparent. The image changes so you can see the Image window background through the color you made transparent (see **Figure 52**).

3. Choose Save Image from the File menu (see **Figure 53**) or press ⌘⌥⑤.

✔ Tips

■ The Transparency tool is available only for GIF format images.

■ Only one color can be transparent.

■ When you make a color transparent, that information is saved with the image file so it is transparent no matter what page it is used in.

■ To restore the transparent color, use the Transparency tool to click the transparent area. The color returns.

■ Use the Transparency tool to make the background color of an image transparent. This greatly improves the appearance of an image with a large background (see **Figure 54**).

■ Anti-aliased images do not work well with the transparency feature. For best results, turn the anti-alias feature in your graphic application off when creating or editing Web page images.

■ Combine transparent image backgrounds with page backgrounds to give your pages professional polish. I tell you about page backgrounds in **Chapter 10**.

Making an Image Color Transparent

To create an interlaced GIF

1. In the Image window, click the Interlace Toggle switch.

2. Choose Save Image from the File menu (see **Figure 53**).

✔ Tips

■ The Interlace Toggle switch appears only for GIF format images.

■ If you look closely, you'll see that horizontal lines appear across the icon for the Interlace Toggle switch to indicate that the image will be saved as an interlaced GIF.

■ To change an interlaced GIF back to a regular GIF, click the Interlace Toggle switch to remove the horizontal lines from the image on its icon.

■ Interlaced GIFs are good for large images that could take more than a few seconds to load. The entire GIF loads as a blurred image that progressively clears until it is completed loaded.

To close the Image window

Choose Close from the File menu (see **Figure 55**).

or

Press ⌘⌘W.

or

Click the Image window's close box.

✔ Tip

■ If you don't save changes before closing the Image window, a dialog box like the one in **Figure 56** will appear. Click Save or press Return or Enter to save changes before closing the window.

Figure 55.
Choose Close from the File menu to close the Image window when it is the active window.

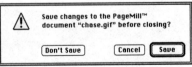

Figure 56. *If you close an Image window before saving changes, a dialog box like this appears.*

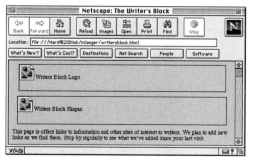

Figure 57. *Alternate text is used to identify images when the images themselves aren't visible in the browser window. This example shows a page viewed with Netscape with its Auto Load Images option turned off.*

Figure 58. *Here's an example of an image with a border around it.*

Figure 59. *Type the text you want to appear in the Alternate Label edit box.*

About Other Object Options

Using the Inspector, you can change other image options:

■ Specify alternate text that will appear when the page is viewed with a text browser or with automatic image loading turned off (see **Figure 57**).

■ Add a border to an image (see **Figure 58**).

To specify alternate text

1. If the Inspector is not displayed, choose Show Inspector from the Window menu (see **Figure 35**) or press ⌃⌘;.

2. In the document window, select the object for which you want to specify alternate text.

3. If necessary, click the Object tab in the Inspector to display the Object options (see **Figure 36**).

4. Click in the Alternate Label edit box to activate it and enter the text you want to appear (see **Figure 59**).

5. Press Return or Enter to complete the entry.

✔ Tips

■ To remove alternate text, follow steps 1 through 3 above. Then clear the contents of the Alternate Label edit box and press Return or Enter to accept the change.

■ Many Web surfers turn off the automatic loading of images simply to speed page loading. You can use the alternate text feature to let these people know what they're missing when they visit your pages.

Specifying Alternate Text

To add an object border

1. If the Inspector is not displayed, choose Show Inspector from the Window menu (see **Figure 35**) or press ⌘;.

2. In the document window, select the object to which you want to add a border.

3. If necessary, click the Object tab in the Inspector to display the Object options (see **Figure 36**).

4. Click in the Border edit box to activate it and enter the number of pixels for the thickness of the border (see **Figure 60**).

5. Press Return or Enter to complete the entry.

Figure 58 shows an image with a border around it.

To remove an object border

1. If the Inspector is not displayed, choose Show Inspector from the Window menu (see **Figure 35**) or press ⌘;.

2. In the document window, select the object from which you want to remove a border.

3. If necessary, click the Object tab in the Inspector to display the Object options (see **Figure 36**).

4. Click in the Border edit box to activate it. Then:

   ▲ Select and delete the edit box contents.

   or

   ▲ Enter 0 (zero).

5. Press Return or Enter to complete the entry.

Figure 60. *Enter the number of pixels for the thickness of the border you want to add to the object.*

✔ Tip

■ If you enter 0 in the Border edit box for an object that is used as a link, its blue border disappears. I tell you about links in **Chapter 7**.

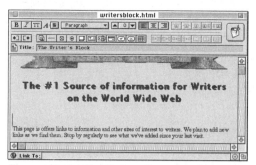

Figure 61. *Position the insertion point where you want the horizontal rule to appear.*

Figure 62. *When you click the Insert Horizontal Rule button, a line appears at the insertion point.*

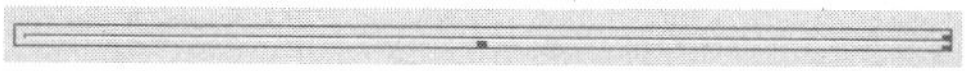

Figure 63. *When you select a horizontal rule, you'll see the same selection box and resizing handles that appear when you select any other object.*

About Horizontal Rules

A *horizontal rule* is a graphic element that is created with HTML tags. Its HTML code is interpreted by the Web browser and displayed as a horizontal line. No special graphic file is required.

✔ Tips

■ A horizontal rule is an excellent graphic tool because it loads just as quickly as text and does not require additional files to display.

■ You can use the text alignment buttons to left align, center, or right align a horizontal rule.

To add a horizontal rule

1. Position the insertion point where you want the horizontal rule to appear (see **Figure 61**).

2. Click the Insert Horizontal Rule button on the button bar.

   or

   Press Control ⌘ 2.

   The horizontal rule appears (see **Figure 62**).

To remove a horizontal rule

1. Click the horizontal rule to select it. A selection box and resizing handles appear (see **Figure 63**).

   or

   Position the insertion point immediately to the right of the horizontal rule (see **Figure 62**).

2. Press Delete.

   The horizontal rule disappears.

To format a horizontal rule by dragging

1. Click the horizontal rule to select it. A selection box and resizing handles appear (see **Figure 63**).

2. Drag a resizing handle to change the length (see **Figure 64**) or thickness or both of the horizontal rule. When you release the mouse button, the size changes (see **Figure 65**).

✔ Tip

■ You cannot make a horizontal rule's length exceed the page width if you resize it by dragging a resizing handle.

To format a horizontal rule with the Inspector

1. If the Inspector is not displayed, choose Show Inspector from the Window menu (see **Figure 35**) or press ⌘;.

2. In the document window, click the horizontal rule to select it. A selection box and resizing handles appear (see **Figure 63**).

3. If necessary, click the Object tab in the Inspector to display the Object options for a horizontal rule (see **Figure 66**).

4. To change the width of the line, choose Pixels or Percent from the Width pop-up menu (see **Figure 37**). Then enter a width value in the Width edit box.

5. Enter a thickness, in pixels, in the Size edit box.

6. Press Return or Enter to complete the entries.

Figure 67 shows an example of a 10-pixel thick, 60% wide horizontal rule.

Figure 64. *One way to resize a horizontal rule is to drag one of its resizing handles.*

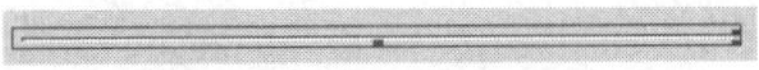

Figure 65. *When you release the mouse button, the rule's size changes.*

Figure 66.
The Inspector's Object panel offers additional control over the size and appearance of a selected horizontal rule.

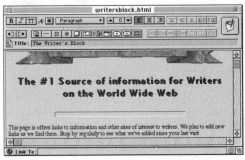

Figure 67. *Here's a short, thick horizontal rule centered with the Center Align Text button.*

Figure 68. *Turn on the No Shade check box to change the default horizontal rule into a black line.*

✔ Tip

■ You can turn on the No Shade check box in the Inspector to remove the three-dimensional shadow effect from a horizontal rule. **Figure 68** shows the horizontal rule from **Figure 67** with the No Shade check box turned on.

Figure 1. *A basic table like this one can present information in a spreadsheet-like format.*

Figure 2. *Tables can also be used to recreate familiar objects, like this calendar.*

About HTML Tables

HTML tables offer unsurpassed control over the positioning of text and objects on the Web pages you create. You can create tables comprised of columns and rows and fill in the intersecting cells with text and graphic elements for a wide range of effects:

- ■ Create simple tables to present data in a spreadsheet-like format (see **Figure 1**).

- ■ Create more complex tables to reproduce information in familiar formats (see **Figure 2**).

- ■ Use tables to lay out page components much as you would with a page layout application (see **Figure 3**).

While creating tables by typing raw HTML commands is tedious, time-consuming, and difficult, creating tables—even complex nested tables—is easy with PageMill. This chapter will show you how.

✔ Tip

- ■ Although most graphic Web browsers recognize and properly interpret the HTML codes for tables, some don't. In addition, no text browser displays table information properly. Keep this in mind when determining how to present information that may be viewed with a variety of browsers. You may prefer using the Preformatted format, which I discuss in **Chapter 4**.

Figure 3. *With a little imagination—and some borderless nested tables like these—you can lay out page components any way you like.*

About Creating Tables

PageMill offers three ways to create tables:

- Use the Insert Table button on the button bar (see **Figure 4**) to insert a table with the number of columns and rows desired.

- Use the Create Table dialog box (see **Figure 5**) to insert a table with the size and some of the formatting options desired.

- Paste in worksheet cells from a Microsoft Excel document (see **Figure 8**) to insert a table with the number of columns and rows and all the table data desired.

✔ Tips

- If you accidentally create a table with the wrong dimensions, use the Undo command to remove the table and then try again.

- You can always add or remove columns or rows to a table after it has been created. I tell you how later in this chapter.

- By default, all columns in a table are the same width. I tell you how to change column width later in this chapter.

- You can insert a table within a table. Simply position the insertion point within a table cell before inserting a table.

Figure 4.
As you drag away from the Insert Table button, a menu grows.

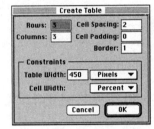

Figure 5.
When you create a table with the Create Table dialog box, you can set more than just the table's size.

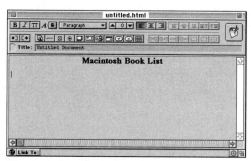

Figure 6. *Begin by positioning the insertion point where you want the table to appear.*

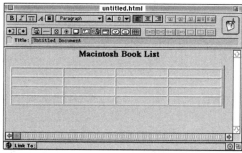

Figure 7. *The table appears at the insertion point.*

To insert a table with the Insert Table button

1. Position the insertion point where you want the table to appear (see **Figure 6**).

2. Position your mouse pointer on the Insert Table button, press the mouse button down, and drag down and to the right. A menu pops up and expands as you drag (see **Figure 4**).

3. When the desired number of columns and rows is indicated by the Insert Table pop-up menu, release the mouse button.

The table appears (see **Figure 7**).

To insert a table with the Create Table dialog box

1. Position the insertion point where you want the table to appear (see **Figure 6**).

2. Click the Insert Table button on the button bar to display the Create Table dialog box (see **Figure 5**).

3. Enter the number of rows and columns desired in the Rows and Columns edit boxes.

4. Enter values for the table formatting options in the appropriate edit boxes.

5. Click OK or press Return or Enter to accept your settings and create the table.

✔ Tip

■ I tell you about table formatting options like those in the Create Table dialog box (see **Figure 5**) later in this chapter.

Inserting a Table

85

To insert Excel worksheet cells as a table

1. In an Excel worksheet document, select the cells you want to turn into a PageMill table (see **Figure 8**).

2. Choose Copy from Excel's Edit menu (see **Figure 9**) or press ⌘C.

3. Switch to or open the PageMill document in which you want to paste the Excel cells.

4. Position the insertion point where you want the table to appear.

5. Choose Paste from PageMill's Edit menu (see **Figure 10**) or press ⌘V.

The table appears (see **Figure 11**).

✔ Tips

■ If you often use Excel to calculate or store information that may be used in Web pages, this is, by far, the easiest way to include that information in PageMill documents.

■ Cell formatting is not carried forward from the Excel document to the PageMill document. This could be a problem if the Excel worksheet includes numbers formatted as dates—they will appear as numbers rather than dates in PageMill. Check the resulting PageMill table carefully and make changes as necessary to cell contents.

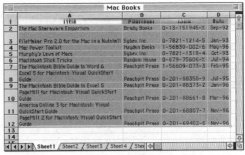

Figure 8. *In an Excel worksheet, select the cells you want to use in a PageMill document.*

Figure 9. *Choose Copy from Excel's Edit menu to copy the selected cells to the Clipboard.*

Figure 10. *Choose Paste from PageMill's Edit menu to paste the copied cells to the PageMill document.*

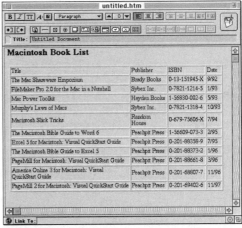

Figure 11. *The Excel cells appear as a PageMill table at the insertion point.*

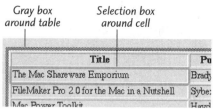

Gray box around table — Selection box around cell

Figure 12. *To select a single cell, click in the cell, then drag to the cell's border.*

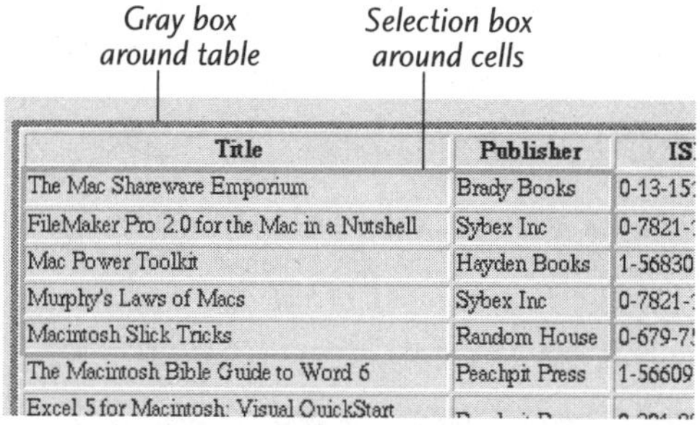

Gray box around table — Selection box around cells

Title	Publisher	IS:
The Mac Shareware Emporium	Brady Books	0-13-15:
FileMaker Pro 2.0 for the Mac in a Nutshell	Sybex Inc	0-7821-:
Mac Power Toolkit	Hayden Books	1-56830
Murphy's Laws of Macs	Sybex Inc	0-7821-:
Macintosh Slick Tricks	Random House	0-679-7:
The Macintosh Bible Guide to Word 6	Peachpit Press	1-56609
Excel 5 for Macintosh: Visual QuickStart		

Figure 13. *To select multiple cells, click in the first cell, then drag to the border of the last cell.*

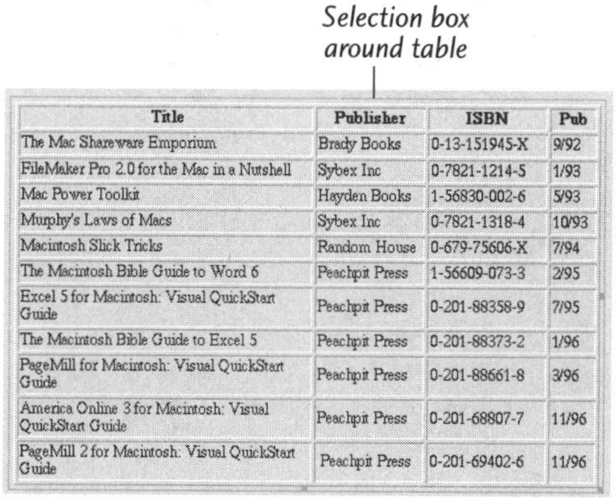

Selection box around table

Title	Publisher	ISBN	Pub
The Mac Shareware Emporium	Brady Books	0-13-151945-X	9/92
FileMaker Pro 2.0 for the Mac in a Nutshell	Sybex Inc	0-7821-1214-5	1/93
Mac Power Toolkit	Hayden Books	1-56830-002-6	5/93
Murphy's Laws of Macs	Sybex Inc	0-7821-1318-4	10/93
Macintosh Slick Tricks	Random House	0-679-75606-X	7/94
The Macintosh Bible Guide to Word 6	Peachpit Press	1-56609-073-3	2/95
Excel 5 for Macintosh: Visual QuickStart Guide	Peachpit Press	0-201-88358-9	7/95
The Macintosh Bible Guide to Excel 5	Peachpit Press	0-201-88373-2	1/96
PageMill for Macintosh: Visual QuickStart Guide	Peachpit Press	0-201-88661-8	3/96
America Online 3 for Macintosh: Visual QuickStart Guide	Peachpit Press	0-201-68807-7	11/96
PageMill 2 for Macintosh: Visual QuickStart Guide	Peachpit Press	0-201-69402-6	11/96

Figure 14. *To select an entire table, click once in the table to display its gray border, then click on the gray border.*

✔ Tips

- When one or more cells is selected, clicking any other cell selects that cell.

- When selecting cells, be careful not to drag a selection. If you accidentally drag cells to a new position, use the Undo command to replace them.

About Selecting Cells & Tables

To make changes to the structure or formatting of a table or its cells, you must first select the table or cells you want to change.

To select a cell

1. Click once within the cell to position the insertion point inside it. A thick gray box appears around the entire table.

2. Press the mouse button down and drag to the border of the cell. A selection border appears around the cell (see **Figure 12**).

To select multiple cells

1. Click once within the top left cell in the intended selection to position the insertion point inside it. A thick gray box appears around the entire table.

2. Press the mouse button down and drag to the border of the bottom right cell in the intended selection. A selection border appears around the cells (see **Figure 13**).

To select an entire table

1. Click once anywhere within a table cell. A thick gray box appears around the entire table.

2. Click once on the gray box around the table. A selection box, complete with resizing handles, appears around the table (see **Figure 14**).

To deselect a table or cell(s)

Click anywhere outside the table. The selection box disappears.

Selecting Cells & Tables

About Entering Information into Cells

You can enter text or objects into table cells by typing, pasting, dragging, or placing it in.

✔ Tips

- Each table cell works like a word processing document that expands vertically to accept what's entered into it.

- You can use standard text editing techniques to edit the contents of a cell. I tell you about editing text in **Chapter 2**.

- By default, each table cell contains a non-breaking space character. Deleting this character in an empty cell changes the appearance of the cell (see **Figures 15** and **16**).

To type text into a cell

1. Click inside the cell to position the insertion point there (see **Figure 17**).

2. Type the text you want to appear in the cell (see **Figure 18**).

✔ Tips

- A cell's width may change depending on the length of the text you type and the contents of other cells (see **Figure 19**). I tell you how to change column width manually later in this chapter.

- To begin a new line within a cell, press ⟨Shift⟩⟨Return⟩. To begin a new paragraph within a cell, press ⟨Return⟩.

- Press ⟨Tab⟩ or ⟨Shift⟩⟨Tab⟩ to select the contents of the next or previous cell in the table. Or hold down ⟨Control⟩ and press ⟨←⟩, ⟨↑⟩, ⟨→⟩, or ⟨↓⟩ to select an adjacent cell in a specific direction. This makes it possible to fill in table cells without using the mouse to click in each cell.

Figure 15. *By default, each table cell has a single space character in it. This gives the appearance of empty cells.*

Figure 16. *As you can see by looking at the first cell in this table, removing all of a cell's contents changes the appearance of the cell.*

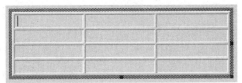

Figure 17. *To type information into a cell, begin by positioning the insertion point inside it.*

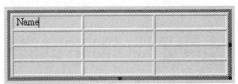

Figure 18. *Then type in the information you want to appear.*

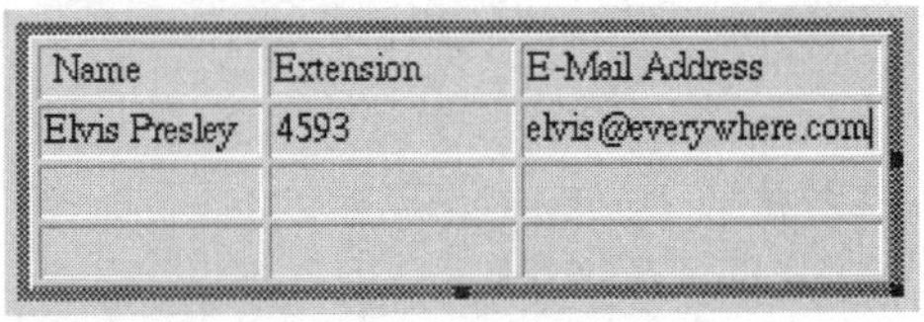

Name	Extension	E-Mail Address
Elvis Presley	4593	elvis@everywhere.com

Figure 19. *If the information you enter is lengthy, the width of columns in your table may change.*

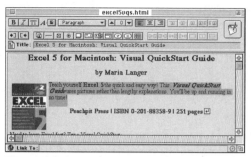

Figure 20. *To paste text into a cell, begin by selecting the text.*

Figure 21. *Choose Copy from the Edit menu to copy the selected text to the Clipboard.*

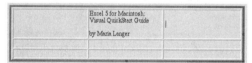

Figure 22. *Position the insertion point in the cell in which you want to paste the text.*

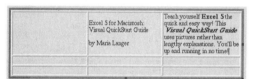

Figure 23. *When you use the Paste command, the text appears in the cell.*

Figure 24. *You can also drag selected objects or text into table cells.*

Figure 25. *When you release the mouse button, the object or text appears in the cell.*

To paste information into a cell

1. Select the information you want to paste into the cell (see **Figure 20**).

2. Choose Copy from the Edit menu (see **Figure 21**) or press ⌘C to copy the information to the Clipboard.

3. Click in the cell in which you want to paste the information to position the insertion point there (see **Figure 22**).

4. Choose Paste from the Edit menu (see **Figure 10**) to paste in the contents of the Clipboard (see **Figure 23**).

✔ Tip

■ This technique works with text (as illustrated here), objects, or form elements. I tell you more about working with multimedia objects in **Chapter 5** and about form elements in **Chapter 9**.

To drag information into a cell

1. Select the information you want to drag into the cell.

2. Position your mouse pointer on the selection, press the mouse button down, and drag toward the destination cell.

3. When a selection box appears inside the destination cell (see **Figure 24**), release the mouse button. The selection appears in the cell (see **Figure 25**).

✔ Tip

■ This technique works with text, objects (as illustrated here), or form elements. I tell you more about working with text in **Chapter 2** and about form elements in **Chapter 9**.

Pasting & Dragging Information into Cells

About Modifying Table Structure

You can modify a table's structure a variety of ways:

- Insert or delete columns or rows.
- Join or split cells.
- Place a table within a table cell to create a *nested table*.
- Delete a table.

✔ Tip

- You can modify a table's structure before or after you have entered information into its cells.

To insert a column

1. Select the column to the left of where you want the new column to go (see **Figure 26**).

   or

   Select a cell in the column to the left of where you want the new column to go.

2. Click the Insert Column button on the button bar.

A new column appears to the right of the selected column or cell (see **Figure 27**).

✔ Tips

- If you select more than one column in step 1 above, clicking the Insert Column button will insert the same number of columns you have selected.

- When you insert a column, the other columns resize and shift to the left to make room for it, depending on how table and cell size options are set.

- Once you insert a new column, you can change its width to make room for information you want to enter into it.

- I tell you how to change table and column width later in this chapter.

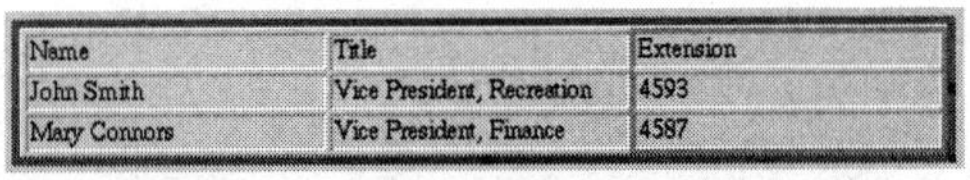

Name	Title	Extension
John Smith	Vice President, Recreation	4593
Mary Connors	Vice President, Finance	4587

Figure 26. *To insert a column, begin by selecting the column or a cell in the column to the left of where you want the new column to go. In this example, the last column is selected.*

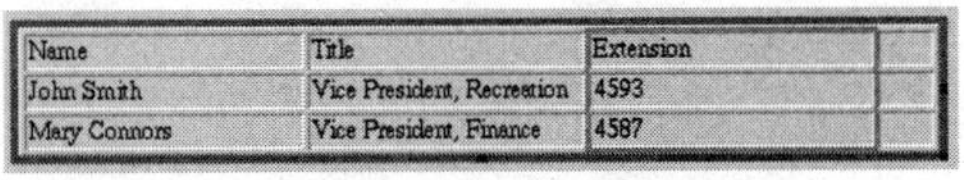

Name	Title	Extension	
John Smith	Vice President, Recreation	4593	
Mary Connors	Vice President, Finance	4587	

Figure 27. *When you click the Insert Column button, a new column appears to the right of the selected column or cell.*

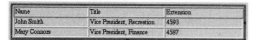

Figure 28. *To insert a row, begin by selecting the row or a cell in the row above where you want the new row to go. In this example, the first row is selected.*

Name	Title	Extension
John Smith	Vice President, Recreation	4593
Mary Connors	Vice President, Finance	4587

Figure 29. *The new row is inserted below the selected row or cell.*

To insert a row

1. Select the row above where you want the new row to go (see **Figure 28**).

   or

   Select a cell in the row above where you want the new row to go.

2. Click the Insert Row button on the button bar.

A new row appears beneath the selected row or cell (see **Figure 29**).

✔ Tips

■ If you select more than one row in step 1 above, clicking the Insert Row button will insert the same number of rows you have selected.

■ When you insert a row, the rows beneath it shift down and the table resizes to make room for it.

To delete columns or rows

1. Select the column or a cell in the column you want to delete.

   or

   Select a row or a cell in the row you want to delete.

2. Click the Delete Column button on the button bar.

   or

   Click the Delete Row button on the button bar.

The selected column or row is deleted.

✔ Tips

■ When you delete a column or row, the column or row's contents are also deleted.

■ You cannot use this method to delete all the columns or rows in a table.

Inserting Rows, Deleting Columns & Rows

To join cells

1. Select two or more cells in the same column or row (see **Figures 30** and **31**).

2. Click the Join Cells button on the button bar.

The cells are joined to form one large cell (see **Figures 32** and **33**).

✔ Tip

■ Text or objects in cells you join appear in the joined cell. Cell contents are not lost.

To split joined cells

1. Position the insertion point within the cell where you want the split to occur (see **Figure 34**).

2. If the cells are in the same row click the Split Cell Vertically button on the button bar.

   or

   If the cells are in the same column click the Split Cell Horizontally button on the button bar.

The cell splits in the location you specified (see **Figure 35**).

✔ Tips

■ You can only split cells that were previously joined. In a way, the Split Cells buttons are like "Unjoin Cells" buttons.

■ The split cells feature can be tricky to use. If you split a joined cell and are disappointed by the results, use the Undo command to undo the split.

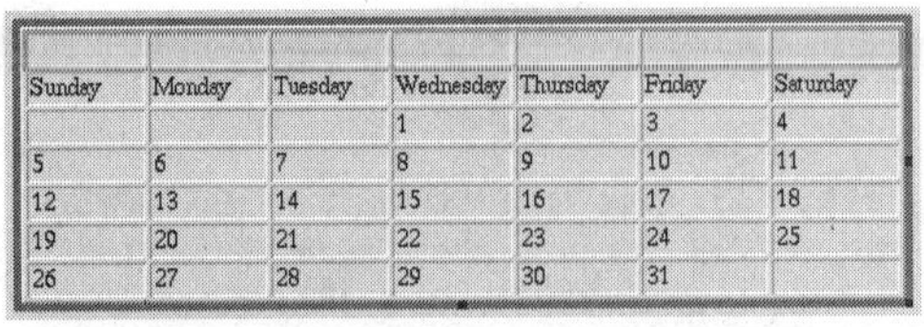

Figure 30. *To join cells, you must begin by selecting the cells you want to join. In this example, seven cells across the top row are selected...*

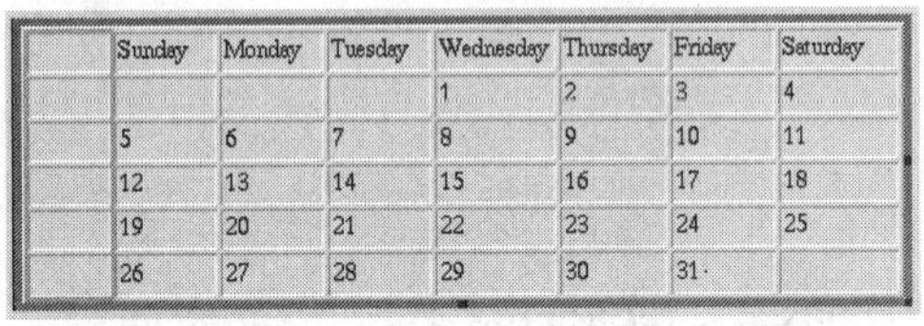

Figure 31. *...and in this example, six cells down the first column are selected.*

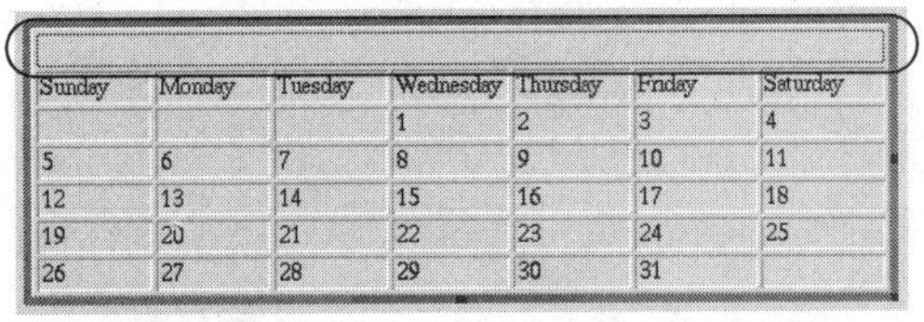

Figure 32. *Here's the table after joining the cells selected in* **Figure 30***...*

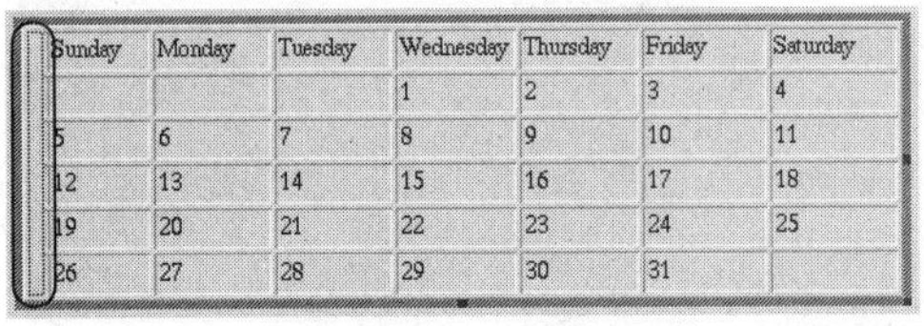

Figure 33. *...and here's the table after joining the cells selected in* **Figure 31***.*

Figure 34. *Position the insertion point where you want the split to occur.*

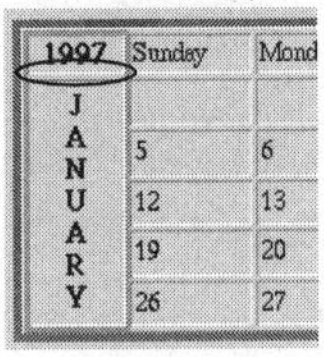

Figure 35. *The cell splits at the insertion point.*

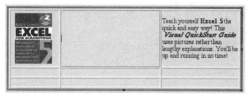

Figure 36. *Begin by positioning the insertion point inside the cell in which you want to insert the table.*

Figure 37.
In this example, a table is being inserted by dragging the Insert Table button.

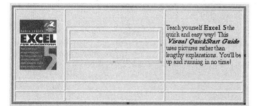

Figure 38. *The table is inserted within the cell you specified.*

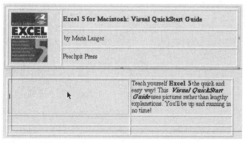

Figure 39. *Another way to insert a table within a table is to simply drag it into a cell.*

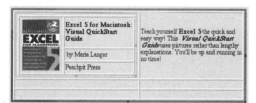

Figure 40. *When you release the mouse button, the table moves into the cell. As you can see in this example, the table resized automatically to fit the cell's width.*

To create a nested table

1. Position the insertion point in the cell in which you want the nested table to appear (see **Figure 36**).

2. Use one of the techniques discussed earlier in this chapter to insert a table with the number of columns and rows you want. **Figure 37** shows an example of inserting a table by dragging the table button.

The table is inserted within the cell (see **Figure 38**).

✔ Tips

■ You can also insert a table within a table by dragging. Select the table you want to insert, then drag it into the cell in which you want it inserted (see **Figure 39**). When you release the mouse button, the table moves (see **Figure 40**).

■ When you insert a table into a cell, one of two things will happen, depending on table width contraint settings (which I discuss on the next page):

   ▲ If the width of the table you insert is based on a percentage measurement, its width will change automatically to fit the cell's width.

   ▲ If the width of the table you insert is based on a pixel measurement, the cell's width will change automatically to accommodate the inserted table's width.

To delete a table

1. Select the entire table.

   or

   Position the insertion point immediately to the right of the table.

2. Press [Delete].

The table and all the information within it disappears.

About Table & Column Width

When you create a table, certain default settings and behaviors are applied to the table and its columns:

- Each new table is set to 450 pixels in width.

- Each column in a table is set to an equal percentage of the entire table width.

You can override table and column width settings by adjusting *width constraints*:

- Set table width as a percentage of the window width or as a fixed width stated in pixels.

- Set column width as a percentage of the table width or as a fixed width stated in pixels.

Figures 41 and **42** illustrate a table with both the table width and columns set as percentages. As you can see, when the window is wider, so are the table and its cells.

✔ Tips

- As mentioned earlier in this chapter, column width can automatically adjust depending on cell contents. Width constraints you set will override any automatic adjustments.

- You can specify table width constraints when you create a table by setting values in the Constraints area of the Create Table dialog box (see **Figure 7**). The controls in this area are the same as those in the Object panel of the Inspector when a table or table cell is selected (see **Figures 48** and **54**)—I tell you about Inspector options for tables and cells on the next two pages.

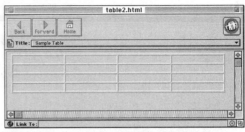

Figure 41. *A table that's 100% of the window width stretches from one side of the window to the other...*

Figure 42. *...even when the window is resized.*

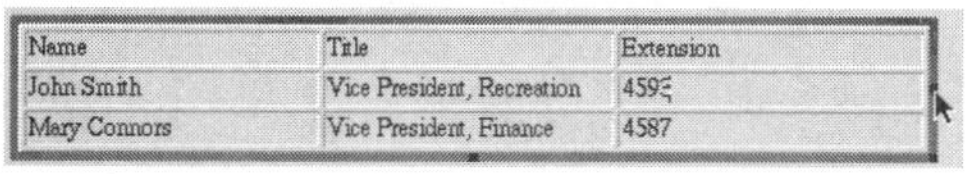

Name	Title	Extension
John Smith	Vice President, Recreation	4593
Mary Connors	Vice President, Finance	4587

Figure 43. *Position the mouse pointer on the selection handle.*

Name	Title	Extension
John Smith	Vice President, Recreation	4593
Mary Connors	Vice President, Finance	4587

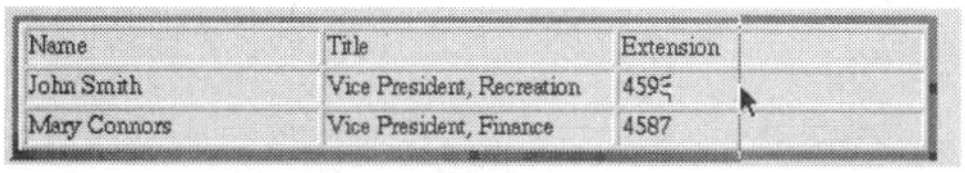

Figure 44. *Drag the handle to change the table width.*

Name	Title	Extension
John Smith	Vice President, Recreation	4593
Mary Connors	Vice President, Finance	4587

Figure 45. *When you release the mouse button, the table and its columns resize.*

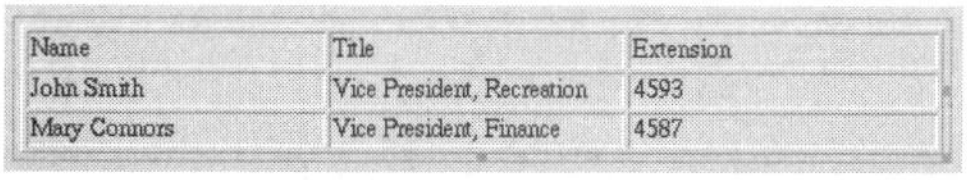

Name	Title	Extension
John Smith	Vice President, Recreation	4593
Mary Connors	Vice President, Finance	4587

Figure 46. *To use the Inspector to change table width, begin by selecting the table.*

Figure 47. *If the Inspector isn't showing, choose Show Inspector from the Window menu.*

Figure 48. *Change the table width by choosing an option from the Width pop-up menu and entering a value in the Width edit box.*

Figure 49. *Choose an option from the pop-up menu.*

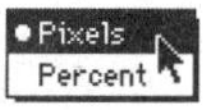

To change table width by dragging

1. Click inside the table. A gray border appears around it.

2. Position the mouse pointer on the selection handle on the right side of the gray box (see **Figure 43**).

3. Press the mouse button down and drag to the right or left. As you drag, a dotted line border moves with the mouse pointer (see **Figure 44**).

4. When the dotted border is in the desired position, release the mouse button. The width of the table and the cells within it change. (see **Figure 45**).

✔ Tip

■ You can also use this technique to set table height—simply drag the bottom selection handle on the gray box. The height of the table and the cells within it change.

To change table width with the Inspector

1. Select the table (see **Figure 46**).

2. If the Inspector is not showing, choose Show Inspector from the Window menu (see **Figure 47**) or press ⌃⌘;. If necessary, click the Object tab to display the Object panel (see **Figure 48**).

3. In the Inspector, choose an option from the Width pop-up menu (see **Figure 49**).

4. Enter a value in the Width edit box and press Return.

Changing Table Width

To change column width by dragging

1. Click inside the table. A gray border appears around it.

2. Position the mouse pointer over the border between the two columns you want to change. The mouse pointer turns into a two-headed arrow (see **Figure 50**).

3. Press the mouse button down and drag to the right or left. As you drag, a dotted line border moves with the mouse pointer (see **Figure 51**).

4. When the dotted border is in the desired position, release the mouse button. The column border shifts, resizing the columns on either side of it (see **Figure 52**).

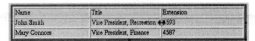

Figure 50. *When you position the mouse pointer on a border between two columns, it changes to a two-headed arrow.*

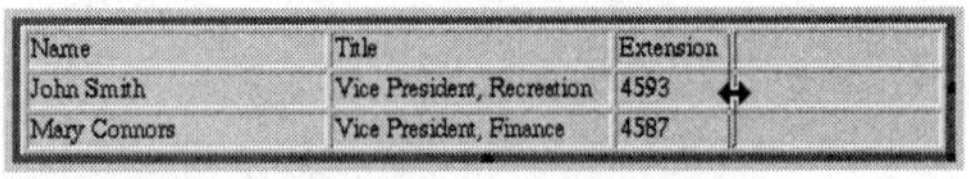

Figure 51. *Drag the border to the right or left.*

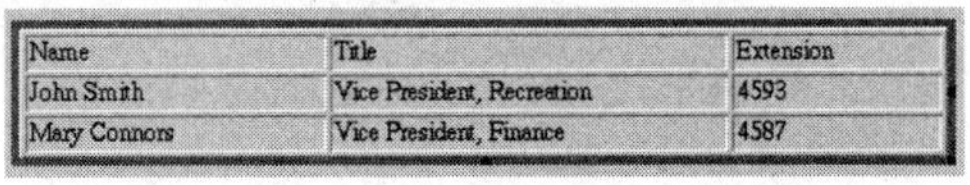

✔ Tips

- You can also use this technique to set row height—simply drag the bottom border of a cell. The height of the cells in the row changes.

- You cannot drag the outside border of a table to change column width.

Figure 52. *When you release the mouse button, the border shifts, thus resizing both columns.*

To change column width with the Inspector

1. Select a cell in the column whose width you want to change (see **Figure 53**).

2. If the Inspector is not showing, choose Show Inspector from the Window menu (see **Figure 47**) or press ⌘; . If necessary, click the Object tab to display the Object panel (see **Figure 48**).

3. In the Inspector, choose an option from the Width Constraint pop-up menu (see **Figure 54**).

4. Enter a value in the Width Constraint edit box and press Return .

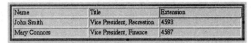

Figure 53. *Select a cell in the column whose width you want to change.*

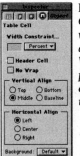

Figure 54. *Change the column width by choosing an option from the Width Constraints pop-up menu and entering a value in the Width edit box.*

✔ Tip

- To allow column width to change automatically based on table size and cell contents, clear the contents of the Width Constraint edit box.

Changing Column Width

About Formatting Cell Contents

You can format the contents of cells just as you format any other document contents. Simply select the text or object you want to format, then use menu commands, button bar buttons, and shortcut keys:

■ Apply physical and logical styles to text. I tell you how in **Chapter 3**.

■ Apply paragraph formatting to text. I tell you how in **Chapter 4**.

■ Change size and alignment for objects. I tell you how in **Chapter 5**.

In addition to these basic formatting techniques, you can also use the Inspector to apply special cell formatting to selected cells:

■ Apply header cell formatting to make the cell's contents stand out.

■ Use no wrap formatting to prevent automatic word wrap within a cell.

■ Change the vertical alignment to shift a cell's contents up or down.

■ Change the horizontal alignment to shift a cell's contents to the right or left.

■ Change a cell's background color.

Figure 55 shows an example of a table with a variety of formatting options applied.

✔ Tip

■ To use the formatting techniques discussed in **Chapters 3**, **4**, and **5**, you must select specific text or an object within a cell. This means you can only apply formatting to the contents of one cell at a time. When using the Inspector to format cells, however, you can select multiple cells and format multiple cells at once.

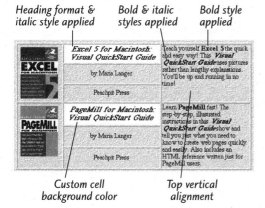

Heading format & italic style applied   Bold & italic styles applied   Bold style applied

Custom cell background color   Top vertical alignment

Figure 55. *Here's an example of a table with a variety of text and cell formatting applied.*

To apply header cell formatting

1. Select the cells to which you want to apply header cell formatting (see **Figure 56**).

2. If the Inspector is not showing, choose Show Inspector from the Window menu (see **Figure 47**) or press ⌘;. If necessary, click the Object tab to display the Object panel (see **Figure 54**).

3. Turn on the Header Cell check box.

✔ Tip

■ Header cell formatting makes cell contents bold and centers them within the cell boundaries (see **Figure 57**).

To apply no wrap formatting

1. Select the cells to which you want to apply no wrap formatting (see **Figure 58**).

2. If the Inspector is not showing, choose Show Inspector from the Window menu (see **Figure 47**) or press ⌘;. If necessary, click the Object tab to display the Object panel (see **Figure 54**).

3. Turn on the No Wrap check box.

✔ Tips

■ No wrap cell formatting prevents automatic word wrap from occurring within a cell (see **Figure 59**).

■ If no wrap formatting is applied to a cell, the only way to break a line of text is to position the insertion point where you want the break to occur and press Return (for a new paragraph) or Shift Return (for a new line in the same paragraph).

Figure 56. *Select the cells to which you want to apply header cell formatting. In this example, the cells containing the days of the week are selected.*

Figure 57. *Header cell contents are bold and centered.*

Figure 58. *Select the cells to which you want to apply no wrap formatting.*

Figure 59. *No wrap formatting prevents automatic word wrap. As this example shows, column width adjusts automatically to accommodate the text.*

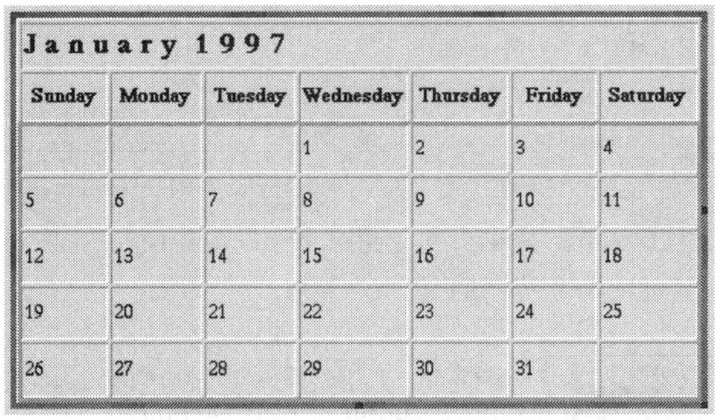

January 1997						
Sunday	Monday	Tuesday	Wednesday	Thursday	Friday	Saturday
			1	2	3	4
5	6	7	8	9	10	11
12	13	14	15	16	17	18
19	20	21	22	23	24	25
26	27	28	29	30	31	

Figure 60. *Select the cells you want to align. In this example, the cells containing the numbered days of the month are selected.*

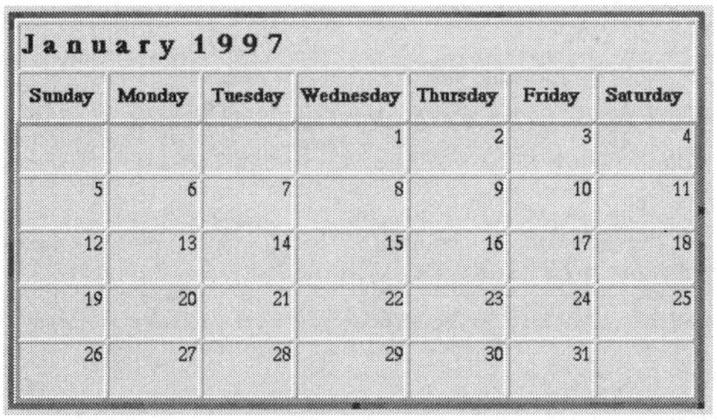

January 1997						
Sunday	Monday	Tuesday	Wednesday	Thursday	Friday	Saturday
			1	2	3	4
5	6	7	8	9	10	11
12	13	14	15	16	17	18
19	20	21	22	23	24	25
26	27	28	29	30	31	

Figure 61. *The selected cells here have Top vertical and Right horizontal alignment applied.*

To change a cell's vertical & horizontal alignment

1. Select the cells whose alignment you want to change (see **Figure 60**).

2. If the Inspector is not showing, choose Show Inspector from the Window menu (see **Figure 47**) or press ⌘;. If necessary, click the Object tab to display the Object panel (see **Figure 54**).

3. To change vertical alignment, select one of the radio buttons in the Vertical Align area of the Inspector.

   or

   To change horizontal alignment, select one of the radio buttons in the Horizontal Align area of the Inspector.

Figure 61 shows an example of cells with Top vertical alignment and Right horizontal alignment applied.

✔ Tip

■ Horizontal cell alignment (discussed here) applies alignment to everything in the cell. Horizontal paragraph alignment (discussed in **Chapter 4**) only applies alignment to selected paragraphs. If a cell contains multiple paragraphs, you can use paragraph alignment to align individual paragraphs the way you want them.

Changing Cell Alignment

To change cell background color with a Color Wheel

1. Select the cells whose background color you want to change (see **Figure 62**).

2. If the Inspector is not showing, choose Show Inspector from the Window menu (see **Figure 47**) or press ⌘;. If necessary, click the Object tab to display the Object panel (see **Figure 54**).

3. Choose Custom from the Background pop-up menu (see **Figure 63**) in the Inspector.

4. Use the Color Wheel that appears to select a color (see **Figure 64**).

5. Click OK or press Return or Enter to apply the new color (see **Figure 65**).

To change cell background color with the Color Panel

1. Select the cells whose background color you want to change (see **Figure 62**).

2. If the Inspector is not showing, choose Show Inspector from the Window menu (see **Figure 47**) or press ⌘;. If necessary, click the Object tab to display the Object panel (see **Figure 54**).

3. If the Color Panel is not showing, choose Show Color Panel from the Window menu (see **Figure 66**).

4. Drag a color swatch from the Color Panel (see **Figure 67**) to the Background pop-up menu. When you release the mouse button, the color is applied.

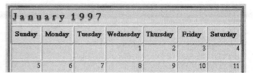

Figure 62. *Select the cells whose background color you want to change.*

Figure 63. *Choose Custom from the Background pop-up menu.*

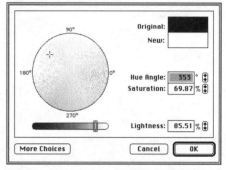

Figure 64. *Use a standard Color Wheel to select a new color for the cell background.*

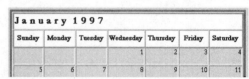

Figure 65. *The color you selected is applied.*

Figure 66. *Choose Show Color Panel from the Window menu.*

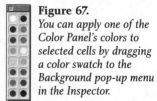
Figure 67. *You can apply one of the Color Panel's colors to selected cells by dragging a color swatch to the Background pop-up menu in the Inspector.*

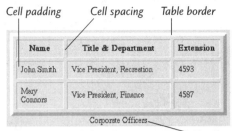

Cell padding   Cell spacing   Table border

Figure 68. *Table formatting options.*   *Caption*

About Formatting Tables

The Inspector's Object panel offers options to format a selected table:

■ Add a caption above or below the table.

■ Set the table's *border*—the thickness of the line around the table.

■ Set the table's *cell spacing*—the amount of space between table cells.

■ Set the table's *cell padding*—the amount of space between a cell's border and contents.

Figure 68 illustrates the table formatting options you can change with the Inspector. The border, cell spacing, and cell padding options were all set to 5.

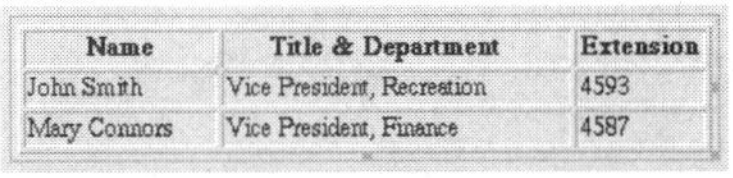

Figure 69. *Select the table to which you want to add a caption.*

To add a caption

1. Select the table to which you want to add a caption (see **Figure 69**).

2. If the Inspector is not showing, choose Show Inspector from the Window menu (see **Figure 47**) or press ⌘;. If necessary, click the Object tab to display the Object panel (see **Figure 48**).

3. Turn on the Caption check box.

4. Select one of the Caption radio buttons to indicate whether the caption should be above or below the table.

5. Click above or below the table to deselect it.

6. Triple-click the word *caption* above or below the table to select it (see **Figure 70**).

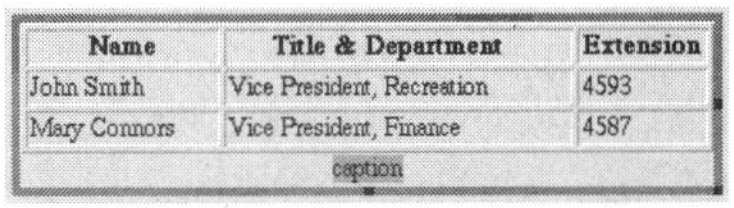

Figure 70. *Triple-click the word* caption *to select it.*

7. Type the text you want to appear in the caption (see **Figure 71**).

✔ Tip

■ To remove a caption, follow steps 1 and 2 above, then turn off the Caption check box.

Figure 71. *Type the text you want to appear in the caption.*

To adjust table border, cell spacing, & cell padding

1. Select the table you want to format (see **Figure 69**).

2. If the Inspector is not showing, choose Show Inspector from the Window menu (see **Figure 47**) or press ⌘⌥;. If necessary, click the Object tab to display the Object panel (see **Figure 48**).

3. To change the thickness of the border, enter a value in the Border edit box.

   or

   To change the amount of space between cells, enter a value in the Cell Spacing edit box.

   or

   To change the amount of space between a cell's border and contents, enter a value in the Cell Padding edit box.

Figures 68, **72**, and **73** show examples of the kinds of effects you can obtain with borders, spacing, and padding.

✔ Tips

■ You can enter a value from 0 to 50 in the Border, Cell Spacing, and Cell Padding edit boxes. The default values are 1, 2, and 0 respectively.

■ You can make any combination of changes to borders, spacing, and padding.

■ A table's border has a three dimensional appearance. The higher you set the border value, the more three dimensional the table will look. **Figure 73** shows an exaggerated example with the border set to the maximum value of 50.

■ To create a multicolumn effect like the page illustrated in **Figure 3**, set the table's border to 0.

Figure 72. *Here's one table formatting combination…*

Figure 73. *…and here's another.*

Figure 1. *This example shows several links from a "Home" page to other pages, an e-mail address, and an Adobe Acrobat PDF file on the same site.*

About Links

The real power of World Wide Web publishing lies in its ability to link your Web pages to each other and to other pages and references anywhere on the Internet. When properly set up, someone browsing your pages can click a hypertext or graphic link to display another page—even one that's on a server halfway across the world! **Figure 1** shows an example of links to several pages, an e-mail address, and an Adobe Acrobat PDF format file on the same site.

When working with links, there are two kinds of documents:

■ The *source* document is the one containing the clickable link.

■ The *destination* or *referenced* document is the one that is displayed when you click a link.

A link works by including the address or *URL* (Uniform Resource Locator) of the destination document within HTML codes associated with text or an image on the source page. While that may sound complex, with PageMill, it's easy since PageMill automatically prepares the HTML codes for you.

✔ Tips

■ You can recognize linked text or a linked graphic on a Web page by the colored underline or border around it.

■ Although the default link color is blue, it can be changed. I tell you how in **Chapter 10**.

About URLs

In order to create a link, you must provide a URL to the destination document. A URL is a document's address or location on the World Wide Web. Just as every file on your hard disk has a pathname, every file on the World Wide Web has a URL. But rather than all files being stored on a single hard disk, they're stored on hard disks all over the world.

There are two ways to include a URL in a Web page document:

■ An *absolute* reference includes the entire pathname to the referenced location.

■ A *relative* reference includes the pathname to the referenced location from the source document.

Figure 2 illustrates both the absolute and relative URLs for a destination page.

If a link's URL refers to a document that does not exist, anyone following that link will see an error message like the one in **Figure 3**. Links to locations that can't be found are often called *broken links*.

✔ Tips

■ I tell you more about URLs in the **Introduction** chapter of this book.

■ You must use an absolute reference to create a link to a location outside your Web site.

■ Relative references to pages on your own Web site are less likely to "break" if you move your pages from one directory or server to another.

■ Although URLs most often refer to Web pages, they can also refer to other kinds of documents or Internet connections. **Table 1** provides a list of some of the URL types supported by PageMill. I tell you more about other types of links later in this chapter.

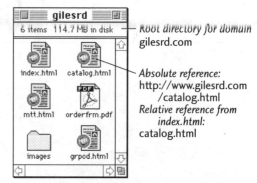

Root directory for domain
gilesrd.com

Absolute reference:
http://www.gilesrd.com
/catalog.html
Relative reference from
index.html:
catalog.html

Figure 2. *As this illustration shows, an absolute URL is the complete pathname to a destination file while a relative URL is the destination file's location from the source document. When referring to* catalog.html *from* index.html, *therefore, the relative reference includes only the file name.*

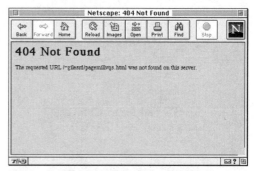

Figure 3. *When you click a link to a URL that cannot be found, your browser displays an error message like this.*

URL Type	Description
http://	Opens a Web page
file://	Opens a file
news:	Opens a Usenet newsgroup
mailto:	Sends an e-mail message
ftp://	Connects to an FTP server
gopher://	Connects to a Gopher server
telnet://	Connects to a server via Telnet

Table 1. *Some of the URL types PageMill supports.*

Page icon —

Figure 4. *The Page icon stores information about the location of a page.*

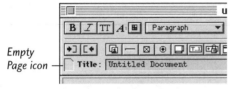

Empty
Page icon —

Figure 5. *If a document has not yet been saved, its Page icon area will be empty.*

Figure 6.
Position the insertion point where you want the anchor to appear.

Figure 7.
Choose Anchor from the Insert Invisible submenu under the Edit menu.

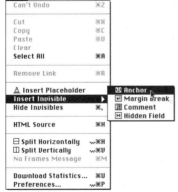

Figure 8.
The anchor appears at the insertion point.

About PageMill's Page Icons

PageMill stores information about a page location in the Page icon near the top left corner of the window (see **Figure 4**). One way to create a link is to drag the Page icon from one page to another.

✔ Tip

■ If the page has not yet been saved, the Page icon area will be empty (see **Figure 5**). You must save the page before you can drag its Page icon.

About Anchors

Normally, when you create a link to a page, clicking the link displays the top of the page. When you create a link to an *anchor*, however, clicking the link displays a specific location on the page.

✔ Tip

■ Anchors are especially useful on long pages. Create a table of contents at the top of the page with links to anchors for topics throughout the page to provide access to topics without scrolling.

To create an anchor

1. Position the insertion point where you want the anchor to appear (see **Figure 6**).

2. Choose Anchor from the Insert Invisible submenu under the Edit menu (see **Figure 7**).

The anchor appears at the insertion point (see **Figure 8**).

✔ Tips

■ If you can't see an anchor after inserting one, choose Show Invisibles from the Edit menu or press ⌘,.

■ Anchors do not appear in Preview mode.

About Page Icons & Anchors

To move an anchor

Drag the anchor to a new position within the page. Any links that reference the anchor will automatically reference it in its new position.

To name an anchor

1. Select the anchor you want to name (see **Figure 9**).

2. If the Inspector is not showing, choose Show Inspector from the Window menu (see **Figure 10**) or press ⌘⌘;.

3. If necessary, click the Inspector's Object tab to display Anchor options (see **Figure 11**).

4. In the Name edit box, type the name you want to use for the anchor (see **Figure 12**) and press Return.

✔ Tip

■ It is not necessary to name the anchors you create. You may find it helpful, however, if you plan to edit the HTML code PageMill creates. I tell you about editing HTML in **Chapter 11**.

To delete an anchor

1. Select the anchor you want to delete (see **Figure 9**).

2. Press Delete. The anchor disappears.

✔ Tip

■ If you delete an anchor that is referenced by a link, the link will no longer function.

Figure 9.
Select the anchor you want to rename or delete.

Figure 10.
Choose Show Inspector from the Window menu.

Figure 11.
The Inspector's Object tab displays Anchor options when an anchor is selected.

Figure 12. *Enter a new name for the anchor in the Name edit box.*

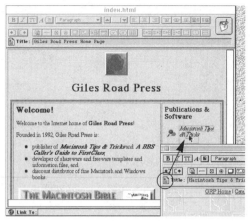

Figure 13. *This example shows a Page icon being dragged onto selected text.*

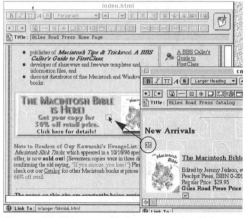

Figure 14. *This example shows an anchor being dragged onto a selected image.*

Figure 15. *Here's the linked text after the Page icon was dropped on it in* **Figure 13.**

Figure 16. *Here's the linked image after the anchor was dropped on it in* **Figure 14.**

About Adding Links

PageMill offers several methods for adding links to text and images:

- Use drag and drop to create links to pages you create.
- Use the Copy and Paste commands to copy links on one page to other pages.
- Type a URL into the Link Location bar.
- Use the Place command's Open dialog box to link to a local or remote URL.

To add a link by dragging

1. In the source document, select the text or image that you want to use as a link.

2. Drag the Page icon for the destination document onto the selection (see **Figure 13**).

   or

   Drag the anchor for the destination location onto the selection (see **Figure 14**).

   or

   Drag the icon for the destination document from a Finder window onto the selection in the PageMill window.

   or

   Drag a selected link from another PageMill window onto the selection.

   or

   Drag a selected link from the Pasteboard onto the selection.

When you release the mouse button, the selection gets a blue underline (if it's text; see **Figure 15**) or a blue border (if it's an image; see **Figure 16**) to indicate that it's a link.

Adding Links by Dragging

✔ Tips

■ If you drag a Page Icon onto another page without dropping it on a selection, PageMill creates the link for you (see **Figure 17**). You can edit the link just as you would any other text. I tell you how to edit text in **Chapter 2**.

■ When you select a link, the destination address appears in the Link Location Bar at the bottom of the page window (see **Figure 18**). You can copy the link by dragging the URL icon to another location.

■ Selected text on inactive pages appears with a selection border around it (see **Figure 19**).

■ To create a link to an anchor on the same page by dragging, hold down ⌘ while dragging the anchor into position. This creates a link to the anchor rather than moving the anchor.

■ When you drag text or an image containing a link from the Pasteboard to a document window, the link is pasted into the document along with the text or image. I tell you more about the Pasteboard in **Chapters 1**, **2**, and **5**.

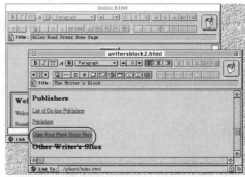

Figure 17. *Here's a link created by dropping a Page icon from a destination page into an empty area of a source page.*

URL icon   Link Location bar

Figure 18. *When a link is selected, its destination URL appears in the Link Location bar.*

Figure 19. *A selection on an inactive page appears with a border around it.*

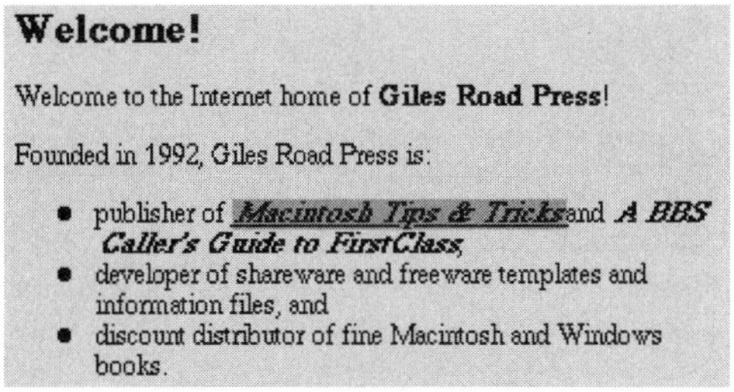

Welcome!
Welcome to the Internet home of Giles Road Press!
Founded in 1992, Giles Road Press is:
publisher of Macintosh Tips & Tricks and A BBS Caller's Guide to FirstClass,
developer of shareware and freeware templates and information files, and
discount distributor of fine Macintosh and Windows books.

Figure 20. *Select the link you want to copy.*

Figure 21. *Choose Copy from the Edit menu.*

Edit
Undo Create Link ⌘Z
Cut ⌘X
Copy ⌘C
Paste ⌘V
Clear
Select All ⌘A
Remove Link ⌘R
Insert Placeholder
Insert Invisible
Hide Invisibles ⌘,
HTML Source ⌘H
Split Horizontally
Split Vertically
No Frames Message ⌘M
Download Statistics... ⌘U
Preferences...

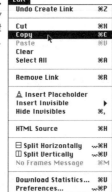

Figure 22. *Position the insertion point where you want the link to appear.*

Publications
Other Writer's Sites
Writer's Resources on the Web
Inkspot

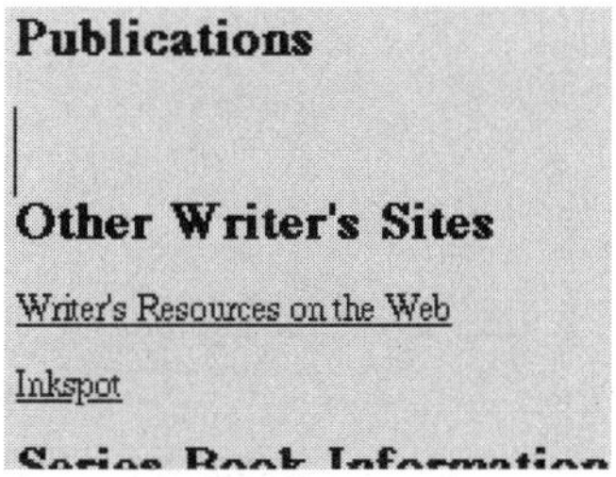

Figure 23. *Choose Paste from the Edit menu.*

Edit
Undo Paragraph ⌘Z
Cut ⌘X
Copy ⌘C
Paste ⌘V
Clear
Select All ⌘A

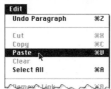

Figure 24. *The linked text appears at the insertion point.*

Publications
Macintosh Tips & Tricks
Other Writer's Sites
Writer's Resources on the Web
Inkspot

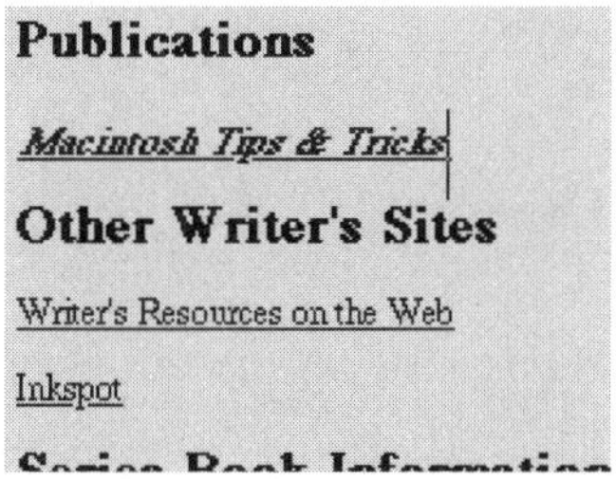

To add a link with the Copy & Paste commands

1. Select the linked text or image (see **Figure 20**) you want to copy.
2. Choose Copy from the Edit menu (see **Figure 21**).

   or

   Press [⌘C].
3. Position the insertion point in the document where you want the link to appear (see **Figure 22**).
4. Choose Paste from the Edit menu (see **Figure 23**).

   or

   Press [⌘V].

The text or image, including its link, appears at the insertion point (see **Figure 24**).

✔ Tips

- You can also use the Cut and Paste commands to move a link.
- Do not use Copy and Paste to copy an anchor. Doing so will create a duplicate of the anchor, not a link.
- I tell you how to use Copy, Cut, and Paste for text in **Chapter 2** and for images in **Chapter 5**.

To add a link by typing in the Link Location bar

1. In the source document, select the text or image that you want to use as a link (see **Figure 25**).

2. Click in the Link Location bar at the bottom left side of the window.

   or

   Press (Enter).

   This activates the Link Location bar (see **Figure 26**).

3. Enter the URL for the destination (see **Figure 27**) and press (Return).

The selected text or image turns into a link (see **Figure 28**).

✔ Tips

■ When typing a link, be sure to enter it correctly. If it has not been entered correctly, it will not work. I tell you how to test links in **Chapter 11**.

■ You can also use the Copy and Paste commands to paste the URL for a page into the Link Location bar.

■ PageMill offers several shortcuts for typing common URL components into the Link Location bar:

▲ To quickly enter the URL protocol, type its first letter and press (Tab). To enter *http://*, for example, press (H) and then (Tab).

▲ To quickly enter the document type, type its first letter and press (Tab). To enter *www.* for example, press (W) and then press (Tab).

▲ To quickly enter the domain, type its first letter and press (Tab). To enter *com*, for example, press (C) and then (Tab).

Figure 25. *Select the text or image you want to use as a link.*

Figure 26. *When you click in the Link Location bar, it becomes active and an insertion point appears within it.*

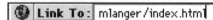

Figure 27. *Enter the URL for the destination. In this example, the URL is a relative reference to another page on the same server.*

Figure 28. *When you press* (Return)*, the selected text or image becomes a link. In this example, you can tell that the image is a link because it has a border around it.*

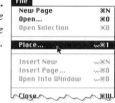

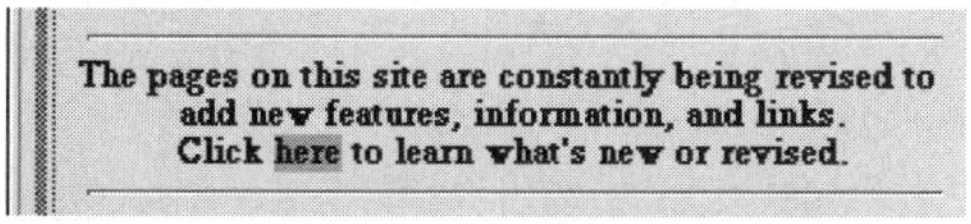
The pages on this site are constantly being revised to
add new features, information, and links.
Click here to learn what's new or revised.

Figure 29. *Select the text or image you want to use as a link.*

Figure 30. *Choose Place from the File menu.*

File
New Page ⌘N
Open... ⌘O
Open Selection
Place... ⌘1
Insert New
Insert Page...
Open Info Window
Close ⌘W

gilesrd
Hard Disk
linkinfo.html
links.html
mtt.html
navbar.html
new.html
orderfrm.html
orderfrm.pdf
Eject
Desktop
Cancel
Link To
Place
Object Type: All
Remote URL:

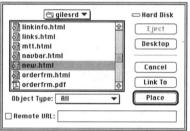

Figure 31. *Use the Open dialog box to locate and select the file to which you want to link...*

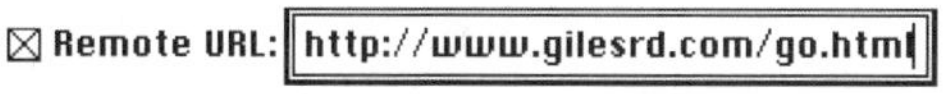
Remote URL: http://www.gilesrd.com/go.html

Figure 32. *...or enter the URL for a remote file in the Remote URL edit box.*

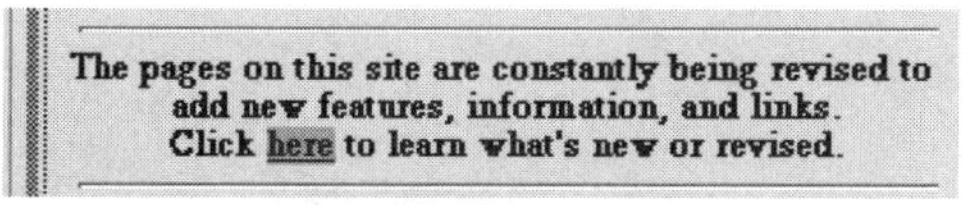
The pages on this site are constantly being revised to
add new features, information, and links.
Click here to learn what's new or revised.

Figure 33. *The selected text or image becomes a link.*

To add a link with the Place command

1. In the source document, select the text or image that you want to use as a link (see **Figure 29**).
2. Choose Place from the File menu (see **Figure 30**).

   or

   Press Control ⌘ 1.

   or

   Click the Place Object button on the button bar.
3. Use the Open dialog box that appears to locate and select the file to which you want to link (see **Figure 31**).

   or

   Turn on the Remote URL check box and enter the complete URL for the file to which you want to link in the edit box beside it (see **Figure 32**).
4. Click the Link To button. The selected text or image becomes a link (see **Figure 33**).

✔ Tips

- In step 3, you can use the Object Type pop-up menu to narrow down the list of files that appear in the Open dialog box (see **Figure 31**) by type.
- When typing a link, be sure to enter it correctly. If it has not been entered correctly, it will not work. I tell you how to test links in **Chapter 11**.
- If you use the Place command to add a link without first selecting text or an image, PageMill creates the entire link for you, using the name or URL of the link as the linked text. You can edit the link just as you would any other text. I tell you how to edit text in **Chapter 2**.

To edit a link

1. Select the text or image containing the link (see **Figure 28** or **33**).

2. Activate the Link Location bar by clicking it or pressing Enter.

3. Use standard editing techniques to change the contents of the Link Location bar, then press Return to complete the entry.

✔ Tips

■ To select a text link, triple-click it.

■ You can also change a link by linking something else to the linked text or image.

To remove a link

1. Select the text or image containing the link (see **Figure 28** or **33**).

2. Choose Remove Link from the Edit menu (see **Figure 34**).

   or

   Press ⌘R.

   or

   Press Enter or click in the Link Location bar to activate it, press Delete to delete its contents, and press Return to complete the entry.

✔ Tips

■ Deleting text or an image containing a link also deletes the link.

■ Deleting a link does not delete the file that was linked.

Figure 34.
To remove a link from selected text or images, choose Remove Link from the Edit menu.

Editing & Removing Links

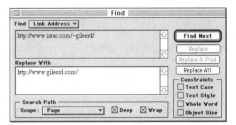

Figure 35. *Here's an example of the Find dialog box all set up to replace one URL with another.*

Figure 36. *Use the Find pop-up menu to tell PageMill to look in link addresses rather than page content to match the Find window's search string.*

About Finding & Replacing URLs

PageMill's find and replace features can be used to locate and/or change the URLs for links throughout a Web page document. You use the Find dialog box (see **Figure 35**) to specify your find and, if applicable, replacement URL. Then use buttons within the Find dialog box or on the Search menu to locate and/or replace URLs as specified.

I discuss the find and replace features in detail in **Chapter 2**. They work the same way for URLs. Just remember to choose Link Address from the Find pop-up menu (see **Figure 36**) at the top of the Find dialog box before beginning the search.

✔ Tips

■ I provide step-by-step instructions for using the find and replace features in **Chapter 2**.

■ To replace only part of a URL, make sure the Whole Word check box is turned off in the Find dialog box (see **Figure 35**).

■ To delete a URL throughout a document, leave the Replace With scrolling window empty. Then replace every occurrence of the URL with nothing, thus deleting it.

Finding & Replacing URLs

About Other Links

When it comes to creating links, you're not limited to linking to the pages you create with PageMill. Using the Link Location bar, you can also create links to:

- **Web pages on other sites.** These external links give the people who browse your pages access to more information than you offer.

- **E-mail addresses.** When a link to an e-mail address is clicked, the Web browser opens an addressed e-mail form (see **Figure 37**), making it convenient to send an e-mail message.

- **Files.** When a link to a file is clicked, the browser software downloads the file to the user's computer. This is a great way to distribute software and information for use offline.

- **FTP and Gopher servers.** These servers offer access to files and database information.

- **Newsgroups.** Providing easy access to specific Usenet newsgroups is a great way to add information to your site without adding files.

Table 2 provides examples of real URLs to a variety of destinations.

✔ Tips

- No matter what kind of link you create, its URL must be entered correctly for it to work.

- Links are often case-sensitive—especially links to files on UNIX servers. Be sure you enter URLs with correct capitalization or the link may not work.

- Check all external links on a regular basis to make sure they're still valid. I tell you how to check external links in **Chapter 11**.

Figure 37. *A link to an e-mail address opens an e-mail form like this one.*

External Pages:
http://www.peachpit.com/
http://info.apple.com/
http://www.adobe.com/
http://www.intac.com/~gilesrd/
http://www.intac.com/~gilesrd/mlanger/

E-Mail Addresses:
mailto:tell@peachpit.com
mailto:info@solutions.apple.com
mailto:MariaL1@aol.com

Files:
ftp://ftp.dartmouth.edu.pub/mac/
    Fetch_3.0.hqx
http://www.intac.com/~gilesrd/mlanger/
    PageMillVQS.pdf

FTP Servers:
ftp://info.apple.com/
ftp://ftp.adobe.com/

Gopher Servers
gopher://info.hed.apple.com/
gopher://mac-gopher.mic.ucla.edu/

Newsgroups:
news:alt.comedy.standup
news:rec.pets.dogs

Table 2. *Here's a list of real Web pages, e-mail addresses, and files that you can try on your Web pages. Remember, although this list was tested and known to be valid when this book went into production, the Internet is constantly changing— URLs that were valid today could become invalid tomorrow. If one of these links doesn't work when you try it, you may not be doing anything wrong— that URL may just be out of date.*

About Image Maps

An image map lets you use one image to link to multiple destinations. You insert the image in a PageMill document, then create "hotspots" on the image, each of which is associated with a different address. PageMill automatically creates the HTML-encoded map files for you.

There are two kinds of image maps:

■ A *client-side* image map stores all hotspot and link information within the Web page document. When a user clicks a hotspot, the browser gets the link URL right from the Web page.

■ A *server-side* image map stores all hotspot and link information in a separate image map file that is stored on the Web server. When a user clicks a hotspot, the browser must open and search through the corresponding image map file to get the link URL.

✔ Tips

■ Although client-side image maps are easier to create and use and offer quicker access to linked pages, not all browsers support them. Fortunately, Netscape Navigator 2.0 or later and Microsoft Internet Explorer 2.0 or later, the two most popular Web browsers, do support client-side image maps.

■ A server-side image map may require a special program called a Common Gateway Interface (CGI) to operate. If you're not sure whether you need a CGI script to use a server-side image map, ask your System Administrator or Webmaster.

To create a client-side Image map

1. Select an image file on the page.
2. Use drawing tools to add hotspots with links to the image.
3. Save the file.

✔ Tips

- Creating and editing client-side image maps is sometimes referred to as *in-line* editing because it's done on the page.
- I tell you how to create hotspots later in this chapter.
- I tell you how to save files in **Chapter 1**.

To create a server-side image map

1. Set or check preferences for your server's image map format (see **Figure 38**) and root folder (see **Figure 39**).
2. Open an image on the page in the Image window.
3. Use drawing tools to add hotspots with links to the image.
4. Save the edited image.
5. Use the Inspector to set the image as an image map and specify a location for the image map file on the server.

✔ Tips

- I tell you about setting preferences in **Chapter 12**. If you're not sure how to set these options, ask your System Administrator or Webmaster.
- I tell you how to save images in the Image window in **Chapter 5**.
- I tell you how to create hotspots and how to use the Inspector to set server-side image map options later in this chapter.

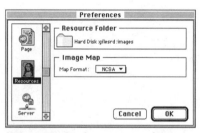

Figure 38. *Set the image map format in the Resources section of the Preferences dialog box.*

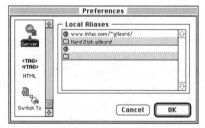

Figure 39. *Set the location of the root directory in the Server section of the Preferences dialog box.*

Creating Image Maps *(sidebar)*

About Hotspots

Hotspots are locations on an image that are linked to URLs. When a user clicks a hotspot on an image map, the destination URL is loaded into his browser.

Hotspots are created with drawing tools. The drawing tools are the same for both types of image maps. The only difference is where they appear:

■ For client-side image maps, the drawing tools appear on the page window's button bar (see **Figure 40**).

■ For server-side image maps, the drawing tools appear in the Image window (see **Figure 41**).

To display the drawing tools for a client-side image map

Double-click the image you want to use as an image map.

A gray box appears around the image. The drawing tools, which are used to create and edit hotspots, appear on the button bar where the table editing buttons normally appear (see **Figure 40**).

To display the drawing tools for a server-side image map

Hold down the ⌘ key and double-click the image you want to use as an image map.

or

Click the image you want to use as an image map once to select it, then choose Open Selection from the File menu or press ⌘D.

The image opens in the Image window (see **Figure 41**). The drawing tools appear along the left side of the window.

Figure 40. *Double-click an image to display the drawing tools for a client-side image map.*

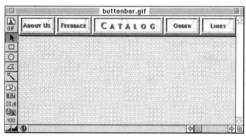

Figure 41. *Open the image in an Image window to display the drawing tools for a server-side image map.*

To add hotspots to an image

1. Click the hotspot tool that most closely matches the shape of the hotspot you want to draw:

   ▲ The Rectangle Hotspot tool draws rectangular or square hotspots.

   ▲ The Circle Hotspot tool draws round hotspots.

   ▲ The Polygon Hotspot tool draws multisided hotspots to your specifications.

2. Move the mouse pointer, which should appear as a cross hair pointer, to the area where you want to draw a hotspot.

3. To use the Rectangle or Circle Hotspot tool, drag to "draw" the shape (see **Figure 42**).

   or

   To use the Polygon Hotspot tool, click to position the corners of the polygon (see **Figure 43**), then click on the starting point to close the polygon.

   When you complete the shape, it appears in blue with a number beneath it (see **Figure 44**).

✔ Tips

■ To draw a square hotspot, click the Rectangle Hotspot tool and hold down (Shift) while you drag.

■ To change the size or shape of a hotspot, click it to select it and drag its resizing handles (see **Figure 45**).

■ To move a hotspot, position the mouse pointer in the middle of the hotspot, press the mouse button down, and drag to a new position.

■ To delete a hotspot, click it to select it and press (Delete) or choose Clear from the Edit menu.

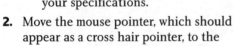

Figure 42. To use the Rectangle Hotspot tool, simply drag to "draw" the hotspot shape.

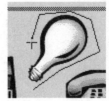

Figure 43. To use the Polygon Hotspot tool, click to position corners. To close the shape, simply click on the starting point.

Figure 44. *Here are four completed hotspots.*

Figure 45. A selected hotspot has resizing handles you can drag to resize it.

■ The number under each hotspot corresponds to its stacking order. If two or more spots overlap, the one with the lowest number is the one that will be activated when the overlapping area is clicked.

Figure 46.
One way to add a link to a hotspot is to drag a Page icon onto it.

To add a link to a hotspot by dragging

To link a page to hotspot, drag the Page icon for the destination page onto the hotspot (see **Figure 46**).

or

To link an anchor to a hotspot, drag the anchor for the destination onto the hotspot.

or

To link an image to a hotspot, drag the image icon from an Image view window or from a Finder window onto the hotspot.

The name of the link appears in blue over the hotspot (see **Figure 47**).

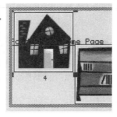

Figure 47.
The name of the linked page appears in blue on top of the hotspot.

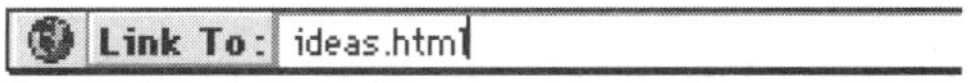

To add a link to a hotspot by typing

1. Click the hotspot to select it.
2. Activate the Link Location bar by clicking in it or pressing [Enter].
3. Type the URL for the destination (see **Figure 48**) and press [Return].

The name of the link appears in blue over the hotspot (see **Figure 49**).

Figure 48. *Another way to add a link is to select the hotspot and enter the link's URL in the Link Location bar.*

To create a default link

1. Click on the image anywhere except on a hotspot so no hotspot is selected.
2. Activate the Link Location bar by clicking in it or pressing [Enter].
3. Type the URL for a default destination and press [Return] to complete the entry.

The name of the link appears in blue in the lower left corner of the image (see **Figure 49**). This is the destination that will be displayed if someone clicks the image but misses the hotspots.

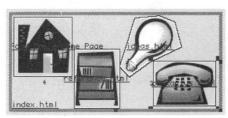

Figure 49. *Here's what the image from Figures 40 and 44 looks like with all hotspots linked. When you create a default link, its name or URL appears in the bottom left corner of the image.*

Adding Links to Hotspots

To remove a link from a hotspot

1. Click the hotspot containing the link to select it.

2. Activate the Link Location bar by clicking in it or pressing [Enter].

3. Press [Delete] and then [Return] to clear the contents of the Link Location bar.

The name of the link disappears from the hotspot.

To change the stacking order of hotspots

1. Click the hotspot you want to change to select it (see **Figure 50**).

2. Click the Shuffle Hotspot tool to display a menu of four stacking options (see **Figure 51**):

   ▲ Bring To Front assigns number 1 to the hotspot, thus putting it on the top of the stack.

   ▲ Send To Back assigns the highest number to the spot, thus putting it on the bottom of the stack.

   ▲ Shuffle Forward lowers the number of the spot by one, thus bringing it up one layer.

   ▲ Shuffle Backward raises the number of the spot by one, thus sending it back one layer.

When you make your selection, the numbers under each of the hotspots change as necessary (see **Figure 52**).

✔ Tip

■ Stacking order is only important if the hotspots on an image map overlap.

Figure 50. *In this example, one hotspot (#1) is overlapping two others, making it impossible to click either of the two smaller spots.*

Figure 51. *Use the Shuffle Hotspot pop-up menu to change the stacking order of overlapping hotspots.*

Figure 52. *By moving the large hotspot to the back, the other two spots are accessible. The hotspot numbers change accordingly.*

Figure 53.
Make hotspots more visible by changing their color.

Figure 54. *Here are the hotspots from* **Figure 44** *colored yellow instead of blue.*

Figure 55.
And here are the same hotspots with the labels turned off.

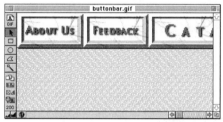

Figures 56 & 57. *You can change the view to zoom in (above) or zoom out (below).*

✔ Tips

■ You can only change magnification in the Image window.

■ The zoom percentage is indicated above the magnification icon (see **Figures 56** and **57**).

■ Magnification percentages range from 12 to 800 percent.

To change the hotspot color

1. Click the Hotspot Color icon to display a menu of fourteen colors (see **Figure 53**).

2. Choose a color that contrasts from the dominant color of the image.

The color changes for all hotspots and URL text in the active Image window.

Figures 49 and **54** illustrate the same image with the default blue hotspot color (see **Figure 49**) and a bright yellow color (see **Figure 54**).

✔ Tip

■ Changing the hotspot color does not affect the way images that contain hotspots appear on Web pages since hotspot outlines are invisible.

To toggle the display of hotspot labels

Click the Show Hotspot Label button.

The labels disappear (see **Figure 55**).

✔ Tip

■ If you look closely, you'll see that the X in the button's check box disappears when label display is turned off.

To change the Image window's magnification

To enlarge the view of the image (see **Figure 56**), click the large mountains on the magnification icon.

or

To reduce the view of the image (see **Figure 57**), click the small mountains on the magnification icon.

Changing Hotspot View Options

121

About Additional Server-Side Image Map Settings

Server-side image maps require that you perform two additional steps after the image map has been created:

■ Set the image's behavior as a map.

■ Specify the image map (and possibly CGI) location.

To set an image as a map

1. If necessary, save the image and close the Image window for the image.

2. In the PageMill window, click the image to select it.

3. If the Inspector is not showing, choose Show Inspector from the Window menu (see **Figure 10**) or press ⌘;.

4. If necessary, click the Object tab to display Image options (see **Figure 58**).

5. Click the Map radio button in the Behavior area (see **Figure 59**) to select it.

✔ Tip

■ You must select the Map radio button as instructed above for a server-side image map to function correctly. This option is turned on automatically for a client-side image map.

Figure 58.
Use the Object panel of the Inspector to set the behavior of an image.

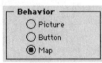

Figure 59.
Select the Map radio button to set an image as a server-side image map. This is done automatically by PageMill for client-side image maps.

Setting an Image as a Map

Link To: http://www.intac.com/~gilesrd/images/buttonbar.map

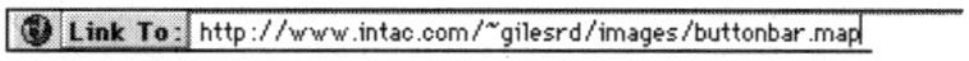

Figure 60. *Enter the absolute URL of the image map file...*

Link To: /images/buttonbar.map

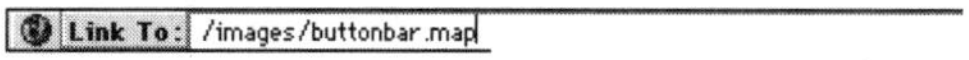

Figure 61. *...or the relative URL of the image map file...*

Link To: http://www.intac.com/cgi-bin/imagemap/~gilesrd/images/buttonbar.map

Figure 62. *...or the absolute URL of the CGI and image map file...*

Link To: /cgi-bin/imagemap/~gilesrd/images/buttonbar.map

Figure 63. *...or the relative URL of the CGI and the image map file.*

To set the image map location

1. In the PageMill window, click the image to select it.
2. Activate the Link Location bar by clicking in it or pressing (Enter).
3. Enter the URL for the image map file (see **Figure 60**) and press (Return).

✔ Tips

■ You must set the image map location as instructed above for a server-side image map. Do not perform these steps for a client-side image map.

■ The pathname entry varies depending on the Web server software. The most common options are:

▲ Absolute URL of the image map file (see **Figure 60**).

▲ Relative URL of the image file (see **Figure 61**).

▲ Absolute URL of the CGI script name and image map (see **Figure 62**).

▲ Relative URL of the CGI script name and image map (see **Figure 63**).

■ If you're not sure what to enter as a pathname for the map, check with your System Administrator or Webmaster. Or find another image map that works and look at its URL to guide you.

■ If you do not set the correct location for the image map (and, if applicable, CGI script) a server-side image map will not work.

Setting the Image Map Location

This frame displays a table of contents

This frame displays pages listed in the table of contents.

Figure 1. *Frames split a Web browser window into separate sections, each of which can contain a different Web page.*

This frame displays a navigation bar for the site.

About Frames

The frames feature of HTML makes it possible to divide a Web browser window into multiple parts called *frames*. Each frame can contain a separate Web page and have its own scroll bars. By using frames, you can display more than one Web page at a time—in the same Web browser window. **Figure 1** shows an example.

✔ Tips

■ Frames are often used in situations when the same information—like the table of contents and navigation bar shown in **Figure 1**—must appear in a certain position in every window.

■ A link within a frame can be set so that its destination page opens in a specific frame of the window, in the window without frames, or in a new window. I give you general information about links in **Chapter 7** and information about using links with frames later in this chapter.

■ Not all Web browsers support frames. Netscape Navigator 2.0 or later and Microsoft Internet Explorer 3.0 or later, the two most popular Web browsers, do support frames. I tell you how to edit a No Frames Message for browsers which cannot support frames at the end of this chapter.

About Frames

About Framesets

Information about how frames should appear within a Web browser window is stored in a special kind of Web page document called a *frameset*. You build a frameset by creating frames in a regular Web page document window. When you save the frameset, individual settings for each of the individual frames are saved within the frameset file.

PageMill offers two ways to create frames:

- Drag window borders to split the window horizontally, vertically, or both.

- Use commands under the Edit menu to split a selected frame horizontally, vertically, or both.

✔ Tips

- A frameset can include any number of frames.

- The more frames you include in a window, the less information can appear in that window due to the amount of space needed for scroll bars and frame borders. If you include too many frames in a window, the window will look cluttered and the frame contents may not display properly.

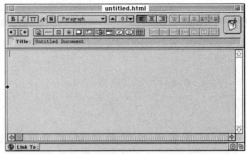

Figure 2. *Position the mouse pointer on the left edge of the window.*

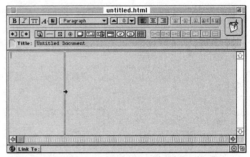

Figure 3. *Drag toward the center of the window.*

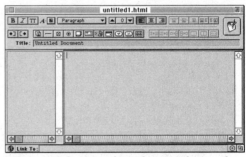

Figure 4. *When you release the mouse button, the window splits.*

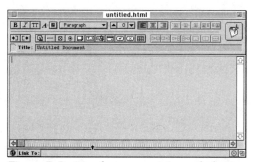

Figure 5. *Position the mouse pointer on the bottom edge of the window.*

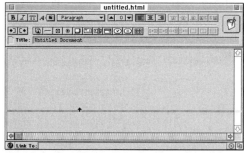

Figure 6. *Drag toward the center of the window.*

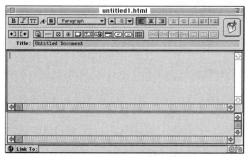

Figure 7. *When you release the mouse button, the window splits.*

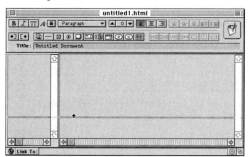

Figure 8. *Hold down both the* ⌘ *and* Option *keys to create a split across frames.*

To create a frame by dragging

1. Hold down Option and position the mouse pointer at the left, bottom, right, or top edge of the window. The mouse pointer should turn into a black arrow pointing into the document window (see **Figures 2** and **5**.)

2. Press the mouse button down and drag in the direction of the arrow. A thick line indicating the frame edge moves along with the mouse (see **Figures 3** and **6**).

3. When the thick line indicates the desired frame width (see **Figure 3**) or height (see **Figure 6**), release the mouse button. The frame border appears (see **Figures 4** and **7**).

✔ Tips

■ You can use the instructions above to split an existing frame. Simply hold down Option while positioning the mouse pointer on an outside edge of the frame. Drag when the arrow pointer appears.

■ To create a frame that spans the entire width (see **Figures 8** and **9**) or height of the window, hold down ⌘ Option while dragging as instructed above.

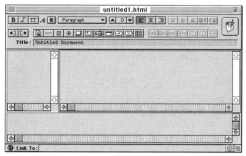

Figure 9. *The resulting frameset looks like this.*

Creating Frames by Dragging

To create a frame with Edit menu commands

1. To split a window into two frames, position the insertion point inside the window (see **Figure 10**).

2. To split the window or frame horizontally (see **Figure 12**), choose Split Horizontally from the Edit menu (see **Figure 11**) or press Control ⌘ H.

   or

   To split the window or frame vertically (see **Figure 13**) choose Split Vertically from the Edit menu (see **Figure 11**) or press Control ⌘ V.

   The window splits accordingly (see **Figures 12** and **13**).

✔ Tip

■ You can use the instructions above to split an existing frame. Simply position the insertion point within the frame you want to split. Then choose Split Horizontally or Split Vertically from the Edit menu (see **Figure 11**) to split the frame.

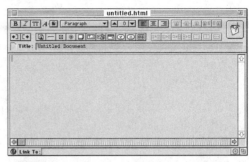

Figure 10. *Position the insertion point within the window or frame.*

Figure 11. *The Split Horizontally and Split Vertically commands split the selected window or frame into two frames.*

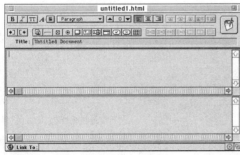

Figure 12. *Choosing Split Horizontally splits the window or frame in half horizontally.*

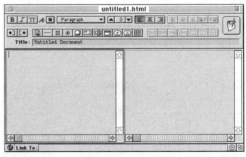

Figure 13. *Choosing Split Vertically splits the window or frame in half vertically.*

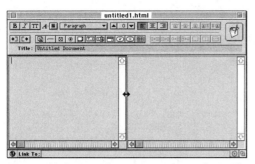

Figure 14. *Position the mouse pointer on the inside border of the frame you want to remove.*

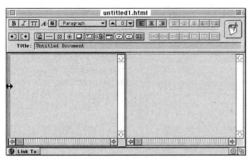

Figure 15. *Drag the inside border to the outside border.*

Figure 16. *A dialog box like this confirms that you want to remove the frame.*

Figure 17. *Immediately after creating a frame, you can use the Undo command to remove it.*

Figure 18. *If you try to remove an unsaved frame, a dialog box like this appears, offering to save its contents.*

To remove a frame

1. Position the mouse pointer on the inside border of the frame you want to remove. The mouse pointer turns into a two-headed arrow (see **Figure 14**).

2. Press the mouse button down and drag to the outside border of the frame (see **Figure 15**).

3. When you release the mouse button, a dialog box like the one in **Figure 16** appears. Click OK or press (Enter) to remove the frame.

✔ Tips

- If the last thing you did was create a frame, you can choose Undo Create Frame from the Edit menu (see **Figure 17**) or press (⌘Z) to remove it. I tell you more about using the Undo command in **Chapter 2**.

- If you try to remove an unsaved frame, a dialog box like the one in **Figure 18** may appear. Click Save to save the frame before removing it. I tell you more about saving framesets and frames later in this chapter.

Removing Frames

About Entering Information into Frames

Each frame in a frameset can contain a different Web page. There are two ways to specify what should appear in a specific frame:

■ Enter text and objects in the frame just as you would any other web page document.

■ Use the Insert Page command to insert an existing Web page document into the frame.

✔ Tips

■ I tell you how to enter, edit, and format text and objects in Web pages throughout this book. The same techniques apply when entering information into a frame.

■ If you try to insert an existing page or a new page into an unsaved frame, a dialog box like the one in **Figure 18** may appear. Click Save to save the frame's current contents before replacing it with another Web page document. I tell you more about saving framesets and frames later in this chapter.

To insert an existing page into a frame

1. Position the insertion point in the frame in which you want to insert the existing page (see **Figure 19**).

2. Choose Insert Page from the File menu (see **Figure 20**) or press (Control)(⌘)(O).

3. Use the Open dialog box that appears (see **Figure 21**) to locate and open the Web page you want to insert.

The page opens in the selected frame (see **Figure 22**).

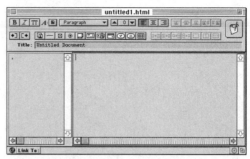

Figure 19. *Position the insertion point in the frame in which you want to insert the page.*

Figure 20. *Choose Insert Page from the File menu to insert an existing Web page into a frame.*

Figure 21. *Use the Open dialog box to locate and open the page you want to insert.*

Figure 22. *The page opens in the selected frame.*

Figure 23.
To open the contents of a frame in its own window, choose Open Into Window from the File menu.

To work with a frame's contents in a separate window

1. Position the insertion point in the frame you want to open in its own window (see **Figure 22**).

2. Choose Open Into Window from the File menu (see **Figure 23**) or press Control ⌃⌘D.

   The page opens in its own window (see **Figure 24**).

To create a new page in a frame

1. Position the insertion point in the frame in which you want to create a new page.

2. Choose Insert New from the File menu (see **Figure 25**) or press Control ⌃⌘N.

   The contents of the frame are cleared out to make a new page.

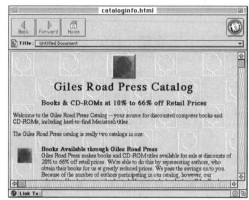

Figure 24. *The frame's contents open in a new window.*

Figure 25.
To create a new page in a frame, choose Insert New from the File menu.

Working with Frame Contents

About Frame Options

The Inspector lets you set a variety of options for the frames you create:

- Give the frame a name that makes sense to you.

- Specify the frame width or height in pixels, as a percentage of window width or height, or relative to the other frames in the frameset.

- Set frame margin width and height.

- Specify whether scrollbars should appear in the frame.

- Set an anchor for the frame.

- Specify whether frames are resizable by users in their Web browsers.

✔ Tip

- You can also change the width or height of a frame by dragging. I tell you how later in this section of the chapter.

To set options for a frame

1. Position the insertion point in the frame for which you want to set options.

2. If the Inspector is not showing, choose Show Inspector from the Window menu (see **Figure 26**) or press ⌘;.

3. If necessary, click the Frame tab in the Inspector to display the Frame options (see **Figure 27**).

4. Make changes in the Inspector as discussed throughout this part of the chapter.

Figure 26.
To display the Inspector, choose Show Inspector from the Window menu.

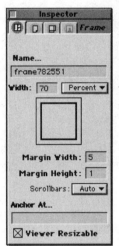

Figure 27.
The Frame panel of the Inspector gives you access to a variety of frame setting options.

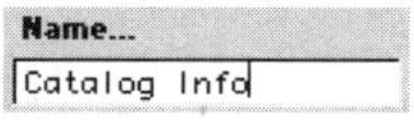

Figure 28. *Enter the name you want to use in the Name edit box.*

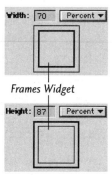

To rename a frame

1. Enter a name in the Name edit box of the Inspector (see **Figure 28**).

2. Press ⟨Return⟩ to complete the entry.

✔ Tip

■ As shown in **Figure 27**, the names PageMill automatically gives frames aren't easy to remember. Give each frame a name that makes sense to you.

Figures 29 & 30. *If necessary, click the Frames Widget to display Width (top) or Height (bottom) options. As you can see here, the appearance of the Widget changes depending on which option is selected.*

Frames Widget

To resize a frame with the Inspector

1. If necessary, click a box in the Frames Widget to display Width (see **Figure 29**) or Height (see **Figure 30**) options.

2. Choose an option from the Width or Height pop-up menu (see **Figure 31**) in the Inspector:

   ▲ *Pixels* enables you to set width or height as an exact measurement.

   ▲ *Percent* enables you to set width or height as a percentage of the window size.

   ▲ *Relative* enables you to set width or height relative to other frames in the frameset. For example, in a three-column frameset, if you set one column to 200 pixels and the other two columns to 1 and 3 relative, the first column would be 200 pixels wide and the remaining width would be divided between the other two columns, with the third column three times the width of the second.

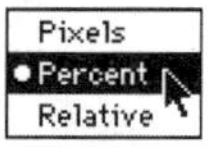

Figure 31. *The option you choose from this pop-up menu determines how the measurement you enter is interpreted.*

✔ Tip

■ If the total height or width of your entries is less than or greater than the size of the window, the frames are sized proportionally.

3. Enter a measurement in the Width or Height edit box (see **Figures 29** and **30**) and press ⟨Return⟩.

To resize a frame by dragging

1. Position the mouse pointer on the inside border of the frame whose width or height you want to change. The mouse pointer turns into a two-headed arrow (see **Figure 32**).

2. Press the mouse button down and drag in a direction of the arrow to increase or decrease the size of the frame. A thick line indicating the frame edge moves along with the mouse (see **Figure 33**).

3. When the thick line indicates the desired frame width (see **Figure 33**) or height, release the mouse button. The frame resizes (see **Figure 34**).

✔ Tip

■ When you resize a frame, the adjacent frame(s) may also resize. You can see this in **Figures 32** and **34**—when the left frame's width is increased, the right frame's width is automatically decreased.

Figure 32. *Position the mouse pointer on the inside edge of the frame.*

Figure 33. *Press the mouse button and drag.*

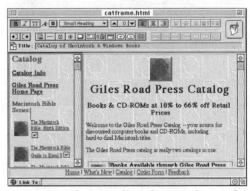

Figure 34. *When you release the mouse button, the frame resizes.*

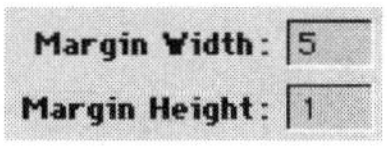

Figure 35. *Enter values in the Margin Width and Margin Height edit boxes.*

Margin Width: 5
Margin Height: 1

Figure 36. *In this example, the right frame's margin width and height are set to 20. Compare this illustration to the one in* **Figure 34** *to see how this differs from the default values.*

Figure 37. *Choose an option from the Scrollbars pop-up menu.*
Yes
No
Auto

✔ Tip

■ If a frame contains only a small amount of text or an object, you can specify a frame size in pixels and turn off scrollbars to create a fixed menu or navigation bar. The bottom frame of the frameset in **Figure 36** is a good example.

To set frame margin width & height

1. To change the amount of space between the left and right edges of the frame and the contents of the frame, enter a value in the Margin Width edit box (see **Figure 35**).

    or

    To change the amount of space between the top and bottom edges of the frame and the beginning and end of the contents of the frame, enter a value in the Margin Height edit box (see **Figure 35**).

2. Press Return to complete the entry.

✔ Tips

■ Margin height is set in pixels. The smallest acceptable value is 1.

■ The default Margin Width setting is 5 and the default Margin Height setting is 1.

■ **Figure 36** shows an example with a frame's Margin Width and Margin Height set to 20.

To set scrollbar display options

Choose an option from the Scrollbars pop-up menu (see **Figure 37**):

■ *Yes* displays both horizontal and vertical scrollbars all the time for the frame. The left frame in **Figure 33** has the Scrollbar option set to Yes.

■ *No* never displays either horizontal or vertical scrollbars for the frame. The bottom frame in **Figure 36** has the Scrollbar option set to No.

■ *Auto* displays a horizontal or vertical scrollbar (or both) only when needed. The two top frames in **Figure 36** have the Scrollbar option set to Auto.

To set a frame anchor

1. Follow the steps in Chapter 7 to insert and rename an anchor (see **Figure 38**).

2. In the Frame panel of the Inspector, enter the name of the anchor in the Anchor At edit box (see **Figure 39**) and press [Return] to complete the entry.

   or

   Drag the anchor from the frame into the Anchor At edit box in the Frame panel of the Inspector.

✔ Tip

■ When you set a frame anchor, the anchor appears at the top of the frame when the frameset first opens. This enables you to specify an exact page location to appear within a frame.

To specify whether a frame can be resized in a browser

Turn the Viewer Resizable check box (see **Figure 40**) on or off as follows:

■ To enable users to resize a frame while viewing the frameset with a Web browser, make sure the Viewer Resizable check box is turned on.

   or

■ To prevent users from resizing a frame while viewing the frameset with a Web browser, turn off the Viewer Resizable check box.

✔ Tips

■ The Viewer Resizable check box is turned on by default.

■ With the Viewer Resizable check box turned on, a user can resize a frame by dragging its border (see **Figure 41**) in a Web browser window. Frame width changes made in a Web browser window are not saved.

Figure 38. *Insert and rename an anchor where you want the page to open in the frame.*

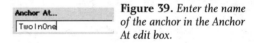

Figure 39. *Enter the name of the anchor in the Anchor At edit box.*

Figure 40. *This check box setting determines whether a user can resize a frame while viewing it.*

Figure 41. *If the Viewer Resizable check box is turned on for a frame, a user can resize the frame by dragging its border in the browser window.*

Setting Frame Anchors & Resizability

About Target Frames

Most Web pages include links that, when clicked, display other Web pages. Unlike a regular Web page, however, a frameset has multiple frames in which a linked page can appear.

PageMill lets you specify a destination or *target frame* for any link in a frame. Your choices are:

- *Default*, which displays the linked page in the same window or frame as the link.

- *New window*, which creates a new browser window to display the linked page.

- *Parent frameset*, which displays the linked page with the "top-level" frameset—the main frameset for the window containing the link. This option applies when a frame contains another frameset.

- *Same frame*, which displays the linked page in the same frame as the link.

- *Same window*, which displays the linked page in the same window as the link.

Or you can select a specific frame in the current frameset to display the linked page.

✔ Tips

- I tell you how to create and edit text and graphic links in **Chapter 7**. You should be familiar with what links are and how they work before attempting to create target frames.

- You can set a default target for all links in a frame in the Inspector. I tell you how in **Chapter 10**.

To set a target frame

1. Select the link for which you want to specify a target frame.

2. Position the mouse pointer on the link, press the mouse button down and hold it down until the mouse pointer turns into a target icon and a pop-up menu appears (see **Figure 42**).

   or

   Position the mouse pointer on the target icon in the lower right corner of the frameset window, press the mouse button down and hold it down until the mouse pointer turns into a target icon and a pop-up menu appears (see **Figure 43**).

3. Choose the desired option from the pop-up menu (see **Figure 44**).

✔ Tips

- An easy way to select a text link is to triple-click it.

- To select a specific frame of the current frameset, choose it from the pop-up menu (see **Figure 45**).

- When you choose an option from the Frame Target pop-up menu, your choice is written to the frame file. There's no on-screen indication of the choice.

- Be sure to test your target frames before publishing the frameset on the Web. I tell you how to test pages in **Chapter 11**.

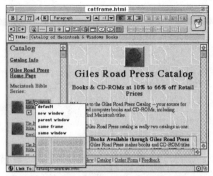

Figure 42. *The Frame Target pop-up menu appears at the selected link...*

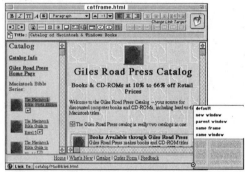

Figure 43. *...or at the target icon in the corner of the frameset window.*

Figure 44.
Select a location option from the Frame Target pop-up menu...

Figure 45.
...or select a specific frame in the current frameset from the Frame Target pop-up menu.

Figure 46.
Use commands
under the File
menu to save
framesets and
save and print
frames.

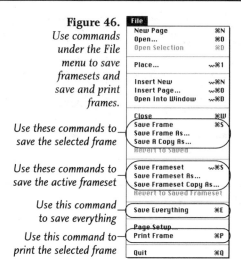

Use these commands to
save the selected frame

Use these commands to
save the active frameset

Use this command
to save everything

Use this command to
print the selected frame

About Saving & Printing Framesets & Frames

When you work with framesets and frames, you're working with multiple documents at the same time:

■ The frameset is the document that contains instructions regarding frame size and other settings.

■ The frames are the documents that contain the Web page data that displays in the frames.

The File menu (see **Figure 46**) includes commands to save framesets and frames and to print frames.

✔ Tips

■ PageMill will not allow you to close a frameset or frame without saving changes to it. If you try to close an unsaved frameset or frame, a dialog box like the ones in **Figure 18** or **47** will appear, offering you a chance to save the frame.

Figure 47. *PageMill displays a dialog box like this when you try to close an unsaved frameset.*

■ A frameset document includes information about the Web pages that will appear in each frame. Before saving changes to a frameset, be sure that the Web pages you want to appear in each frame are displayed.

■ I tell you more about saving files in **Chapter 1**.

To name a frameset

1. Enter a name for the frameset in the Title edit box near the top of the window (see **Figure 48**).

2. Press [Return] to complete the entry.

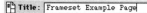

Figure 48. *Enter a name for the frameset in the Title edit box.*

✔ Tip

■ The frameset name is what appears in the title bar of a Web browser window when the frameset is displayed.

To save a frameset for the first time

1. Choose Save Frameset from the File menu (see **Figure 46**) or press [Control] [⌃] [⌘] [S].

   or

   Choose Save Frameset As from the File menu (see **Figure 46**).

2. Use the Save As dialog box that appears (see **Figure 49**) to select a destination folder and enter a name for the file.

3. Click the Save button or press [Return].

To save changes to a saved frameset

Choose Save Frameset from the File menu (see **Figure 46**) or press [Control] [⌃] [⌘] [S].

The frameset is saved with the same name in the same location.

To save a copy of a frameset

1. To save a copy of the frameset and continue working with the copy, choose Save Frameset As from the File menu (see **Figure 46**).

   or

   To save a copy of the frameset and continue working with the original, choose Save Frameset Copy As from the File menu (see **Figure 46**).

2. Use the Save As dialog box that appears (see **Figure 50**) to select a destination folder and enter a name for the file.

3. Click the Save button or press [Return].

✔ Tips

- You may find it helpful to include the word *frame* or *frameset* in the name of a frameset. This makes it easy to distinguish between framesets and regular Web page documents on your hard disk.

Figure 49. *Use the Save As dialog box to save a frameset.*

Figure 50. *When you choose the Save Frameset Copy As or Save A Copy As command, PageMill suggests a name that is based on the original's name.*

- The Save Frameset command is only available if the frameset contains unsaved changes.

To save a frame for the first time

1. Position the insertion point anywhere in the frame you want to save.

2. Choose Save Frame from the File menu (see **Figure 46**) or press ⌘⌥S.

    or

    Choose Save Frame As from the File menu (see **Figure 46**).

3. Use the Save As dialog box that appears (see **Figure 51**) to select a destination folder and enter a name for the file.

4. Click the Save button or press Return or Enter.

To save changes to a saved frame

Choose Save Frame from the File menu (see **Figure 46**) or press ⌘⌥S.

The frame is saved with the same name in the same location.

✔ Tip

■ The Save Frame command is only available if the frame contains unsaved changes.

To save a copy of a frame

1. To save a copy of the frame and continue working with the copy, choose Save Frame As from the File menu (see **Figure 46**).

    or

    To save a copy of the frame and continue working with the original, choose Save A Copy As from the File menu (see **Figure 46**).

2. Use the Save As dialog box that appears (see **Figure 49**) to select a destination folder and enter a name for the file.

3. Click the Save button or press Return or Enter.

Figure 51. *Use the Save As dialog box to save a frame.*

To save all changed framesets & frames

1. Choose Save Everything from the File menu (see **Figure 46**).

   or

   Press ⌘⌘E.

2. A Save As dialog box (see **Figures 49** and **51**) appears for each frameset or frame that has not yet been saved. Use it to select a destination folder and enter a name for the file. Then click Save or press [Return] or [Enter]. Repeat this step as necessary until all files have been saved.

To revert to the saved frameset or frame

1. To restore the frameset to the way it was the last time you saved it, choose Revert to Saved Frameset from the File menu (see **Figure 52**).

   or

   To restore a frame to the way it was the last time you saved it, position the insertion point within the frame and choose Revert to Saved from the File menu (see **Figure 52**).

2. A dialog box appears, asking you to confirm that you want to revert to the last saved version of the file (see **Figure 53**). Click Revert.

All changes you made to the frameset or frame since the last time it was saved are reversed.

✔ Tip

■ When you revert a frameset, you may see a dialog box like the one in **Figure 18** that asks whether you want to save changes to a frame. Click Save to save changes to the frame before reverting to the saved frameset.

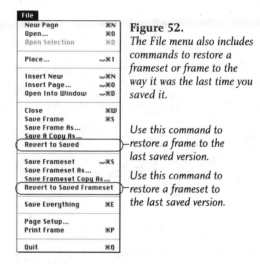

Figure 52.
The File menu also includes commands to restore a frameset or frame to the way it was the last time you saved it.

Use this command to restore a frame to the last saved version.

Use this command to restore a frameset to the last saved version.

Figure 53. *PageMill confirms that you really do want to revert to the saved frameset.*

Figure 54. *Choose Print Frame from the File menu to print the contents of a selected frame on its own page.*

To print a frame

1. Position the insertion point in the frame you want to print.

2. Choose Print Frame from the File menu (see **Figure 54**).

or

Press ⌘P.

3. In the Print dialog box that appears (see **Figure 55**), set the number of copies, page range, and paper source.

4. To print the page's background (which I tell you about in **Chapter 10**), be sure to turn on the Print Page Background check box.

5. If the dialog box includes an Options button, click it to view and change other options if desired. When you're finished with that dialog box, click OK or press Return or Enter to save your settings.

6. Click Print or press Return or Enter to print.

✔ Tips

■ The Print Frames command is the same as the Print command for regular Web page documents.

■ You cannot print multiple frames in a frameset they way they appear on screen.

■ The way the Print dialog box appears (see **Figure 55**) depends on your printer and the printer driver you selected in Apple's Chooser.

■ I tell you more about printing, including how to set page options, in **Chapter 1**.

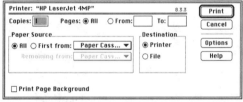

Figure 55. *Use the Print dialog box to set options before you print.*

Printing Frames

About the No Frames Message

As mentioned earlier in this chapter, not all browsers can properly display frames. You can use the No Frames Message to tell users with browsers that don't support frames that the page they are viewing includes frames.

To edit the No Frames Message

1. Choose No Frames Message from the Edit menu (see **Figure 56**) or press ⌘⌘Ⓜ.

2. A No Frames Message window appears (see **Figure 57**). Edit the contents of the window so it displays the text you want to appear (see **Figure 58**).

3. When you finish making changes, click the No Frames Message window's close box to dismiss it.

Figure 59 shows an example of the way the No Frames Message in **Figure 58** appears when viewed in a browser that does not support frames.

✔ Tip

■ If desired, you can include links in the No Frames Message window (see **Figure 60**). This is a great way to offer easy access to one or more alternate pages (see **Figure 61**). I tell you how to add links in **Chapter 7**.

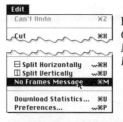

Figure 56.
Choose No Frames Message from the Edit menu.

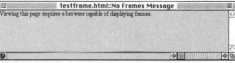

Figure 57. *The default No Frames Message states that a different browser is required to view the page.*

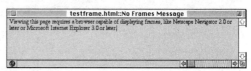

Figure 58. *You can edit the default message to be more specific.*

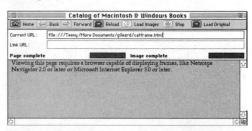

Figure 59. *Here's the message in **Figure 58** viewed with America Online's old browser.*

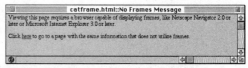

Figure 60. *You can also include links to other pages that don't use frames.*

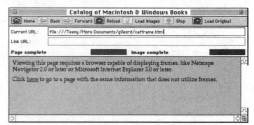

Figure 61. *Here's the message in **Figure 60** viewed with America Online's old browser.*

CREATING FORMS

9

About Forms

Forms are Web pages with special objects designed to gather information. You create a form by adding any combination of the following form objects to a Web page:

- *Check boxes*, which can be used to select multiple items from a list.

- *Radio buttons*, which let users choose from a variety of options.

- *Text areas*, which accept long passages of text.

- *Text fields*, which accept short strings of text.

- *Password fields*, which let users enter passwords.

- *Pop-up menus* and *selection list fields*, which let users choose from a variety of options.

- *Submit button*, which sends data on completed forms to be processed.

- *Reset button*, which clears all entries so the user can start over.

- *Hidden fields*, which can store predefined information that is used when processing the form.

Figure 1 shows an example of a form that uses many of these objects.

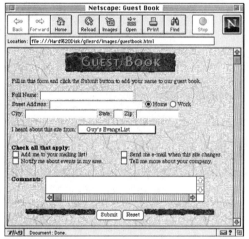

Figure 1. *Here's a form that combines many form elements.*

✔ Tip

- In order to use a form, you need a program called a CGI. I tell you more about CGIs at the end of this chapter.

About Creating Forms

With PageMill, you create forms by placing form objects, text, and images on a page.

- Form objects (see **Figure 2**) collect input from the user. Each one must have a unique name and/or value that is recognized by the CGI with which the form will be used.

- Text labels or descriptions (see **Figure 3**) identify the kind of information requested by each form object. Text can be formatted as desired. I tell you about entering and formatting text in **Chapters 2**, **3**, and **4**.

- Graphic objects (see **Figure 1**) and objects like horizontal rules add visual appeal to your forms. I tell you about working with graphic objects in **Chapter 5**.

✔ Tips

- PageMill supports only one form per page.

- You can copy form objects within a form or from one form to another using the Copy and Paste commands or by holding down Option while dragging a selected object. I discuss copying techniques in **Chapter 2**.

- To delete a form object, simply select it and press Delete or choose Clear from the Edit menu.

- Use the basic text and image entry, formatting, and editing techniques discussed in **Chapters 2** through **5** to modify and reorganize your forms as needed.

- To align text and fields in a form, consider using the Preformatted format (see **Figure 4**) or tables (see **Figures 5** and **6**). I discuss the Preformatted format in **Chapter 4** and tables in **Chapter 6**.

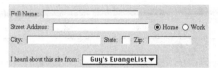

Figure 2. *Form objects like the text fields, radio buttons, and pop-up menu shown here gather information.*

Figure 3. *Without text labels beside each of these check boxes, how would the user know what to check?*

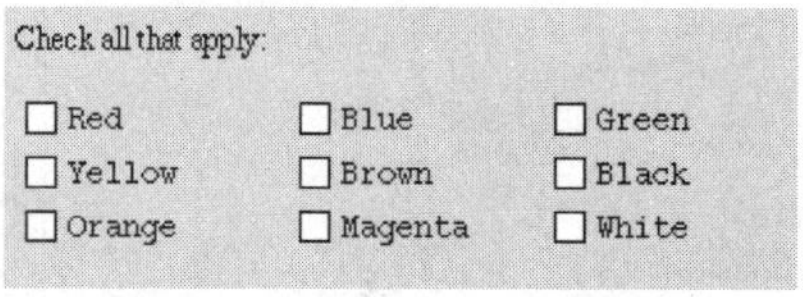

Figure 4. *One way to align form objects is to use the Preformatted format, which features a monospaced typeface.*

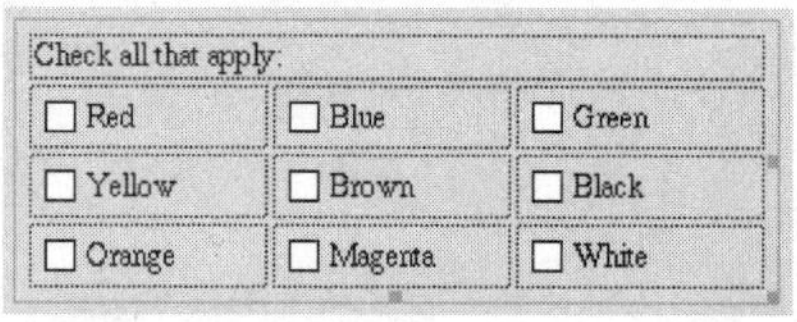

Figure 5. *To align form objects, put them in a table.*

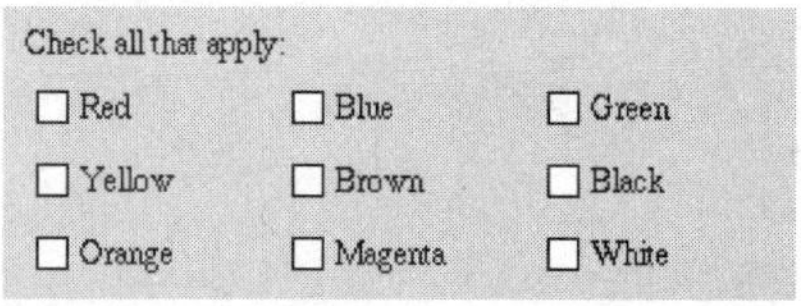

Figure 6. *When the borderless table from Figure 5 is viewed in Preview mode, the form objects are neatly lined up.*

About Creating Forms

About Check Boxes

Check boxes are used when you want to provide a list and let the user select more than one option. Unlike radio buttons, which I discuss later in this chapter, a user can turn on any number of check boxes in a group.

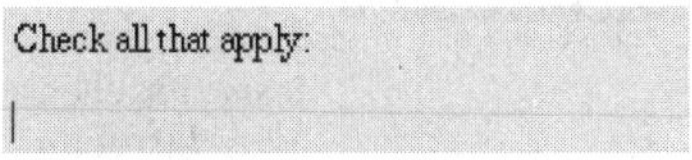

To add a check box

Check all that apply:

Figure 7. *Position the insertion point where you want the check box to appear.*

1. Position the insertion point where you want the check box to appear (see **Figure 7**).

2. Click the Insert Checkbox button on the button bar.

   or

   Press ⌃⌘ Control 3.

   A check box appears at the insertion point (see **Figure 8**).

Check all that apply:

☐

Figure 8. *The check box appears at the insertion point.*

3. Type in a label or descriptive text for the check box.

4. Repeat steps 1 through 3 for each check box you want to add.

When you're finished, your check boxes might look something like the ones in **Figure 9**.

Check all that apply:

☐ Add me to your mailing list!
☐ Notify me about events in my area.
☐ Send me e-mail when this site changes.

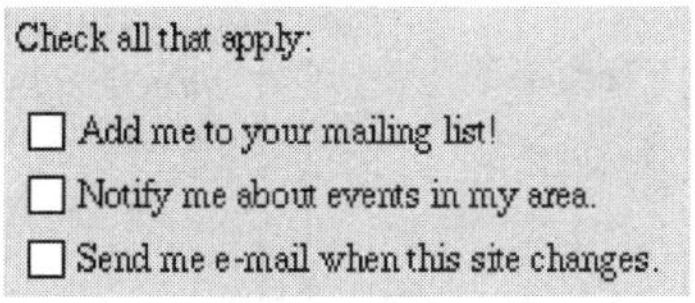

Figure 9. *Finished check boxes.*

Adding Check Boxes

To specify check box settings

1. Select the check box for which you want to specify settings (see **Figure 10**).

2. If the Inspector is not showing, choose Show Inspector from the Window menu (see **Figure 11**) or press ⌘; to display it.

3. If necessary, click the Inspector's Object tab to display the Checkbox options (see **Figure 12**).

4. To name the check box, enter a name in the Name edit box.

5. To set a value for the check box, enter a value in the Value edit box.

6. To set the check box so it is turned on by default, turn on the Checked check box.

✔ Tip

■ The Name and Value you assign to a check box must meet the requirements of the CGI that will process the form. Consult the CGI documentation for specifics.

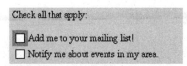

Figure 10. *Click a check box to select it.*

Figure 11. *To display the Inspector, choose Show Inspector from the Window menu.*

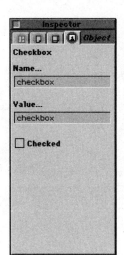

Figure 12. *Use the Inspector to set check box options like name and value and whether the check box is automatically turned on by default.*

About Radio Buttons

Radio buttons are used when you want to provide a list and let the user select exactly one option. Unlike check boxes, which I discuss on the previous pages, a user must select one—and only one—radio button in a group.

To add a group of radio buttons

1. Position the insertion point where you want the first radio button to appear (see **Figure 13**).

2. Click the Insert Radio Button button on the button bar.

   or

   Press ⌘ Control 4.

   A radio button appears at the insertion point (see **Figure 14**).

3. Type in a label or descriptive text for the radio button.

4. Click the radio button to select it (see **Figure 15**).

5. Use the Copy and Paste commands to place a copy of the button where you want another radio button to appear.

   or

   Hold down Option and drag the first radio button to where you want another radio button to appear.

   A radio button appears where you pasted or Option-dragged the first radio button (see **Figure 16**). Note that only one of the radio buttons is turned on.

6. Type in a label or descriptive text for the new radio button.

7. Repeat steps 4 through 6 for each radio button you want to add to the group.

When you're finished, your radio buttons might look something like the ones in **Figure 17**.

This address is my

Figure 13. *Position the insertion point where you want the radio button to appear.*

This address is my ◉

Figure 14. *The radio button appears at the insertion point.*

This address is my ◉ Home

Figure 15. *Select the first radio button.*

This address is my ○ Home ◉

Figure 16. *Clone or copy it to create a second radio button in the group.*

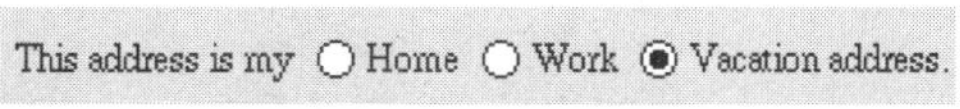

This address is my ○ Home ○ Work ◉ Vacation address

Figure 17. *When you're finished making radio buttons for a group, only one will be selected.*

✔ Tip

■ You must copy or *clone* radio buttons to create a group. If you use the Insert Radio Button button for each one, they will not be part of the same group.

To specify radio button settings

1. Select the radio button for which you want to specify settings (see **Figure 15**).

2. If the Inspector is not showing, choose Show Inspector from the Window menu (see **Figure 11**) or press ⌘; to display it.

3. If necessary, click the Inspector's Object tab to display the Radio Button options (see **Figure 18**).

4. To name the radio button, enter a name in the Name edit box.

5. To set a value for the radio button, enter a value in the Value edit box.

6. To set the radio button so it is selected by default, turn on the Checked check box.

✔ Tips

■ The Name and Value you assign to a radio button must meet the requirements of the CGI that will process the form. Consult the CGI documentation for specifics.

■ All radio buttons in a group have the same name. If you change the name of one radio button in a group, be sure to change the names of the others so they match.

■ To make radio buttons that you inserted separately into a group of radio buttons, change their names so they're all the same.

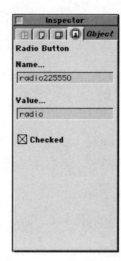

Figure 18.
Use the Inspector to set radio button options like name and value and whether the radio button is automatically selected by default.

Figure 19. *A text area accepts multiple-line text entries.*

Full Name: Maria Langer

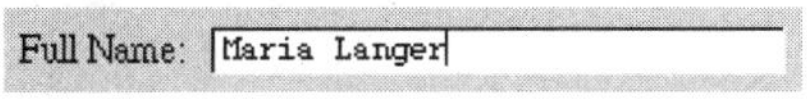

Figure 20. *A text field accepts only one line of text.*

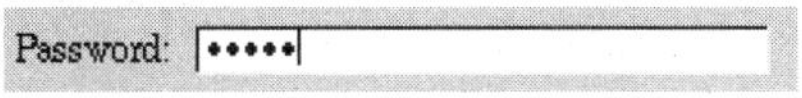

Password: •••••

Figure 21. *A password field echoes its contents with bullets or asterisks.*

Secret Code:

Figure 22. *Position the insertion point where you want the object to appear.*

Secret Code:

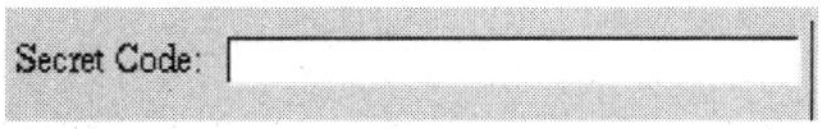

Figure 23. *The object you chose appears at the insertion point.*

About Text Input Objects

Text input form objects collect typed input from users. There are three kinds of text objects:

■ A text area (see **Figure 19**) accepts multiple-line text entries. It is designed for lengthy input.

■ A text field (see **Figure 20**) accepts a single line of text. It is designed for short input.

■ A password field (see **Figure 21**) accepts a single line of text. It is specially designed for password entry since input is echoed back as bullet or asterisk characters.

To add a text input object

1. Position the insertion point where you want the object to appear. In most cases, this will be right after or under a typed-in label or descriptive text (see **Figure 22**).

2. Click one of the following button bar buttons or press one of the following Command key equivalents:

   ▲ To insert a text area, click the Insert Text Area button or press ⌘ Control 5.

   ▲ To insert a text field, click the Insert Text Field button or press ⌘ Control 6.

   ▲ To insert a password field, click the Insert Password Field button or press ⌘ Control 7.

   The object you inserted appears at the insertion point (see **Figure 23**).

3. Repeat steps 1 and 2 for each input object you want to add.

Adding Text Input Objects

To resize a text area by dragging

1. Click once on the text area to select it. A selection box and three resizing handles appear around it (see **Figure 24**).

2. Position the mouse pointer on one of the resizing handles, press the mouse button down, and drag.

   ▲ To change the width of the text area, drag the right side resizing handle.

   ▲ To change the height of the text area, drag the bottom resizing handle.

   ▲ To change the width and height of the text area, drag the corner resizing handle.

   As you drag, an outline of the text area appears to indicate the final size (see **Figure 25**).

3. When the text area is the desired size, release the mouse button. The text area resizes to your specifications (see **Figure 26**).

To resize a text field or password field by dragging

1. Click on the text field or password field to select it. A selection box appears around it and one resizing handle appears on its right side (see **Figure 27**).

2. Position the mouse pointer on the resizing handle, press the mouse button down, and drag to the left or right. As you drag, an outline of the field appears to indicate the final size (see **Figure 28**).

3. When the field is the desired size, release the mouse button. The field resizes to your specifications (see **Figure 29**).

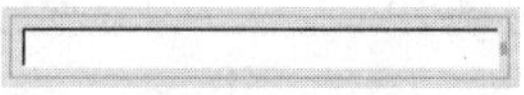

Figure 24. *Click a text area once to select it.*

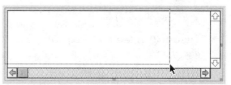

Figure 25. *Drag one of its resizing handles to make it bigger or smaller.*

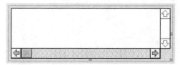

Figure 26. *When you release the mouse button, the size changes.*

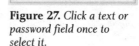

Figure 27. *Click a text or password field once to select it.*

Figure 28. *Drag its resizing handle to make it longer or shorter.*

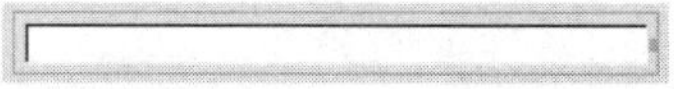

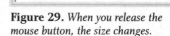

Figure 29. *When you release the mouse button, the size changes.*

Resizing Text Input Objects by Dragging

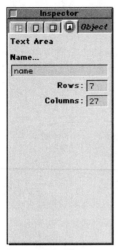

Figure 30. *The Inspector's Text Area options, ...*

Figure 31. *...Text Field options, ...*

Figure 32. *...and Password Field options.*

To resize a text input object with the Inspector

1. Click once on the text area, text field, or password field to select it.

2. If the Inspector is not showing, choose Show Inspector from the Window menu (see **Figure 11**) or press ⌘; to display it.

3. If necessary, click the Inspector's Object tab to display the Text Area (see **Figure 30**), Text Field (see **Figure 31**), or Password Field (see **Figure 32**) options.

4. Enter values in the Rows, Columns, Size, or Max Length edit box(es).

✔ Tips

- All sizes are expressed in terms of characters.

- When you make a change to one of the size-related values in the Inspector, the size of the selected input object changes accordingly. The same holds true when you change the size of an object by dragging it—the values in the Inspector change accordingly.

- If you specify a Max Length value for a Text Field or Password Field, the field will not get any larger than the number of characters you specify.

Resizing with the Inspector

To specify a default value for a text input object

1. Double-click the object for which you want to specify a default value. A dark border appears around it and an insertion point appears inside it (see **Figure 33**).

2. Enter the value you want to appear (see **Figure 34**).

Figure 33. *Double-click the object in which you want to enter a default value.*

Figure 34. *Enter the value you want to use as a default.*

✔ Tip

■ Default text can be used when a field has a common response or when you want to provide hints on how text should be entered (see **Figure 34**).

To name a text input object

1. Select the text input object you want to name (see **Figures 24** and **27**).

2. If the Inspector is not showing, choose Show Inspector from the Window menu (see **Figure 11**) or press ⌘; to display it.

3. If necessary, click the Inspector's Object tab to display the Text Area (see **Figure 30**), Text Field (see **Figure 31**), or Password Field (see **Figure 32**) options.

4. Enter a name in the Name edit box.

✔ Tip

■ The Name you assign to a text input area must meet the requirements of the CGI that will process the form. Consult the CGI documentation for specifics.

Specifying Text Input Object Options

Figure 35. *Position the insertion point where you want the pop-up menu to appear.*

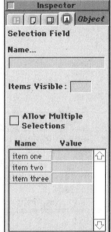

Figure 36. *A pop-up menu with PageMill's default values appears.*

Figure 37. *Click once on the pop-up menu to select it.*

Figure 38. *Use the Inspector to specify settings for pop-up menus and list-selection fields.*

Figure 39. *The number of items you specified appears in a scrolling list.*

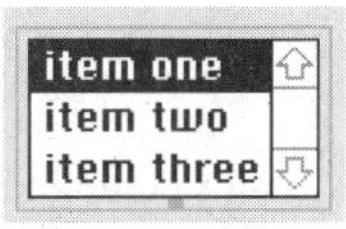

Figure 40. *Another way to turn a pop-up menu into a list selection field is to drag its resizing handle.*

✔ Tip

- Another way to turn a pop-up list into a list selection field is to select it and drag its bottom resizing handle (see **Figure 40**).

About Selection Fields

PageMill offers two types of selection fields:

- A pop-up menu, which enables the user to choose one option from a menu you provide.

- A list-selection field, which enables the user to choose one or more options from a scrolling list you provide.

To add a pop-up menu

1. Position the insertion point where you want the pop-up menu to appear. In most cases, this will be right after or under a typed-in label or descriptive text (see **Figure 35**).

2. Click the Insert Popup button in the button bar or press ⌘ Control 8. The pop-up menu appears at the insertion point (see **Figure 36**).

To add a list-selection field

1. Follow steps 1 and 2 above.

2. Click once on the pop-up menu you created to select it (see **Figure 37**).

3. If the Inspector is not showing, choose Show Inspector from the Window menu (see **Figure 11**) or press ⌘ ; to display it.

4. If necessary, click the Inspector's Object tab to display the Selection Field options (see **Figure 38**).

5. Enter the number of menu items you want to appear in the scrolling list in the Items Visible edit box and press Return.

The pop-up list expands to show the number of items you specified. A scroll bar appears on the right side of the box (see **Figure 39**). The field will now function as a list-selection field.

To specify selection field options

1. Double-click the pop-up menu or list-selection field for which you want to specify options. The menu or list opens to display the default options (see **Figures 41a** and **41b**).

2. Select all the default options by dragging the mouse over them, choosing Select All from the Edit menu (see **Figure 42**), or pressing ⌃⌘A.

3. Type in the values you want. Be sure to press ⟨Return⟩ after each one. When you're finished, your list might look like the one in **Figure 43a** or **43b**.

4. Click elsewhere in the page window to close the menu options (see **Figures 44a** and **44b**).

✔ Tips

■ The list expands to accept as many entries as you need to include.

■ The width of the pop-up menu or list-selection field is determined by the number of characters in the longest entry for the field.

■ You can also use this technique to edit the values in a pop-up menu or list selection field if you need to change them.

Specifying Selection Field Options

Figure 41a. *Double-click a pop-up menu…*

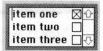

Figure 41b. *…or list-selection field to edit it.*

Figure 42. *Choose Select All from the Edit menu to select all the options in the list.*

Figure 43a. *Enter the options you want to appear on the pop-up menu…*

Figure 43b. *…or list-selection field.*

Figure 44a. *Here's the pop-up menu from Figure 43a…*

Figure 44b. *…and here's the list-selection field from Figure 43b.*

Figure 45a.
Drag the triangle into position beside the default option on the pop-up menu…

```
Guy's EuangeList
Maria Langer
Macintosh Tips & Tricks ▼
Another Web Site
A Friend
Can't Remember
```

Figure 45b.
…or turn on the check box beside the default option in a list-selection field.

```
Guy's EuangeList      □ ⬆
Maria Langer          □
Macintosh Tips & Tricks ⊠
Another Web Site      □
A Friend              □
Can't Remember        □ ⬇
```

Figure 46a.
The default pop-up menu option is the one that appears when the menu is closed.

```
Macintosh Tips & Tricks ▼
```

Figure 46b.
The default list-selection field option is the one that is automatically highlighted or selected when the field appears on a form.

```
Guy's EuangeList      ⬆
Maria Langer          ▤
Macintosh Tips & Tricks
```

To set a default selection field option

1. Double-click the pop-up menu or list-selection field for which you want to set a default option. The list opens to display the options (see **Figures 43a** and **43b**).

2. To change the default option for a pop-up menu, drag the triangle into position beside the option you want (see **Figure 45a**).

   or

   To change the default option for a list-selection field, turn on the check box for the option you want (see **Figure 45b**).

3. Click elsewhere in the page window to close the menu options.

The entry you set as the default appears on the pop-up menu (see **Figure 46a**) or list-selection field (see **Figure 46b**).

✔ Tips

- Although you can use this technique to set any option as the default, the default option in a pop-up menu or list-selection field is usually the first one.

- You can set multiple default options for a list-selection field if the Allow Multiple Selections check box is turned on in the Inspector (see **Figure 38**) for the field. I tell you about specifying selection field settings on the next page.

To specify selection field settings

1. Select the pop-up menu or list-selection field for which you want to specify settings (see **Figures 47a** and **47b**).

2. If the Inspector is not showing, choose Show Inspector from the Window menu (see **Figure 11**) or press ⌃⌘; to display it.

3. If necessary, click the Inspector's Object tab to display the Selection Field options (see **Figure 48**).

4. To name the field, enter a name in the Name edit box.

5. To allow users to select more than one option in a list-selection field, turn on the Allow Multiple Selections check box.

6. To set a value for a pop-up menu or list-selection field option, enter it in the appropriate Value edit box.

✔ Tips

■ The Name and Values you assign to a pop-up menu or list-selection field must meet the requirements of the CGI that will process the form. Consult the CGI documentation for specifics.

■ You must turn on the Allow Multiple Selections check box before you can specify multiple default options. I tell you how to specify default options on the previous page.

Figure 47a. *Click the pop-up menu…*

Figure 47b. *…or list-selection field once to select it.*

Figure 48. *Use the Inspector to set options for a pop-up menu or list-selection field.*

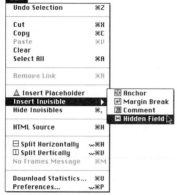

Figure 49. *Choose Hidden Field from the Insert Invisible submenu under the Edit menu.*

Figure 50. *A hidden field appears as a purple H icon on the page.*

Figure 51. *Click the hidden field icon to select it.*

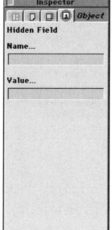

Figure 52. *Use the Inspector's Hidden Field options to give a hidden field a Name and Value.*

✔ Tip

- The Name and Value you assign to a hidden field must meet the requirements of the CGI that will process the form. Consult the CGI documentation for specifics.

About Hidden Fields

A hidden field is a special kind of field that the form user never sees. You use a hidden field to include information required by the CGI that remains the same for every processed form and is not entered by the user.

✔ Tips

- It doesn't matter where you place a hidden field, since it will never appear to the user. Just make sure you put it on the same page as the form!

- A form can contain as many hidden fields as required by the CGI that will process the form.

To add a hidden field

1. Make sure the insertion point is in the page containing the form to which you want to add a hidden field.

2. Choose Hidden Field from the Insert Invisible submenu under the Edit menu (see **Figure 49**).

The hidden field appears as a purple H icon on the page (see **Figure 50**).

To specify hidden field options

1. Click the hidden field icon once to select it (see **Figure 51**).

2. If the Inspector is not showing, choose Show Inspector from the Window menu (see **Figure 11**) or press ⌘; to display it.

3. If necessary, click the Inspector's Object tab to display the Hidden Field options (see **Figure 52**).

4. To name the field, enter a name in the Name edit box.

5. To set a value for the field, enter it in the Value edit box.

Adding Hidden Fields

About Submit & Reset Buttons

Forms usually include two special buttons:

■ The Submit button sends the information from the form to the CGI on the server.

■ The Reset button clears all entries in the form so the user can start fresh.

To add a Submit or Reset button

1. Position the insertion point where you want the button to appear.

2. Click one of the following buttons or press one of the following Command key equivalents:

   ▲ To add a Submit button, click the Insert Submit Button button or press ⌘ Control 9.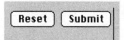

   ▲ To add a Reset button, click the Insert Reset Button button or press ⌘ Control 0.

The button you inserted appears at the insertion point (see **Figure 53**).

✔ Tips

■ You should only have one Submit button on a form.

■ Submit and Reset buttons are normally placed together on a form.

■ In most cases, Submit and Reset buttons are placed at the bottom of a form, right after the last input area.

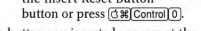

Figure 53. *The Reset and Submit buttons, which are standard equipment for forms, are usually placed together.*

Figure 54. *Double-click the button to edit it.*

To change the name of a button

1. Double-click the button. A dark border appears around it and an insertion point appears inside it (see **Figure 54**).

2. Edit the name of the button by selecting it and typing your changes (see **Figure 55**). The button resizes to accommodate the text inside it.

3. Click elsewhere in the page window to accept your changes.

Figure 55. *As you enter new text to appear on the button, the button resizes to accommodate it.*

To use an image as a Submit button

1. Select the image you want to use as a Submit button (see **Figure 56**).

2. If the Inspector is not showing, choose Show Inspector from the Window menu (see **Figure 11**) or press ⌘; to display it.

3. If necessary, click the Inspector's Object tab to display the Image options (see **Figure 57**).

4. Select the Button radio button in the Behavior area of the Inspector.

A blue border appears around the image to indicate that it is a button.

Figure 56. *Click once on the image you want to use as a Submit button to select it.*

Figure 57. *Use the Behavior area of the Inspector's Object tab for the selected image to set the image as a button.*

✔ Tip

■ I tell you more about working with images in **Chapter 5**.

About CGIs

Forms work with programs called CGIs (Common Gateway Interfaces) that run on the Web server. When a user fills in a form and clicks the Submit button, the information gathered by the form is processed by the CGI. The CGI can do almost anything with the data, such as:

- Send the data to someone via e-mail.
- Add the data to a database maintained in another application.
- Use the data to form the basis of a database search, perform the search, and display the results.
- Use the data to create a Web page.

✔ Tips

- The CGI's functionality (not the form itself) determines how the data is used.
- If you do not have a CGI to process data collected with a form, the form is useless.
- CGIs can be created with AppleScript (on Apple Servers) or other programming languages or purchased from third party vendors.

To specify a CGI for a form

1. If the Inspector is not showing, choose Show Inspector from the Window menu (see **Figure 11**) or press ⌘;) to display it.

2. If necessary, click the Inspector's Form tab to display its options (see **Figure 58**).

3. Enter the pathname for the CGI in the Action edit box.

4. Choose Get or Post from the pop-up menu beneath the Action edit box (see **Figure 59**).

Figure 58.
Use the Inspector's Form panel to set up a CGI.

Figure 59. *Choose Get or Post from this pop-up menu.*

✔ Tip

- If you're not sure what to enter in the Action edit box or choose from the pop-up menu beneath it, ask your Webmaster or System Administrator.

SETTING PAGE ATTRIBUTES 10

About Page Attributes

PageMill makes it easy to set options that affect the entire page, like:

- Page title, which appears in the title bar of a Web browser when the page is viewed.

- Base font size, which determines the default font size for the page.

- Base target, which determines the window or frame in which a linked page will open when its link is clicked in a frame.

- Colors—including body text, background, normal link, active link, and visited link colors—which determine the color of page elements.

- Background image, which puts a texture or image behind page text.

Most of these settings are made in the Inspector (see **Figure 1**).

Figure 1.
Use the Inspector to set most of the page attributes.

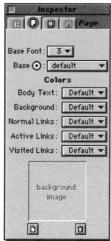

✔ Tips

- It is not necessary to set any of these options for your pages.

- To change default color and background options for all your pages, set options in Page Preferences (see **Figure 2**). This makes it easy to give your pages a consistent look and feel that can set them apart from other pages on the Web. I tell you how to set preferences in **Chapter 12**.

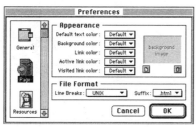

Figure 2. *By changing settings in the Appearance area of the Page Preferences dialog box, you can set default colors and backgrounds for all the pages you create with PageMill.*

About the Page Title

The page title is the name of the page as it appears on the World Wide Web. When you specify a page name, that name appears in the title bar of Web browser windows (see **Figure 3**).

Figure 3. *When you give your page a title, that title appears in the title bar of Web browsers like Netscape Navigator.*

✔ Tips

- The page title is not the same as the page name. The page name, which you specify when you save a file, is subject to the file naming restrictions of your Web server. The page title, however, can be almost anything you like. I tell you about saving files in **Chapter 1**.

- A page title is used as a link name if you create a link by dragging a Page icon into another page window. I tell you about creating links in **Chapter 7**.

- A page title is also used as entry text when someone "bookmarks" your page while viewing it with a Web browser. By making the title descriptive, you make the bookmark name descriptive, too.

To add a page title

1. Click in the Title edit box near the top of the page window to activate it (see **Figure 4**).

2. Type the title you want to assign and press [Return] or [Enter].

The title you entered appears in the Title edit box (see **Figure 5**).

Figure 4. *Activate the Title edit box.*

To edit or remove a page title

1. Click in the Title edit box to activate it.

2. To edit the title, make changes as desired and press [Return] or [Enter].

   or

   To remove the title, select the title, press [Delete] to delete it, and press [Return] or [Enter].

Figure 5. *Enter the title you want to assign and press [Return].*

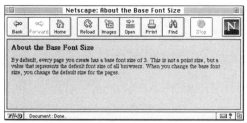

Figure 6a. *Here's a page with a base font of 3 when viewed in Netscape Navigator.*

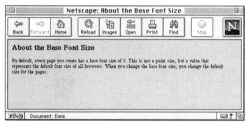

Figure 6b. *Here's the same page, with the base font set to 2.*

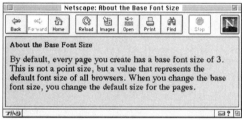

Figure 6c. *And here's the same page with the base font set to 5. The paragraph with a base font of 5 is larger than the heading with Heading 3 formatting applied.*

Figure 7.
To display the Inspector, choose Show Inspector from the Window menu.

Figure 8.
Use the Base Font pop-up menu to select a new relative font size.

About the Base Font Size

By default, every page you create has a base font size of 3. This is not a point size, but a value that represents the default font size of all browsers. When you change the base font size, you change the default size for the page.

Figures 6a, **6b**, and **6c** illustrate three different base font sizes. If you have trouble seeing the size differences in these illustrations, examine the word wrap differences—more text fits on each line with the smaller base font sizes.

✔ Tips

- Not all browsers recognize HTML font size tags. Netscape Navigator 2.0 or later and Microsoft Internet Explorer 3.0 or later do.

- Change the base font only when you want to change the appearance of all text that is not formatted with a heading format. I tell you more about changing font size for selected characters in **Chapter 3** and about headings in **Chapter 4**.

To set the base font size

1. If the Inspector is not showing, choose Show Inspector from the Window menu (see **Figure 7**) or press ⌘ ; .

2. If necessary, click the Page tab to display the Page panel's options (see **Figure 1**).

3. Choose a relative font size from the Base Font pop-up menu (see **Figure 8**). Select a lower number to make the font size smaller and a higher number to make the font size larger.

The size of any text that is not formatted with a heading format changes to reflect the size you selected. (I tell you about heading formats in **Chapter 4**.)

Setting the Base Font Size

About the Base Target

Clicking a link on a page that is displayed within a frameset can display the destination page in a variety of locations. You can use the Base Target pop-up menu in the Page panel of the Inspector (see **Figure 1**) to set the default location. Your choices are:

- *Default*, which displays the linked page in the same window or frame as the link.

- *New window*, which creates a new browser window to display the linked page.

- *Parent window*, which displays the linked page with the "top-level" frameset—the main frameset for the window containing the link.

- *Same frame*, which displays the linked page in the same frame as the link.

- *Same window*, which displays the linked page in the same window as the link.

✔ Tips

- Settings in the Base Target pop-up menu affect only those pages which are displayed within frames and are used only if a clicked link does not have its own target frame setting.

- I tell you how to create and edit text and graphic links in **Chapter 7**.

- I tell you how to set the target frame for individual links in **Chapter 8**.

To set the base target

1. If the Inspector is not showing, choose Show Inspector from the Window menu (see **Figure 7**) or press ⌘;.

2. If necessary, click the Page tab to display the Page panel's options (see **Figure 1**).

3. Choose an option from the Base Target pop-up menu (see **Figure 9**).

Figure 9.
Use the Base Target pop-up menu to set a default location to display a linked page when the link is clicked from within a frame.

About Page Color Options

The Page panel of the Inspector (see **Figure 1**) lets you change the color of a number of page elements:

- *Body Text* sets the color of text on the page that is not a link. The default color is black.

- *Background* sets the color of the page background. The default color is gray.

- *Normal Links* sets the color of links that have not been visited. The default color is blue.

- *Active Links* sets the color of links as they are clicked. The default color is red.

- *Visited Links* sets the color of links that have been visited. The default color is purple.

✔ Tips

- You can override the color of any body text that is not a link by selecting it and applying a color. I tell you how to apply colors to text in **Chapter 3**.

- Background color is not used if the page has a background image—unless part of that image is transparent. I tell you about background images later in this chapter and about making parts of images transparent in **Chapter 5**.

- For an interesting effect, try white or light colored text on a black or dark colored background (see **Figure 10**).

- If the background color is similar to text or link colors, text will be difficult to read (see **Figure 11**).

- Most color options can be overridden by color settings in the user's browser. This means that a user may not view the page the way you intended it to appear if you change colors.

Figure 10. *For an interesting effect, try light colored text on a dark colored background.*

Figure 11. *If text color and background color are too close, text can be difficult to read.*

To set colors

1. If the Inspector is not showing, choose Show Inspector from the Window menu (see **Figure 7**) or press ⌃⌘;.

2. If necessary, click the Page tab to display the Page panel's options (see **Figure 1**).

3. Choose Custom from the Body Text, Background, Normal Links, Active Links, or Visited Links pop-up menu (see **Figure 12**).

4. Use the Color Wheel that appears to select a new color (see **Figure 13**) and click OK or press Return or Enter. The change takes affect immediately.

5. Repeat steps 3 and 4 for each element whose color you want to change.

✔ Tip

■ Another way to change a color in the Page panel of the Inspector is to drag a color from the Color panel onto the pop-up menu for the element whose color you want to change. I tell you about the Color panel in **Chapter 1**.

To restore the default color

1. If the Inspector is not showing, choose Show Inspector from the Window menu (see **Figure 7**) or press ⌃⌘;.

2. If necessary, click the Page tab to display the Page panel's options (see **Figure 1**).

3. Choose Default from the Body Text, Background, Normal Links, Active Links, or Visited Links pop-up menu (see **Figure 12**). The change takes affect immediately.

Figure 12. *The pop-up menu to change a color looks the same for all elements.*

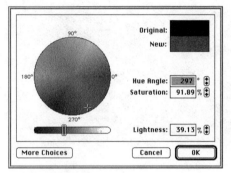

Figure 13. *Use a Color Wheel to select the color you want.*

Figure 14. *Default colored text disappears against a dark background...*

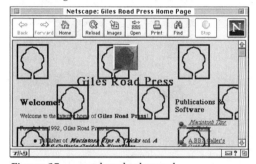

Figure 15. *...or a busy background.*

Figure 16. *By lightening and reducing contrast, the text shows through...*

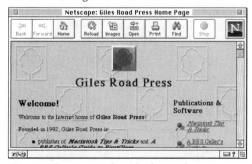

Figure 17. *...even on busy backgrounds.*

About Background Images

A background image is an image that is used as a background pattern or texture behind the text and other images on a Web page. A background image can add professional polish to a Web page.

✔ Tips

■ For best results, use small background images. They take less time to load so your pages display more quickly.

■ You can speed up page loading by using a limited number of background images on the Web pages at your site. Since Web browsers cache recently downloaded page and image files, they don't need to download the same files repeatedly during the session.

■ Be sure the color of a background image contrasts with the color of page text. If the colors are too similar, page text will be illegible (see **Figure 14**). To remedy this problem, either change the color of the background image or the text. I tell you how to change text color later in this chapter.

■ Try not to use "busy" images for backgrounds. Images with too many rich colors make poor backgrounds because text and other images on top of them are difficult to see clearly (see **Figure 15**).

■ You can make an otherwise unsuitable image more appropriate for use as a background pattern by lightening it and reducing its contrast in a graphics application like Adobe Photoshop (see **Figures 16** and **17**).

■ You can use the Transparency tool in the Image window to make the background of an image transparent before using it as a background image. I tell you how to work with Images in **Chapter 5**.

To add a background image with the Inspector

1. If the Inspector is not showing, choose Show Inspector from the Window menu (see **Figure 7**) or press ⌘ ;.

2. If necessary, click the Page tab to display the Page panel's options (see **Figure 1**).

3. With the PageMill application active, drag an image file icon from the Finder to the background image well in the Inspector (see **Figure 18**).

   or

   Drag an image from the PageMill window to the background image well in the Inspector (see **Figure 19**).

   or

   Click the tiny page icon beneath the background image well in the Inspector and use the Open dialog box (see **Figure 20**) to locate and open the image you want to use as a background.

The image fills the background image well in the Inspector and becomes a repeating pattern in the background of the page (see **Figure 21**).

To add a background image with the Page icon

With the PageMill application active, drag an image file icon from the Finder to the Page icon near the top left corner of the PageMill window (see **Figure 22**).

or

Drag the Image icon from PageMill's Image window to the Page icon near the top left corner of the PageMill window (see **Figure 23**).

When you release the mouse button, the image becomes a repeating pattern in the background of the page.

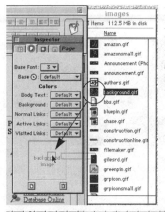

Figure 18. *Drag the Finder icon for an image into the background image well in the Inspector…*

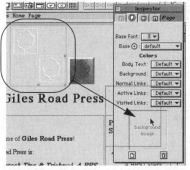

Figure 19. *…or drag an image from the PageMill window to the background image well…*

Figure 20. *…or use the Open dialog box to open and select an image.*

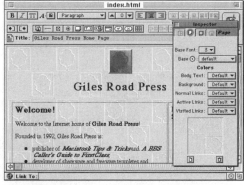

Figure 21. *The image becomes a background pattern.*

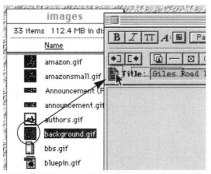

Figure 22. *Drag the Finder icon for an image onto the Page icon...*

Figure 23. *...or drag the Image icon from the Image window onto the Page icon.*

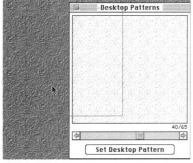

Figure 24. *Drag the pattern onto the desktop...*

Figure 25. *...to create a picture clipping file.*

To use a desktop pattern as a background image

1. Open the Desktop Patterns control panel.

2. In the Desktop Patterns window that appears, use the scroll bar to display the pattern you want to use as a background image.

3. Drag the image you want out of the Desktop Patterns window and onto the desktop (see **Figure 24**) or into a Finder folder icon or window.

   A picture clipping icon appears (see **Figure 25**). This is a file containing a PICT version of the desktop pattern.

4. Follow the steps on the previous page to use the picture clipping file as a background.

✔ Tips

- To follow the above steps, you must have System 7.5 or later properly installed on your Macintosh.

- Desktop patterns make excellent background images for Web pages since they're small and make seamless patterns. Use them as they are or open them in a graphics application like Adobe Photoshop to change brightness and contrast.

To remove a background image

Click the tiny trash can icon beneath the background image well in the Inspector (see **Figure 1**).

The image and background disappear.

Using a Desktop Pattern as a Background

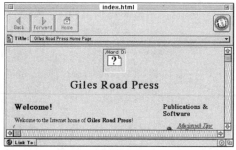

Figure 1. *Use PageMill's Preview mode to find missing images...*

Figure 2. *...or incorrect URLs.*

Figure 3. *Open pages with several Web browsers to avoid surprises. In this example, version 1.1 of the America Online Web Browser failed to display form fields and buttons or animate a GIF.*

Figure 4. *Use a Web browser and Internet connection to test external links.*

About Testing Pages

Even after you've put the finishing touches on your Web pages, they may not be ready for installation on your Web server. There's one last thing you need to do: test them.

The testing process should include the following procedures:

- Use PageMill's Preview mode to view pages and test all local links. This is how you can learn about missing images (see **Figure 1**) or incorrect URLs on your site (see **Figure 2**).

- Open the pages with a variety of Web browsers to make sure they look the way you expect them to. This is how you can avoid formatting and incompatibility surprises (see **Figure 3**).

- Use your favorite Web browser to test remote links. This is how you can learn about incorrect URLs for pages that aren't on your site (see **Figure 4**).

✔ Tip

- In reality, the testing process never ends. Even if you never change a thing on your Web site, other sites change regularly. If your pages include external links, it's important that you test them regularly. That's the only way you can be sure that the linked pages are still available on an ever-changing Internet.

About Testing Pages in PageMill's Preview Mode

PageMill's Preview mode gives you an idea of how your Web pages will look when viewed with a Web browser (see **Figure 5**). It also lets you test links and some multimedia objects, like animated GIFs and QuickTime movies.

✔ Tip

■ Don't depend solely on PageMill's Preview mode to test your pages. Since the appearance of a Web page varies depending on the browser used to view it, it's a good idea to open your pages with one or more popular Web browsers—like Netscape Navigator and Microsoft Internet Explorer. I tell you more about testing pages with Web browsers later in this chapter.

■ You can use PageMill to test local links—those links on your Web site—but you must use a Web browser and a connection to the Internet to test remote links—those links on other Web sites. I tell you about testing local and remote links later in this chapter.

■ As you uncover problems with your pages, you can switch back to Edit mode to fix them. The information throughout this book should help you solve any problems you might encounter.

■ I tell you about links in **Chapter 7** and about multimedia objects in **Chapter 5**.

■ You can set an option in the General Preferences dialog box (see **Figure 6**) to automatically open all pages in Preview mode. I tell you about setting Preferences in **Chapter 12**.

Figure 5. *Preview mode gives you an idea of how your pages will look when viewed with a typical Web browser.*

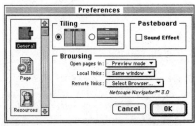

Figure 6. *Set options in the General Preferences dialog box to specify the mode in which pages should be opened, the window in which links should appear, and the browser that should be used to check remote links.*

Figure 7. *In Edit mode, click the Toggle Preview Mode button to switch to Preview Mode.*

To view a page in Preview mode

In Edit mode, click the Toggle Preview Mode button (see **Figure 7**) or press `Control` ⌃ ⌘ `Spacebar`.

Figure 8. *When you're in Preview mode, the Toggle Preview Mode button looks like this.*

✔ Tip

■ The Toggle Preview Mode button looks like the one in **Figure 7** only if the page is currently displayed in Edit mode. Once you're in Preview mode, the Toggle Preview Mode button changes to look like the one in **Figure 8**.

To check page appearance in Preview mode

Use the scroll bars to scroll through the page and examine it for problems. Some areas you should concentrate on are:

▲ Text formatting and legibility.

▲ Images and their borders (if any).

▲ Multimedia objects like animated GIFs and QuickTime movies.

▲ Table and table cell dimensions and borders.

▲ Frame layout and dimensions.

✔ Tips

■ It's a good idea to resize the window once or twice to see how changes in window size affect word wrap, tables, and frames.

■ In order to display QuickTime movies in Preview mode, you must have the QuickTime plug-in properly installed. I tell you about QuickTime and the QuickTime plug-in in **Chapter 5**.

■ I tell you about text formatting in **Chapters 3** and **4**, about images and multimedia objects in **Chapter 5**, about tables in **Chapter 6**, and about frames in **Chapter 8**.

Viewing Pages with Preview Mode

To check links in Preview mode

1. Position the mouse pointer on a link. The mouse pointer turns into a pointing finger and the URL for the link appears in the Link Location bar at the bottom of the window (see **Figure 9**).

2. Click the link once. One of three things will happen:

   ▲ If the link you clicked is a local link, the linked page appears in the Preview mode window.

   ▲ If the link you clicked is a remote link but viewing remote files is disabled, a dialog box like the one in **Figure 10** appears. Click OK to dismiss it.

   ▲ If the link you clicked is a remote link, viewing remote files is enabled, and you have access to the Internet, PageMill will launch a Web browser, connect to the Internet, and display the linked page.

3. Repeat steps 1 and 2 to check all links.

✔ Tips

■ You can set options in the General Preference dialog box (see **Figure 6**) to specify local and remote link viewing options. I tell you how to set preferences in **Chapter 12**.

■ You can use buttons (see **Figure 11a**) and a pop-up menu (see **Figure 11b**) at the top of the Preview mode window to move backward and forward through the pages you check.

■ To navigate forward and backward through links in a frameset, position your mouse pointer in a blank area of the page window and press the mouse button down until a menu like the one in **Figure 12** appears. Choose an option to navigate in the frame.

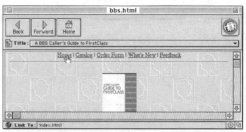

Figure 9. *When you point to a link, the mouse pointer turns into a pointing finger and the link URL appears in the Link Location bar at the bottom of the screen.*

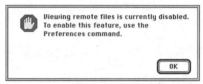

Figure 10. *If the remote file viewing option is disabled, you'll see a dialog box like this when you click a link to a remote file.*

Click to view the previous page.   Click to view the home page.

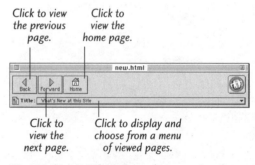

Click to view the next page.   Click to display and choose from a menu of viewed pages.

Figures 11a & 11b. *To move from one viewed page to another, click buttons (above) or choose a page from a pop-up menu (above and below).*

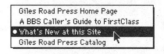

Figure 12. *Use a pop-up menu to navigate from one page to another within a frame.*

About Testing Pages with a Web browser

As mentioned earlier in this chapter, PageMill's Preview mode is not the same as a Web browser. Only by viewing pages with specific browsers can you really see what the pages will look like to the people who view them.

Figures 13, **14**, and **15** show examples of the page from **Figure 5** when viewed with a number of popular browsers in the same size window. Note the differences.

✔ Tips

■ You do not need an Internet connection to open and view a Web page file on your hard disk with a Web browser.

■ Test your pages with as many Web browsers as you can to get a good idea of all the appearance possibilities and see how certain older browsers display incompatible formatting options like tables, horizontally aligned graphic objects, and frames.

■ You must use a Web browser to view and test certain multimedia objects, like Java Applets.

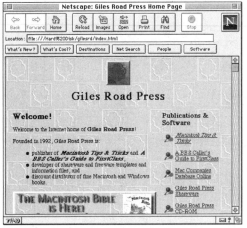

Figure 13. *Here's what the page in* **Figure 5** *looks like when viewed with Netscape Navigator 3.0,…*

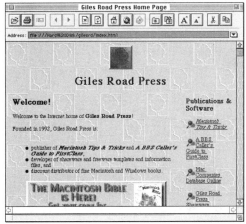

Figure 14. *…here it is when viewed with Microsoft Internet Explorer 2.0,…*

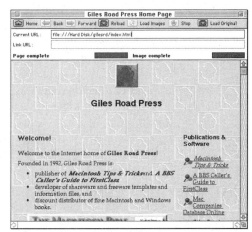

Figure 15. *…and here it is when viewed with the America Online Browser 1.1.*

To open a page with a Web browser

In the Finder, drag the icon for the page you want to view on top of the application icon for the Web browser with which you want to view it (see **Figure 16**). If the program isn't already running, it will launch.

or

Launch the Web browser application with which you want to view the page and use the Open or Open File command under its File menu (see **Figure 17**) to locate and open the page you want to view.

A window containing the page will appear.

✔ Tip

■ If you use either of the above techniques to load a web page that you're currently working with in PageMill, be sure to save the page in PageMill before opening the page with your Web browser.

To open a page with a Web browser from within PageMill

1. If necessary, activate the window containing the page you want to view with a Web browser.

2. Choose the browser you want to use to view the file from the Switch to submenu under the Window menu (see **Figure 18**).

   If the program isn't already running, it will launch. A window containing the page will appear.

✔ Tip

■ To take advantage of the Switch to menu feature, you must configure it. Specify which programs should appear by setting Switch To Preferences (see **Figure 19**). I tell you how to set preferences in **Chapter 12**.

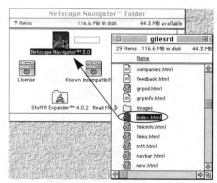

Figure 16. *Drag the icon for the file you want to view onto the icon for the browser with which you want to view it.*

Figure 17.
Most browsers, like Netscape Navigator shown here, have an Open or Open File command under the File menu. You can use this command to open a page file on disk.

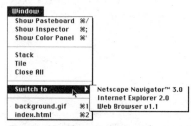

Figure 18. *Choose a browser from the Switch to submenu under the Window menu.*

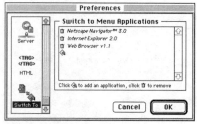

Figure 19. *Use the Switch To Preferences dialog box to configure the Switch to submenu.*

To test appearance & links with a Web browser

1. To test appearance, use the scroll bars to scroll through the page and examine it for problems. Some areas you should concentrate on are:

   ▲ Text formatting and legibility.

   ▲ Images and multimedia objects.

   ▲ Compatibility issues affecting the display of text, tables, forms, and frames.

2. To test links, click each link to display linked pages.

✔ Tips

■ When testing appearance, it's a good idea to resize the window once or twice to see how changes in window size affect word wrap, tables, and frames.

■ Your browser can test local links without connecting to the Internet. If you try to test a remote link, however, your browser may attempt to connect to the Internet.

■ Each remote link that is successfully tested will turn purple or the custom color you may have specified for visited links.

■ If you discover problems with your pages, you can switch back to PageMill and use its Edit mode to fix them. Be sure to save changes to the page before using your browser's Reload button or command to re-check the page— otherwise the unchanged version will load and you won't see your changes.

Testing Pages with a Web Browser

About Download Statistics

Each element of each page or frameset must be downloaded from your Web site to a user's computer before the entire page is displayed. PageMill's Download Statistics feature provides information about the amount of time it will take users to download and display your pages.

To view Download Statistics

1. If necessary, activate the window containing the page whose Download Statistics you want to view.

2. Choose Download Statistics from the Edit menu (see **Figure 20**) or press ⌘ ⌘ U.

3. A window like the one in **Figure 21** or **22** appears. It provides size and download time information for a selected object (if applicable), the page (or frame), and the frameset (if applicable).

4. If desired, choose a connect speed from the kbps pop-up menu (see **Figure 23**) to see download time information at a different speed (see **Figure 24**).

5. When you are finished using the Download Statistics window, click OK or press Return or Enter to dismiss it.

✔ Tips

■ For best results, try to keep your page sizes small and quick to download. Remember, not everyone has a direct connection to the Internet. Many people won't wait more than 10 or 15 seconds for a page to load.

■ You can keep page size small (and download times low) by limiting the size and number of images and other multimedia objects in your pages.

Viewing Download Statistics

Figure 20. *Choose Download Statistics from the Edit menu.*

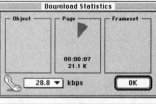

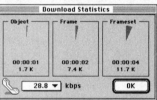

Figures 21 & 22. *Here's what the Download Statistics window looks like for a page (top) and for a frameset with an object within a frame selected (bottom).*

Figure 23. *Use the kbps pop-up menu to change the speed at which the page size is evaluated to calculate download times.*

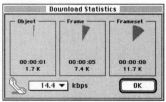

Figure 24. *Here are the Download Statistics from* **Figure 22** *with the connection speed changed to 14.4 kbps.*

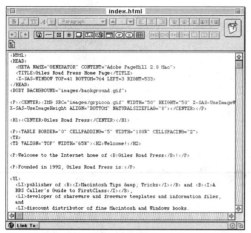

Figure 25. *PageMill's Source View lets you view and edit the HTML underlying a Web page. Here's the beginning of the code for the page in* **Figure 5**.

About Editing HTML

Underlying every Web page is programming code written using HTML (HyperText Markup Language) tags. PageMill, which supports HTML version 3.2, automatically generates the HTML code for the pages you create with it. **Figure 25** shows the HTML source code PageMill has written for the Web page that appears in **Figures 5**, **13**, **14**, and **15**.

PageMill offers several ways you can work with the HTML code it writes:

- ■ Add comments that do not appear on the Web page but are encoded in the underlying HTML.

- ■ Add placeholders that contain HTML code that is not checked or edited by PageMill.

- ■ View and edit actual HTML code using PageMill's Source view (see **Figure 25**).

✔ Tips

- ■ Editing the HTML code that PageMill generates makes it possible to include formatting and features that cannot be automatically included by PageMill.

- ■ **Appendix D** provides a list of all the HTML tags that PageMill supports, as well as some additional tags that might interest advanced PageMill users.

- ■ Although PageMill doesn't support every HTML tag, most browsers don't support them all either. If you use PageMill to create your Web pages and don't add unsupported tags and extensions, you're more likely to produce pages that will appear relatively the same with all browsers.

- ■ You can use PageMill to open pages created by any HTML editor or Web publishing tool. If PageMill encounters tags it does not recognize, it displays a question mark.

About Editing HTML

To add a comment

1. In Edit mode, position the insertion point where you want to place the comment (see **Figure 26**).

2. Choose Comment from the Insert Invisible submenu under the Edit menu (see **Figure 27**). A comment icon appears at the insertion point (see **Figure 28**).

3. Click the comment icon once to select it (see **Figure 29**).

4. If the Inspector is not showing, choose Show Inspector from the Window menu (see **Figure 30**) or press ⌘;.

5. If necessary, click the Object tab to display the Comment options (see **Figure 31**).

6. Enter your comment in the Comment scrolling window. When you're finished, it might look something like **Figure 32**.

✔ Tips

■ As you can see in **Figure 32**, text does not automatically word wrap in the Comment scrolling window. You must press Return to begin a new line.

■ To read or edit a comment, follow steps 3 through 5 above.

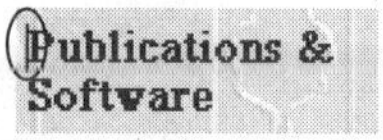

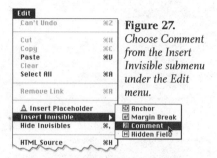

Figure 26. *Position the insertion point where you want to place the comment.*

Figure 27. *Choose Comment from the Insert Invisible submenu under the Edit menu.*

Figure 28. *A comment icon appears at the insertion point.*

Figure 29. *Click the comment icon once to select it.*

Figure 30. *If the Inspector is not showing, choose Show Inspector from the Window menu to display it.*

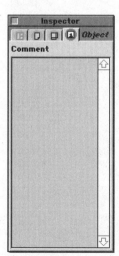

Figure 31. *Enter your comment in this scrolling window.*

Figure 32. *When you're finished, it might look like this.*

Adding Comments

Figure 33. *Position the insertion point where you want the placeholder to appear.*

Figure 34. *Choose Insert Placeholder from the Edit menu.*

Figure 35. *A placeholder icon appears.*

Figure 36. *Click the placeholder icon to select it.*

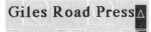

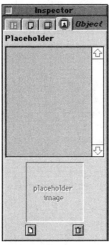

Figure 37. *Enter HTML code in this scrolling window.*

Figure 38. *When you're finished, it might look like this.*

To add a placeholder

1. In Edit mode, position the insertion point where you want the placeholder to appear (see **Figure 33**).

2. Choose Insert Placeholder from the Edit menu (see **Figure 34**). A placeholder icon appears at the insertion point (see **Figure 35**).

3. Click the placeholder icon once to select it (see **Figure 36**).

4. If the Inspector is not showing, choose Show Inspector from the Window menu (see **Figure 30**) or press ⌘;.

5. If necessary, click the Object tab to display the Placeholder options (see **Figure 37**).

6. Enter HTML code in the Placeholder scrolling window. When you're finished, it might look something like **Figure 38**.

✔ Tips

- As you can see in **Figure 38**, text does not automatically word wrap in the Placeholder scrolling window. You must press Return to begin a new line.

- If desired, you can click the page icon beneath the placeholder image well in the Inspector (see **Figures 37** and **38**) and use the Open dialog box that appears to select an image to appear in place of the default placeholder icon.

- The placeholder icon (or any image you use to replace it) appears only in PageMill.

- Placeholders offer a good way to insert Java scripts into your Web pages because they protect the scripts, which cannot be interpreted properly by PageMill, from possible editing by PageMill's HTML checking routines.

- To read or edit the contents of a placeholder, follow steps 3 through 5 above.

Adding a Placeholder

To view & edit HTML source

1. If necessary, activate the window containing the page whose HTML code you want to view.

2. Choose HTML Source from the Edit menu (see **Figure 39**) or press ⌃⌘H.

3. The HTML source code for the page appears in the window (see **Figure 25**). Make changes as desired right in the window.

4. To return to Edit view, choose HTML Source from the Edit menu or press ⌃⌘H again.

Figure 39.
Choose HTML Source from the Edit menu.

✔ Tips

■ To view the HTML source for a frame, click in the frame to activate it before choosing the HTML Source command as instructed above.

■ You cannot view the HTML source for a frameset from within PageMill. To view the HTML underlying a frameset, you must open its file with a text editor or word processor like SimpleText, Microsoft Word, or Claris MacWrite Pro.

■ Save the page before editing HTML code, just in case something goes wrong during the editing process.

■ The text that appears in HTML Source view is color coded to make it easier to read. You can change the color coding, as well as the HTML syntax for font size and alignment coding in the HTML Preferences dialog box (see **Figure 40**). I tell you how to set preferences in **Chapter 12**.

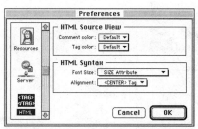

Figure 40. *You can set preferences for HTML view appearance and HTML coding in the Preferences dialog box.*

About Web Page Installation

Once your pages have been created, tested, and perhaps enhanced, they're ready to be installed on your Web server.

■ If your Web server is accessible through an internal network, and you can mount its hard disk on your Macintosh desktop, you can install the page and image files you created by simply dragging them into the proper folders.

■ If your Web server is accessible only by File Transfer Protocol (FTP), you'll need to use a program like Fetch to copy the page and image files from your hard disk into the proper folders on the server's hard disk.

Your Webmaster or System Administrator can provide more information about copying your Web pages and image files to the server.

✔ Tips

■ If you do not install your completed pages on a Web server, they will not be accessible to anyone but you.

■ If your Web server is not connected to the Internet through an Internet Service Provider (ISP), your pages will not be accessible to the World Wide Web.

■ The instructions on the following pages are far from thorough. There are too many possible configurations to discuss them all in this book. Ask your Webmaster or System Administrator for specific instructions if you need more help.

To copy files over a network to a Web server

1. Use the Chooser to mount the Web server's hard disk. Its icon should appear on your desktop (see **Figure 41**).

2. Open the remote root directory on the server's hard disk. (This is the folder in which your page files will reside.)

3. Open the folder on your hard disk where your pages have been saved.

4. Select the files for the pages you want to copy and drag their icons to the window for the remote root directory (see **Figure 42**). A copy progress dialog box appears. Wait until it disappears before you continue.

5. Open the images folder in the remote root directory window. (This is the folder in which your image files will reside.)

6. Select the files for the images you want to copy and drag their icons to the window for the images folder inside the remote root directory. A copy progress dialog box appears. Wait until it disappears before you continue.

7. When you're finished, drag the server's hard disk icon to the trash to unmount it and close all its windows.

✔ Tip

■ It's vital that the relationship between page files, image files, and folders is the same on the server as it is on your hard disk. For example, if image files are inside a folder called Images in the folder containing your Web pages on your hard disk, they must also be inside a folder called Images in the folder containing your Web pages on the server.

Figure 41.
When you mount the server's hard disk, its icon appears on your desktop.

Figure 42. *Drag the file icons to the remote root directory window of the server hard disk to copy them.*

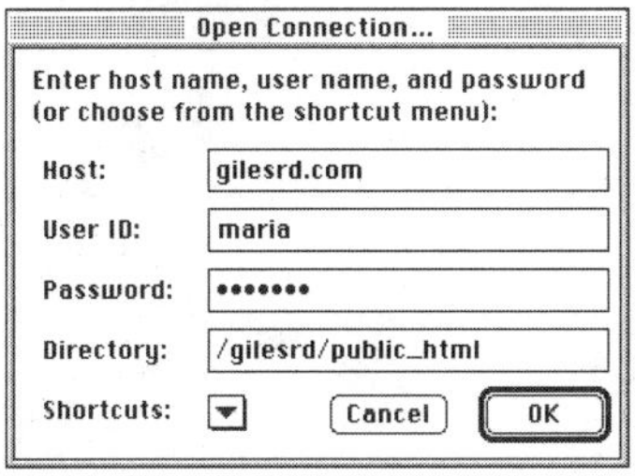

Figure 43.
Use the Open Connection dialog box to connect to the Web server.

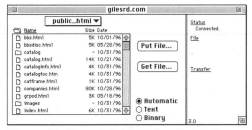

Figure 44. *The main Fetch window displays the contents of the currently open directory.*

Figure 45. *Use this dialog box to select the files you want to copy to the server.*

Figure 46.
Choose Text and Raw Data from the pop-up menus in the Put Files dialog box.

✔ Tip

■ For more information about Fetch or to obtain a copy, check *http://www.dartmouth.edu/pages/ softdev/fetch.html.*

To copy files to a Web server with Fetch

1. Launch Fetch.

2. In the Open Connection dialog box, enter the Host, User ID, Password, and Directory for the remote root directory (see **Figure 43**).

3. Click OK to establish a connection to the Internet. The main Fetch window appears, displaying the contents of the remote root directory (see **Figure 44**).

4. Choose Put Files and Folders from Fetch's Remote menu.

5. In the dialog box that appears, locate and add all the page files you want to copy to the remote root directory (see **Figure 45**). Then click Done.

6. In the Put Files dialog box, choose Text from the Text Files pop-up menu and Raw Data from the Other Files pop-up menu (see **Figure 46**). Then click OK.

7. Wait while the files are copied to the server.

8. In the main Fetch window (see **Figure 44**), locate and open the folder in which your images will be stored.

9. Choose Put Files and Folders from Fetch's Remote menu.

10. In the dialog box that appears, locate and add all the image files you want to copy to the remote root directory. Then click Done.

11. In the Put Files dialog box, choose Text from the Text Files pop-up menu and Raw Data from the Other Files pop-up menu (see **Figure 46**). Then click OK.

12. Wait while the files are copied to the server.

13. When you're finished, choose Quit from Fetch's File menu to quit.

Using Fetch to Copy Files to a Web Server

About PageMill Preferences

PageMill's Preferences dialog box lets you set the way PageMill works:

■ *General* preferences (see **Figure 2**) control window tiling, Pasteboard sound, and browsing.

■ *Page* preferences (see **Figure 8**) control the appearance and format of pages.

■ *Resources* preferences (see **Figure 14**) set the resource folder and image map format.

■ *Server* preferences (see **Figure 17**) maintain local aliases for remote Web servers.

■ *HTML* preferences (see **Figure 19**) set HTML source view colors and syntax options.

■ *Switch To* preferences (see **Figure 22**) customize the Switch to submenu under the Window menu.

✔ Tips

■ Since some preferences affect pathnames used within files, it's a good idea to review and set preferences before you create Web pages with PageMill.

■ Many preference settings apply to pages you create *after* closing the Preferences dialog box—*not* to pages that are open when you change settings.

To open the Preferences dialog box

Choose Preferences from the Edit menu (see **Figure 1**).

or

Press Control ⌘ P.

Figure 1.
To open the Preferences dialog box, choose Preferences from the Edit menu.

To set General preferences

1. In the Preferences dialog box, click the General icon (see **Figure 2**).

2. Set options as follows:

   ▲ To set the way windows arrange when you choose Tile from the Window menu, select a Tiling radio button. The icons beside the radio buttons illustrate how the windows will tile.

   ▲ To toggle a page-flipping sound effect that can play when you change Pasteboard pages, turn the Sound Effect check box under Pasteboard on or off.

   ▲ To set the mode in which pages are opened, choose an option from the Open pages in pop-up menu (see **Figure 3**).

   ▲ To set the window in which a linked page on your hard disk will appear when you click the link in Preview mode, choose an option from the Local links pop-up menu (see **Figure 4**).

   ▲ To set the browser in which a linked page on a remote server will appear when you click the link in Preview mode, choose Select Browser from the Remote links pop-up menu (see **Figure 5**). Then use the Open dialog box that appears (see **Figure 6**) to locate your favorite browser, select it, and click the Open button. The name of the browser appears in the Preferences dialog box (see **Figure 7**).

3. Click OK or press Return or Enter to save your changes.

✔ Tip

■ To disable remote link viewing, choose Disabled from the Remote links pop-up menu (see **Figure 5**).

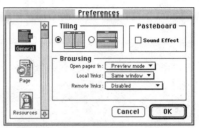

Figure 2. *The General preferences control window tiling, Pasteboard sound, and browsing options. These are the default settings.*

Figure 3. *The Open pages in pop-up menu.*

Figure 4. *The Local links pop-up menu.*

Figure 5. *To specify a browser with which to open linked pages on a remote server, choose Select Browser from the Remote links pop-up menu.*

Figure 6. *Use the Open dialog box to locate and select a browser.*

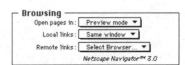

Figure 7. *The name of the browser you selected appears under the pop-up menu.*

Setting General Preferences

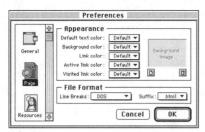

Figure 8. *Page preferences let you set the default options for all pages you create.*

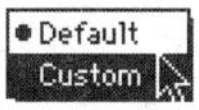

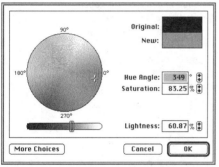

Figure 9. *To change a color, choose Custom from the appropriate pop-up menu.*

Figure 10. *Use a standard Color Wheel like this one to select a custom default color.*

Figure 11.
The background image you select appears in the background image area of the dialog box.

Figure 12.
The Line Breaks pop-up menu.

Figure 13.
The Suffix pop-up menu.

To set Page preferences

1. In the Preferences dialog box, click the Page icon (see **Figure 8**).

2. Set options as follows:

   ▲ To set a default color, choose Custom from the appropriate pop-up menu (see **Figure 9**) in the Appearance area. Then use the Color Wheel that appears (see **Figure 10**) to select a new color. Click OK or press ⌈Return⌋ or ⌈Enter⌋ to accept the new color.

   ▲ To set a default background image, click the left icon below the Background Image well. Then use the Open dialog box that appears to locate and open a background image. The image you selected appears in the dialog box (see **Figure 11**).

   ▲ To set line break formatting for your Web server, choose an option from the Line Breaks pop-up menu (see **Figure 12**).

   ▲ To set the default file suffix for pages you create, choose an option from the Suffix pop-up menu (see **Figure 13**).

3. Click OK or press ⌈Return⌋ or ⌈Enter⌋ to save your changes.

✔ Tips

■ Setting default colors and backgrounds is a great way to enhance consistency among the pages you create.

■ To return any color to the default, choose Default from the appropriate pop-up menu in the Appearance area. I tell you about default page and link colors in **Chapter 10**.

■ If you're not sure how to set the Line Breaks and Suffix options, ask your Webmaster or System Administrator.

Setting Page Preferences

To set Resources preferences

1. In the Preferences dialog box, click the Resources icon (see **Figure 14**).

2. Set options as follows:

   ▲ To set the default location for objects used in Web pages, click the folder icon in the Resource Folder area. Use the Open dialog box that appears to locate and select the folder in which you want objects saved. The path to the folder appears in the Preferences dialog box (see **Figure 15**).

   ▲ Choose the server-side image map format required for your server from the Map Format pop-up menu (see **Figure 16**).

3. Click OK or press [Return] or [Enter] to save your changes.

✔ Tips

■ Set the Resource Folder before creating Web pages. Images converted and saved by PageMill will be saved into this folder.

■ If you're not sure how to set the Map Format option, ask your Webmaster or System Administrator.

■ I tell you about objects (including images) in **Chapter 5** and about image maps in **Chapter 7**.

Figure 14. *The Resources preferences let you set the location of object files and the image map format.*

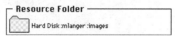

Figure 15. *When you select a new resource folder, its path appears in the Preferences dialog box.*

Figure 16. *The Map Format pop-up menu.*

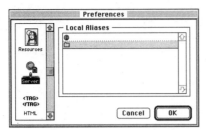

Figure 17. *Use the Server preferences dialog box to set local aliases for remote Web servers.*

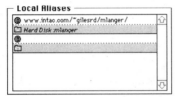

Figure 18. *Here's an example of an entry for a directory on a remote Web server that is mirrored on a local hard disk.*

To set Server preferences

1. In the Preferences dialog box, click the Server icon (see **Figure 17**).
2. Click beside the globe icon to position an insertion point. Then enter the domain name and directory for the Web site.
3. Click the folder icon beneath the globe. Use the Open dialog box that appears to locate and select the folder on your hard disk that will mirror the Web server directory. When you're finished, the entry might look like the one in **Figure 18**.
4. Repeat steps 2 and 4 for each local alias you want to identify.
5. Click OK or press [Return] or [Enter] to save your changes.

✔ Tips

- Set local aliases for any Web pages you create and save on a local hard disk that will later be copied or uploaded to a Web server. This ensures that the correct pathnames are used for local links and multimedia object resources when the files are put on the Web server. I tell you about links in **Chapter 7** and about multimedia objects in **Chapter 5**.

- I tell you about copying or uploading Web page files to a Web server in **Chapter 11**.

To set HTML preferences

1. In the Preferences dialog box, click the HTML icon (see **Figure 19**).

2. Set options as follows:

   ▲ To set the colors for comments and tags in HTML source view, choose Custom from the appropriate pop-up menu (see **Figure 9**) in the HTML Source View area. Then use the Color Wheel that appears (see **Figure 10**) to select a new color. Click OK or press [Return] or [Enter] to accept your changes.

   ▲ To set the way font size is coded by PageMill, choose an option from the Font Size pop-up menu (see **Figure 20**).

   ▲ To set the way alignment is coded by PageMill, choose an option from the Alignment pop-up menu (see **Figure 21**).

3. Click OK or press [Return] or [Enter] to save your changes.

✔ Tips

■ To return either HTML Source View color to the default, choose Default from the appropriate pop-up menu in the HTML Source View area.

■ Although PageMill's Alignment default is <P> Tag, you may get better browser compatibility by choosing <CENTER> Tag from the Alignment pop-up menu (see **Figure 21**). For maximum Netscape Navigator compatibility, choose <DIV> Tag.

■ I tell you about HTML Source View in **Chapter 11**, about font size in **Chapter 3**, and about alignment in **Chapter 4**.

■ I tell you about HTML tags in **Appendix D**.

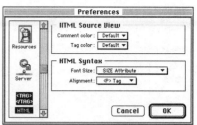

Figure 19. *Use the HTML preferences dialog box to set the way HTML looks and is coded in PageMill.*

Figure 20. *The Font Size pop-up menu.*

Figure 21. *The Alignment pop-up menu.*

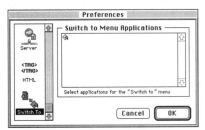

Figure 22. *Use the Switch To preferences dialog box to customize the Switch to submenu.*

Figure 23. *Here's an example of an application added to the Switch to menu...*

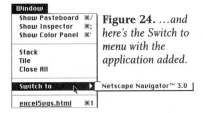

Figure 24. *...and here's the Switch to menu with the application added.*

To add applications to the Switch to submenu

1. In the Preferences dialog box, click the Switch To icon (see **Figure 22**).

2. Click the tiny application icon in the scrolling window.

3. Use the Open dialog box that appears to locate and select an application to add to the Switch to submenu. The name of the application appears in the scrolling window (see **Figure 23**).

4. Repeat steps 2 and 3 for each application you want to add.

5. Click OK or press ⌐Return⌐ or ⌐Enter⌐ to save your changes.

The applications you added appear on the Switch to submenu under the Window menu (see **Figure 24**).

To remove applications from the Switch to submenu

1. In the Preferences dialog box, click the Switch To icon (see **Figure 22**).

2. Click the tiny trash can icon beside the application you want to remove (see **Figure 23**).

3. Click OK or press ⌐Return⌐ or ⌐Enter⌐ to save your changes.

Customizing the Switch To Submenu

About Menus & Shortcut Keys

This appendix illustrates all of PageMill's menus and provides a list of all shortcut keys you can use with PageMill.

To use a shortcut key, hold down the modifier key(s) while pressing the letter, number, or punctuation key corresponding to the command. Using shortcut keys is discussed in **Chapter 1**.

Modifier Keys

Menu Symbol	Keyboard Key	Key Name
⌘	⌘	Command
⇧	Shift	Shift
⌥	Option	Option
⌃	Control	Control

File Menu

Note: *The Save Page, Save Page As, and Print Page commands change depending on what kind of window is open (page or image) and what is selected (page or frame).*

File

New Page	⌘N
Open...	⌘O
Open Selection	⌘D
Place...	⌥⌘1
Insert New	⌥⌘N
Insert Page...	⌥⌘O
Open Into Window	⌥⌘D
Close	⌘W
Save Page	⌘S
Save Page As...	
Save A Copy As...	
Revert to Saved	
Save Frameset	⌥⌘S
Save Frameset As...	
Save Frameset Copy As...	
Revert to Saved Frameset	
Save Everything	⌘E
Page Setup...	
Print Page	⌘P
Quit	⌘Q

File Menu Shortcut Keys

⌘N	New Page
⌘O	Open
⌘D	Open Selection
Control ⌘ 1	Place
Control ⌘ N	Insert New
Control ⌘ O	Insert Page
Control ⌘ D	Open Into Window
⌘W	Close
⌘S	Save Page
⌘S	Save Image
⌘S	Save Frame
Control ⌘ S	Save Frameset
⌘E	Save Everything
⌘P	Print Page
⌘P	Print Frame
⌘Q	Quit

Edit Menu Shortcut Keys

⌘ Z	Undo
⌘ X	Cut
⌘ C	Copy
⌘ V	Paste
⌘ A	Select All
⌘ R	Remove Link
⌘ ,	Show/Hide Invisibles
⌘ H	HTML Source
Control ⌘ H	Split Horizontally
Control ⌘ V	Split Vertically
⌘ M	No Frames Message
⌘ U	Download Statistics
Control ⌘ P	Preferences

Style Menu Shortcut Keys

Shift ⌘ P	Plain
⌘ B	Bold
⌘ I	Italic
Shift ⌘ T	Teletype
Shift ⌘ S	Strong
Shift ⌘ E	Emphasis
Shift ⌘ C	Citation
Shift ⌘ A	Sample
Shift ⌘ K	Keyboard
Shift ⌘ O	Code
Shift ⌘ V	Variable
Shift ⌘ >	Increase Font Size
Shift ⌘ <	Decrease Font Size

Format Menu Shortcut Keys

⌘]	Indent Right
⌘ [	Indent Left
Option ⌘ P	Paragraph
Option ⌘ 6	Smallest Heading
Option ⌘ 5	Smaller Heading
Option ⌘ 4	Small Heading
Option ⌘ 3	Large Heading
Option ⌘ 2	Larger Heading
Option ⌘ 1	Largest Heading
Option ⌘ F	Preformatted
Option ⌘ A	Address
Option ⌘ B	Bullet List
Option ⌘ D	Directory List
Option ⌘ M	Menu List
Option ⌘ N	Numbered List
Option ⌘ E	Definition List
Option ⌘ T	Term List

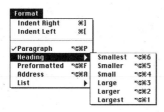

Search Menu Shortcut Keys

⌘ F	Find
⌘ G	Find Next
⌘ L	Replace
⌘ =	Replace & Find Again
⌘ ~	Check Spelling

Window Menu Shortcut Keys

⌘ /	Show Pasteboard
⌘ ;	Show Inspector
⌘ 1 - ⌘ 0	Show Corresponding Window (see menu)

BUTTONS, SWITCHES, & ICONS

About Buttons, Switches, & Icons

You can access many of PageMill's commands and features by clicking buttons, switches, and icons in PageMill windows.

This appendix illustrates all of PageMill's buttons, switches, and icons and, when applicable, provides shortcut keys to access them. (Using shortcut keys is discussed in **Chapter 1** and **Appendix A**.)

Button Bar Buttons & Icons

PageMill's button bar offers a variety of buttons for use with text, multimedia objects, or forms in a page.

B	Bold	⌃⌘B
I	Italic	⌃⌘I
TT	Teletype	Shift ⌃⌘T
A: ▦	Text Color	

Change Format:

Paragraph	Option ⌃⌘P
Preformatted	Option ⌃⌘F
Address	Option ⌃⌘A
Smallest Heading	Option ⌃⌘6
Smaller Heading	Option ⌃⌘5
Small Heading	Option ⌃⌘4
Large Heading	Option ⌃⌘3
Larger Heading	Option ⌃⌘2
Largest Heading	Option ⌃⌘1
Bullet List	Option ⌃⌘B
Directory List	Option ⌃⌘D
Menu List	Option ⌃⌘M
Numbered List	Option ⌃⌘N
Definition List	Option ⌃⌘E
Term List	Option ⌃⌘T

Increase Relative
   Font Size   Shift ⌃ ⌘ >

Relative Font Size

Decrease Relative
   Font Size   Shift ⌃ ⌘ <

Left Align Text[1]

Center Align Text[1]

Right Align Text[1]

Top Align Object[2]

Middle Align Object[2]

Bottom Align Object[2]

Left Align Object[2]

Right Align Object[2]

Indent Right   ⌃ ⌘]

Indent Left   ⌃ ⌘ [

Place Object   Control ⌃ ⌘ 1

Insert Horizontal Rule   Control ⌃ ⌘ 2

Insert Checkbox   Control ⌃ ⌘ 3

Insert Radio Button   Control ⌃ ⌘ 4

Insert Text Area   Control ⌃ ⌘ 5

Insert Text Field   Control ⌃ ⌘ 6

Insert Password Field   Control ⌃ ⌘ 7

Insert Popup   Control ⌃ ⌘ 8

Insert Submit Button   Control ⌃ ⌘ 9

Button Bar Buttons & Icons

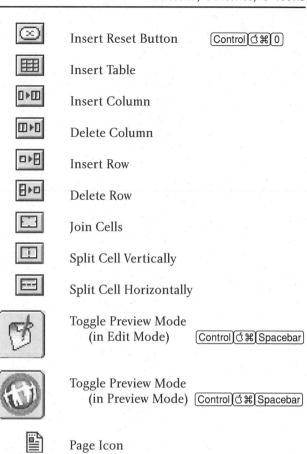

Insert Reset Button   `Control` `⌃⌘` `0`

Insert Table

Insert Column

Delete Column

Insert Row

Delete Row

Join Cells

Split Cell Vertically

Split Cell Horizontally

Toggle Preview Mode
   (in Edit Mode)   `Control` `⌃⌘` `Spacebar`

Toggle Preview Mode
   (in Preview Mode)   `Control` `⌃⌘` `Spacebar`

Page Icon

URL Icon

Button Bar Buttons & Icons

Image Window Buttons, Icons, & Switches

The Image window offers a variety of buttons, icons, and switches for use with images.

Image icon. The image format (GIF or JPEG) appears beneath the icon.

Selection Tool[3]

Rectangle Hotspot[3]

Circle Hotspot[3]

Polygon Hotspot[3]

Transparency Tool

Shuffle Hotspots icon.[3] When clicked, the Shuffle Hotspots pop-up menu appears.

> Bring To Front
> Send To Back
> Shuffle Forward
> Shuffle Back

Hotspot Color icon.[3] When clicked, the Hotspot Color pop-up menu appears.

Hotspot Label Switch[3] (on)

Hotspot Label Switch[3] (off)

Interlace Toggle Switch (on)

Interlace Toggle Switch (off)

Zoom Out

Zoom In

Notes

1 The shortcut keys for text alignment are [Control][⌃⌘][←] to shift text to the left and [Control][⌃⌘][→] to shift text to the right.

2 The shortcut keys for object alignment are [Control][⌃⌘][↑] to shift the object up or to the left and [Control][⌃⌘][↓] to shift the object down or to the right.

3 These buttons, icons, and switches appear on the button bar in place of the table buttons when you double-click an image.

Notes

INSPECTOR REFERENCE

About the Inspector

The Inspector offers a number of panels filled with options to change Frame, Page, Form, and Object settings.

To display the Inspector, choose Show Inspector from the Window menu or press ⌘ ; . Click the Frame, Page, Form, or Object tab to select the panel with which you want to work. The available panels vary depending on what is selected in the PageMill document window.

This appendix provides an illustrated guide to the Inspector's options. I tell you about using the Inspector throughout this book.

Frame Panel Options

Frame panel options, which are discussed in **Chapter 8**, let you specify settings for the name, size, and appearance of a selected frame.

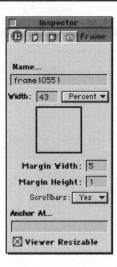

- ■ **Name.** Use this edit box to give the frame a name.

- ■ **Width/Height.** Use this edit box to set the width or height of a frame. The pop-up menu beside it lets you specify whether the width or height should be in pixels, as a percentage of the window size, or relative to other frames in the frameset.

- ■ **Margin Width/Margin Height.** Use these edit boxes to set the number of pixels between the edge of the frame and its contents.

- ■ **Scrollbars.** Use this pop-up menu to set whether the window should have scroll bars all the time, none of the time, or only when needed.

- ■ **Anchor At.** Use this edit box to specify an anchor on the page which should be used when the page is opened into a frame.

- ■ **Viewer Resizable.** Turn this check box on or off to specify whether the frame can be resized by a user viewing the page with a Web browser.

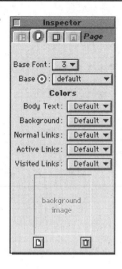

Page Panel Options

Page panel options, which are discussed in **Chapter 10**, let you change the appearance of an active page and its text.

- **Base Font.** Use this pop-up menu to select a default relative font size for all the non-heading text on the page.

- **Base Target.** Use this pop-up menu to select a default target frame for links on the page when the page is viewed in a frameset.

- **Body Text.** Use this pop-up menu to change the color of text on the page that is not a link. The default color is black.

- **Background.** Use this pop-up menu to change the page background. The default color is gray.

- **Normal Links.** Use this pop-up menu to change the color of links that have not been visited. The default color is blue.

- **Active Links.** Use this pop-up menu to change the color of links as they are clicked. The default color is red.

- **Visited Links.** Use this pop-up menu to change the color of links that have been visited. The default color is purple.

- **Background Image.** Drag an image into this "well" to use it as a background image.

- **File Icon.** Click this icon to display an Open dialog box you can use to select an image for a background image.

- **Trash Icon.** Click this icon to remove a background image.

Form Panel Options

Form panel options, which are discussed in **Chapter 9**, let you properly associate a CGI with a form.

■ **Action.** Use the edit box to enter the pathname for a CGI to launch on completion of a form on the page. Use the pop-up menu to select the method of exchanging information with the server: GET or POST. Enter information only if the page includes a form. If you are not sure what to enter, ask your Webmaster or System Administrator.

Form Options

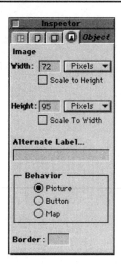

Object Panel Image Options

Image options, which are discussed in **Chapter 5**, let you set the size, alternate text, behavior, and border for an image.

- ◼ **Width.** Use this edit box to specify an image width. Use the pop-up menu beside it to specify whether the measurement is in pixels or a percentage of the original image size. This edit box and pop-up menu will only function if the Scale to Height check box is turned off.

- ◼ **Scale to Height.** Turn on this check box to change the image width in proportion to its height.

- ◼ **Height.** Use this edit box to specify an image height. Use the pop-up menu beside it to specify whether the measurement is in pixels or a percentage of the original image size. This edit box and pop-up menu will only function if the Scale to Width check box is turned off.

- ◼ **Scale to Width.** Turn on this check box to change the image height in proportion to its width.

- ◼ **Alternate Label.** Use this edit box to enter alternate text for the image. The text you enter will appear in text-based browsers or in graphic browsers that have the auto load image option turned off.

- ◼ **Behavior.** Select one of the radio buttons—Picture, Button, or Map—to specify how the image is to be used on the page. The default selection is Picture.

- ◼ **Border.** Enter a measurement, in pixels, to change the width of an image border. By default, this edit box is empty. Entering 0 in this edit box removes any border from an image, even if it is used as a button, map, or link.

Image Options

Object Panel Media Options

Media options, some of which are discussed in **Chapter 5**, let you set the size, name, and value for media elements like QuickTime movies.

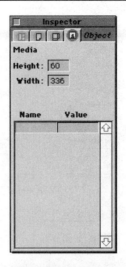

- **Height/Width.** Use these edit boxes to enter a height and width for the media element.

- **Name.** Use this edit box to enter a name for a media element.

- **Value.** Use this edit box to enter a value for a media element.

Object Panel Horizontal Rule Options

Horizontal Rule options, which are discussed in **Chapter 5**, let you change the appearance of a selected horizontal rule.

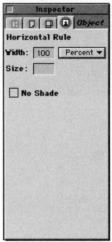

- **Width.** Use this edit box to enter a horizontal width for the horizontal rule. Use the pop-up menu beside it to select whether the measurement should be in pixels or as a percentage of the page width. The default value is 100 percent.

- **Size.** Use this edit box to enter a thickness, in pixels, for the horizontal rule. By default, this edit box is empty.

- **No Shade.** Use this check box to turn a horizontal rule's three dimensional shade effect on or off. With this check box turned on, the rule appears as a plain black line.

Object Panel Break Options

Margin Break options, which are discussed in **Chapter 5**, let you set the alignment for a margin break.

■ **Alignment.** Choose a radio button— Left, Right, or All—to set whether the break affects text at the left margin, the right margin, or both margins.

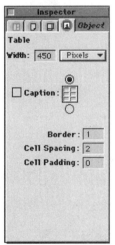

Object Panel Table Options

Table options, which are discussed in **Chapter 6**, let you change the width, caption location, and border, cell spacing, and cell padding settings for a selected table.

■ **Width.** Use this edit box to enter a width for the table. Use the pop-up menu beside it to specify whether the width you enter is in pixels or a percentage of the page width.

■ **Caption.** Turn on the check box to create a caption for the table. Then select one of the radio buttons to place the caption above or below the table.

■ **Border.** Use this edit box to set a border width, in pixels, for the table.

■ **Cell Spacing.** Use this edit box to set the amount of space, in pixels, of the space between table cells.

■ **Cell Padding.** Use this edit box to set the amount of space, in pixels, between the edge of each table cell and the text within it.

Object Panel Table Cell Options

Table cell options, which are discussed in **Chapter 6**, let you change the width constraints, formatting, and alignment of selected cells.

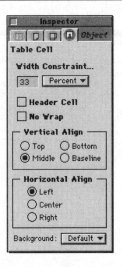

- **Width Constraints.** Use this edit box to set the maximum width for a table cell. Use the pop-up menu beside it to specify whether that width is in pixels or a percentage of the table width.

- **Header Cell.** Use this check box to determine whether a cell should be formatted as a header cell. Header cells are bold and center-aligned.

- **No Wrap.** Use this check box to turn word wrap on or off within a cell.

- **Vertical Align.** Select one of these radio buttons—Top, Middle, Bottom, or Baseline—to specify the vertical alignment of text within a cell. The default setting is middle.

- **Horizontal Align.** Select one of these radio buttons—Left, Center, or Right—to specify the horizontal alignment of text within a cell. The default setting is Left.

- **Background.** Use this pop-up menu to change the color of a cell's background.

Object Panel Anchor Options

Anchor options, which are discussed in **Chapter 7**, let you change the name of an anchor.

- **Name.** Use this edit box to enter a name for the anchor.

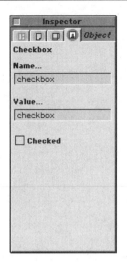

Object Panel Checkbox Options

Checkbox options, which are discussed in **Chapter 9**, let you change the name, value, and default status of a selected check box. The name and value may be dependent on the CGI that will be used with the form, so check CGI documentation when changing these options.

- **Name.** Use this edit box to give the check box a name.

- **Value.** Use this edit box to enter a value for the check box.

- **Checked.** Use this check box to determine whether the check box is turned on by default.

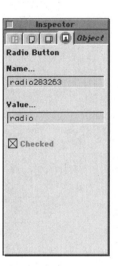

Object Panel Radio Button Options

Radio Button options, which are discussed in **Chapter 9**, let you change the name, value, and default status of a selected radio button. The name and value may be dependent on the CGI that will be used with the form, so check CGI documentation when changing these options.

- **Name.** Use this edit box to give the radio button a name. Each radio button in a group must have the same name.

- **Value.** Use this edit box to enter a value for the radio button.

- **Checked.** Use this check box to determine whether the radio button is selected by default. The default setting for this option is turned on for the last button in a group and turned off for all other buttons in the group. If you change this option for one radio button in a group, it will automatically change for one other button in the group since only one button in a group can be selected at a time.

Checkbox & Radio Button Options

Object Panel Text Area Options

Text Area options, which are discussed in **Chapter 9**, let you change the name and size of a selected text area. The name may be dependent on the CGI that will be used with the form, so check CGI documentation when changing this option.

- **Name.** Use this edit box to give the text area a name.

- **Rows.** Use this edit box to enter the number of text rows that should appear within the text area. The default value is 7.

- **Columns.** Use this edit box to enter the number of character columns that should appear within the text area. The default value is 27.

Object Panel Text Field Options

Text Field options, which are discussed in **Chapter 9**, let you change the name, size, and maximum length of a selected text field. The name may be dependent on the CGI that will be used with the form, so check CGI documentation when changing this option.

- **Name.** Use this edit box to give the text field a name.

- **Size.** Use this edit box to enter the length, in characters, of the text field. The default value is 30.

- **Max Length.** Use this edit box to enter the maximum length, in characters, of an entry in the text field. By default, this edit box is empty.

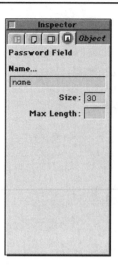

Object Panel Password Field Options

Password Field options, which are discussed in **Chapter 9**, let you change the name, size, and maximum length of a selected password field. The name may be dependent on the CGI that will be used with the form, so check CGI documentation when changing this option.

- **Name.** Use this edit box to give the password field a name.

- **Size.** Use this edit box to enter the length, in characters, of the password field. The default value is 30.

- **Max Length.** Use this edit box to enter the maximum length, in characters, of an entry in the password field. By default, this edit box is empty.

Password Field Options

Object Panel Selection Field Options

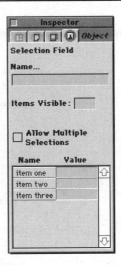

Selection Field options, which are discussed in **Chapter 9**, let you change the name, appearance, and functionality of a selected pop-up menu or selection-list field. The name and values may be dependent on the CGI that will be used with the form, so check CGI documentation when changing these options.

- **Name.** Use this edit box to give the pop-up menu or selection list field a name.

- **Items Visible.** Use this edit box to enter the number of items you want to appear in the selected scrolling list field. This determines the vertical size of the scrolling list. By default, this edit box is empty, which displays the object as a pop-up menu.

- **Allow Multiple Selections.** Use this check box to determine whether the selected scrolling list field should allow more than one selection. By default, this check box is turned off.

- **Value.** Use these edit boxes to assign values to each item in a pop-up menu or list-selection field. By default, these edit boxes are empty.

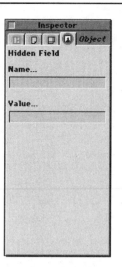

Object Panel Hidden Field Options

Hidden Field options, which are discussed in **Chapter 9**, let you change the name and value of a selected hidden field. The name and value may be dependent on the CGI that will be used with the form, so check CGI documentation when changing these options.

- **Name.** Use this edit box to enter a name for the hidden field.

- **Value.** Use this edit box to enter a value for the hidden field.

Object Panel Submit Button Options

Submit Button options, which are discussed in **Chapter 9**, let you change the name of a selected submit button. The name may be dependent on the CGI that will be used with the form, so check CGI documentation when changing this option.

- **Name.** Use this edit box to give the selected submit button a name.

Object Panel Reset Button Options

Although the Object panel can be displayed for the reset button, which is discussed in **Chapter 9**, there are no options.

Hidden Field, Submit & Reset Button Options

Object Panel Comment Options

Comment options, which are discussed in **Chapter 11**, let you enter comments in your Web page that do not appear in Web browser windows.

- **Comment.** Use this scrolling window to enter any comments you want to include in your Web page document but not display in a browser window.

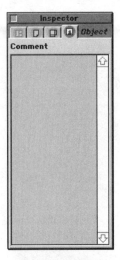

Object Panel Placeholder Options

Placeholder options, which are discussed in **Chapter 11**, let you enter raw HTML code that is not checked or edited by PageMill.

- **Placeholder.** Use this scrolling window to enter the HTML code you want protected from PageMill's error checking and editing functions.

- **Placeholder Image.** Drag an image into this "well" to have it appear as a placeholder image.

- **File Icon.** Click this icon to display an Open dialog box to locate and select a placeholder image.

- **Trash Icon.** Click this icon to discard the placeholder image.

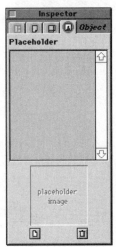

About HTML

HyperText Markup Language (HTML) is a programming language that uses special codes called markup tags to indicate formatting and special elements within a Web page. Web browser software like Netscape Navigator, Microsoft Internet Explorer, NCSA Mosaic, and the Web browsers that are part of America Online interpret HTML tags to display HTML documents as Web pages with formatted text and graphics.

PageMill 2 supports version 3.2 of HTML, as well as several extensions to HTML that are recognized by Netscape, Internet Explorer, and some other browsers. This appendix provides a list of HTML 3.2 markup tags and extensions.

This appendix is intended as a reference for PageMill users, not as an HTML tutorial. For step-by-step, fully illustrated instructions for using HTML, look for *HTML for the World Wide Web: Visual QuickStart Guide*, which is also published by Peachpit Press. For the latest information about HTML and standards, check http://htmlhelp.com/.

HEAD Section Elements

\<HEAD>…\</HEAD>	Defines the HEAD section of the document.
\<TITLE>…\</TITLE>	Defines the page title.
\<DOCTYPE>	Defines the document type.[2]
\<ISINDEX>	Enables primitive searching.[2]
\<META>	Provides meta information for the document.[2]
\<LINK>	Indicates relationships between documents on a site.[2]
\<BASE>	Indicates the location of the document.[2]
\<SCRIPT>…\</SCRIPT>	Specifies an inline script.[1]
\<STYLE>…\</STYLE>	Specifies style information.[1]
\<MULTICOL>	Divides a page into multiple columns.[4]

BODY Section Elements

\<BODY>…\</BODY>	Defines the BODY section of the document.
\<!--…-->	Specifies a comment.[3]
\<!--NOEDIT-->…\<!--/NOEDIT-->	Specifies HTML code to be ignored by PageMill.[3]

Text formatting

<B>...</B>	Applies bold formatting to text.
<I>...</I>	Applies italic formatting to text.
<U>...</U>	Underlines text.
<TT>...</TT>	Displays text with a monospaced font.
<FONT>...</FONT>	Changes the color and/or size of font characters.
<BIG>...</BIG>	Enlarges the font size of text.[2]
<SMALL>...</SMALL>	Reduces the font size of text.[2]
^{...}	Displays text as a superscript.[2]
_{...}	Displays text as a subscript.[2]
<STRIKE>...</STRIKE>	Displays text with a strikethrough font.
<EM>...</EM>	Emphasizes text.
<STRONG>...</STRONG>	Strongly emphasizes text.
<DFN>...</DFN>	Displays text as the definition of a term.
<CODE>...</CODE>	Displays text as a code fragment.
<SAMP>...</SAMP>	Displays text as a sample.
<KBD>...</KBD>	Displays text as keyboard input.
<VAR>...</VAR>	Displays text as a variable.
<CITE>...</CITE>	Displays text as a citation.
<BLINK>...</BLINK>	Flashes text on and off.[4]
<MARQUEE>...</MARQUEE>	Scrolls text across the browser window.[4]
<WBR>	Inserts optional hyphen for line break.[4]

Paragraph formatting

<P>...</P>	Defines a paragraph of text.
 	Inserts a line break within a paragraph.
<NOBR>...</NOBR>	Prevents line break in text.[4]
<DIV>...</DIV>	Aligns a section of a document.
<CENTER>...</CENTER>	Centers a section of a document.
<PRE>...</PRE>	Displays preformatted (monospaced) text.
<BLOCKQUOTE>...</BLOCKQUOTE>	Displays text as an indented quotation.
<ADDRESS>...</ADDRESS>	Displays text as address information.
<UL>...</UL>	Defines an unordered (bulleted) list.
<OL>...</OL>	Defines an ordered (numbered) list.
<DIR>...</DIR>	Defines a directory list.

<MENU>...</MENU>	Defines a menu list.
<LI>...</LI>	Defines a list item.
<DL>...</DL>	Defines a definition list.
<DT>...</DT>	Defines a definition term.
<DD>...</DD>	Defines a definition.
<H1>...</H1>	Displays text as a level 1 (largest) heading.
<H2>...</H2>	Displays text as a level 2 (larger) heading.
<H3>...</H3>	Displays text as a level 3 (large) heading.
<H4>...</H4>	Displays text as a level 4 (small) heading.
<H5>...</H5>	Displays text as a level 5 (smaller) heading.
<H6>...</H6>	Displays text as a level 6 (smallest) heading.

Multimedia objects

<IMG>	Inserts an image.
<LOWSRC>	Specifies a low-resolution proxy image to load before a high-resolution image loads.[4]
<SPACER>	Inserts a space that acts like a transparent GIF.[4]
<HR>	Inserts a horizontal rule.
<EMBED>	Inserts a multimedia object.[3]
<NOEMBED>	Specifies alternative content if multimedia object cannot be displayed.[4]
<APPLET>...</APPLET>	Specifies a Java applet.
<PARAM>	Specifies parameters for a Java applet.
<TEXTFLOW>...</TEXTFLOW>	
	Specifies alternative text if a Java applet cannot be played.

Links

<A>...</A>	Identifies a hyperlink.
<MAP>...</MAP>	Identifies a client-side image map.
<AREA>	Defines a hotspot in an image map.

Tables

<TABLE>...</TABLE>	Defines a table.
<TR>...</TR>	Defines a table row.
<TD>...</TD>	Defines a table cell.
<TH>...</TH>	Defines a header cell.
<CAPTION>...</CAPTION>	
	Defines a table caption.

HTML Reference

Forms

<FORM>...</FORM>   Identifies a form.

<INPUT>...</INPUT>   Identifies an input field or button.

<TEXTAREA>...</TEXTAREA>

                    Identifies a text area field.

<SELECT>...</SELECT>   Identifies a selection list.

<OPTION>...</OPTION>   Defines selection list options.

Frames

<FRAMESET>...</FRAMESET>

                    Defines a frameset.[3]

<FRAME>   Specifies a frame.[3]

Notes

[1]Supported in PageMill 2 through the use of a placeholder.

[2]Supported in PageMill 2 by editing HTML code in HTML Source view.

[3]Extension to HTML 3.2; fully supported by PageMill 2.

[4]Extension to HTML 3.2; supported in PageMill 2 by editing HTML code in HTML Source view.

INDEX

X – Y – Z

Shake up your world, stir up some excitement—web.STIR!

web.STIR ®

Whether you're a Web page designer, multimedia author, or video production artist, Letraset® is pleased to announce a must-have addition to your CD library: web.STIR® Artkit™.

web.STIR is a far-reaching, kitchen-sink, soup-to-nuts collection of our most eye-popping artwork. Four full volumes, each containing 125 or more images:

✔ **Banners & Bars** - Great for headers, footers, highlights, and callouts, these surprising and sophisticated images are readily customized for a wide variety of applications—but always look custom-tailored for each specific need.

✔ **Images & Icons** - Beautiful spot images and GIF animations, from the representational to the modernistic to the utterly abstract, for business or pleasure—or a bit of both!

✔ **Buttons & Bullets** - A veritable treasure chest of fundamental elements for interactive communication—three-dimensional buttons, arrows, and bullets guaranteed to keep visitors active and involved.

✔ **Backgrounds & Dividers** - A terrific compilation of tileable frames, photos, and rules that will bring depth and definition to any layout, enhancing your audience's interest through a subtle separation of visual space.

Built for high quality and engineered for top speed, these are 8-bit, Indexed Color GIF files, ready for immediate use in HTML documents—like the ones you create with Adobe® PageMill™. For Mac and PC alike, they're easily uploaded and downloaded—a movable feast, in short, of vibrantly full-color, unlimited usage images just for you.

- - - - - - - - - - - - ✂ - ✂ - - - - - - - - - - - - - -

Get a FREE web.STIR® Demo Disk!

For a free web.STIR demo disk and brochure, complete the following form and mail or fax it to:
Letraset USA, web.STIR Demo Disk Offer, 40 Eisenhower Drive, Paramus, NJ 07652
Fax: 800-656-6853

Name: _____

Company _____

Address: _____

_____

City: _____ State: _____ Zip: _____

E-Mail Address: _____

Web Address: _____

Would you like to receive information about Letraset's newest graphic arts products?
❑ Yes   ❑ No

More from Peachpit Press

America Online 3 for Macintosh: Visual QuickStart Guide

Maria Langer

Find out everything you need to know about the country's hottest online service provider. *America Online 3 for Macintosh: Visual QuickStart Guide* provides an easy illustrated, step-by-step guide for beginners to get up and running with AOL, and for intermediate users to gain more in-depth understanding of the service. *$17.95 (300 pages w/disk)*

CHAT

Nan McCarthy

Chat is a fast-moving, compelling story of online romance that will appeal to all cyberjunkies and anyone looking for an entertaining story. Bev, a tough-minded book editor, cautiously begins corresponding with Maximilian, a flamboyant copywriter who approaches her after seeing her messages in an online writers forum. Their relationship gradually becomes more intense and their e-mails less inhibited as the story unfolds entirely through their messages to one another. *$7.95 (136 pages)*

Director 5 for Macintosh: Visual QuickStart Guide

Andre Persidsky

Learn how to create animations, movies, and multimedia presentations in Macromedia Director 5 through this generously illustrated *Visual QuickStart Guide.* You'll learn how to use the basic tools and windows such as the Cast window, the Paint window, the Control Panel and the Stage. In addition, you'll learn how to work with sound and tempo, and all the steps you'll need to create your first presentation. *$18.95 (256 pages)*

Excel 5 for Macintosh: Visual QuickStart Guide

Maria Langer

This book will help you take control of one of the most powerful and complex spreadsheet programs. Readers are provided step-by-step instructions and plenty of illustrations in the handy *Visual QuickStart Guide* format. *$16.95 (272 pages)*

HTML for the World Wide Web: Visual QuickStart Guide

Elizabeth Castro

This best-selling book is all you need to start building web pages. It's a primer in basic Hypertext Markup Language, with guidelines on how to format your text, work with images, create links and navigational buttons, and add goodies like tables, forms and sounds to your web site. *$17.95 (192 pages)*

Home Sweet Home Page

Robin Williams with Dave Mark

Best-selling authors Robin Williams and Dave Mark have teamed up to bring you this family-and-friends approach to creating personal Web sites and using them as a collaborative, interactive, and inexpensive means to stay in touch. With a clear, non-technical approach and extensive illustrations, this book offers design examples and ideas you can use to create professional-looking Web pages with a personal flair. *$14.95 (184 pages)*

The Illustrator 6 Book

Deke McClelland

The third edition of this best-selling guide has been completely updated to cover Illustrator 6. The entertaining, informative *Illustrator 6 Book* examines in detail every tool and feature in Illustrator, establishing a groundwork in the basics and then moving on to fully discuss advanced capabilities—including patterns, transformations, imported graphics, and much more. Dozens of step-by-step techniques will provide you with first-hand understanding of features and techniques. *$29.95 (776 pages)*

Illustrator 6 for Macintosh: Visual QuickStart Guide

Elaine Weinmann and Peter Lourekas

Like our other *QuickStart Guides,* this book guides you through the basics of Illustrator with lots of pictures, including a gallery of color illustrations. Learn the basics of how to use the palette tools, create objects, reshape paths, play with type, create gradients, work with layers and masks, and much more. From the authors of our popular *QuarkXPress* and *Photoshop Visual QuickStart* books. *$19.95 (288 pages)*

The Macintosh Bible, 6th Edition

Edited by Jeremy Judson

This classic reference book is now completely updated. *The Macintosh Bible, 6th Edition* is crammed with tips, tricks, and shortcuts that will help you to get the most out of your Mac. Completely revised by 13 editors and over 70 contributors, this is the ultimate reference for all things Mac. It tackles every subject area with a clear vision of what Macintosh users need to know in an engaging, no-nonsense style. Includes a new section on the Internet: getting connected, sending e-mail, surfing the Web, and downloading files. *$29.95 (1,009 pages)*

The Mac Bible Goodies Pack (2 CD-ROMs)

Edited by Victor Gavenda

The Macintosh software universe continues to expand, and we can't fit all the important stuff on just one CD-ROM anymore! Our new *Macintosh Bible* software collection is crammed into 2 CDs. One CD has commercial demos, stock photos, clip art and sounds, and the complete *Macintosh Bible* itself, all accessible through an elegant and intuitive interface. The second CD is devoted to the BMUG collection of shareware, with the finest utilities, games, fonts, Web graphics, movie files, and electronic magazines you'll find anywhere. *$24.95 (2 CD-ROMs)*

The Macintosh Bible Guide to Excel 5

Maria Langer

The Macintosh Bible Guide to Excel 5 gives beginning through advanced readers a no-nonsense, real-world approach to getting the most out of version 5. Now, cross-platform users can enjoy the same features and functions available in the Windows version: new Help Wizards, improved interface, and OLE (Object Linking and Embedding) 2.0 for editing documents. *$24.95 (496 pages)*

The Macintosh Bible Guide to Word 6

Maria Langer

Whether you're a beginning or experienced user of Microsoft Word for the Macintosh, this book will bring you up to speed with version 6. With step-by-step recipes, you'll create newsletters, invitations, display advertising, and more. Provides plenty of details on Word's newest features, including how to add annotations, graphs, and Quick-Time movies to documents. *$24.95 (750 pages)*

The Non-Designer's Design Book

Robin Williams

Robin Williams wrote this one "for all the people who now need to design pages, but who have no background or formal training in design." Follow the basic principles clearly explained in this book and your work is guaranteed to look more professional, organized, unified, and interesting. You'll never again look at a page in the same way. Full of practical design exercises and quizzes. Runner-up for Best Introductory Systems How-to Book in the 10th Annual Computer Press Awards.
$14.95 (144 pages)

The Painter 4 Wow! Book, 2nd Edition

Cher Threinen-Pendarvis

This newly updated, full-color volume uses hundreds of stunning, original illustrations depicting Painter 4's full range of styles and effects. Step-by-step descriptions clearly explain how each piece was created. Users of all levels will find these tips and tricks easy to integrate in their own work. The dual-platform CD includes custom brushes and textures, stock photos, video clips, filters, and try-out versions of some of the hottest graphics programs available. *$44.95 264 pages (w/ CD-ROM)*

The Photoshop 3 Wow! Book Macintosh Edition

Linnea Dayton and Jack Davis

A worldwide bestseller! Full color throughout, this book shows exactly how professional artists employ Photoshop 3 to manipulate scanned images and create an astonishing array of special effects. Each chapter deconstructs an actual piece of art, showing step by step how it was created. Most examples were created for real-world commercial uses. There's also a section showing the effects of scores of filters from Adobe, MetaTools, and other vendors. The companion CD contains Photo CD images and a variety of filters and utilities. Winner of a 1995 Computer Press Award.
$39.95 (288 pages, includes CD-ROM)

Photoshop in 4 Colors, 2nd Edition

Mattias Nyman

Achieve flawless color output from Photoshop the first time with this full-color volume's succinct, practical advice. *Photoshop in 4 Colors* discusses color theory, printing screens, resolution, tonal range, scanning, color correction, color separation, and much more. Plus, it presents clearly illustrated "before and after" images showing the pitfalls and possibilities of color photo manipulation. (Winner, Benjamin Franklin Award.) *$22.95 (80 pages)*

Real World Scanning and Halftones

David Blatner and Steve Roth

Master the digital halftone process–from scanning images to tweaking them on your computer to imagesetting them. Learn about optical character recognition, gamma control, sharpening, PostScript halftones, Photo CD and image-manipulating applications like Photoshop and PhotoStyler. *$24.95 (296 pages)*

Start with a Scan

Janet Ashford and John Odam

Start with a Scan shows designers and illustrators how to transform raw scanned images into high-quality finished illustrations. While the opening section covers the technical basics of scanning, the bulk of the book uses gorgeous four-color illustrations and clear, step-by-step instructions to show you how to take a scan of almost anything and turn it into beautiful artwork using programs such as Photoshop, FreeHand, and Illustrator.
$34.95 (144 pages)

Order Form

USA **800-283-9444** • **510-548-4393** • FAX **510-548-5991**
CANADA **800-387-8028** • **416-447-1779** • FAX **800-456-0536** OR **416-443-0948**
http://www.peachpit.com

Qty	Title	Price	Total
	SUBTOTAL		
	ADD APPLICABLE SALES TAX*		
	SHIPPING		
	TOTAL		

Shipping is by UPS ground: $4 for first item, $1 each add'l.

*We are required to pay sales tax in all states with the exceptions of AK, DE, MT, NH, and OR.
Please include appropriate sales tax if you live in any state not mentioned above.

Customer Information

NAME

COMPANY

STREET ADDRESS

CITY   STATE   ZIP

PHONE (   )   FAX (   )
[REQUIRED FOR CREDIT CARD ORDERS]

Payment Method

❏ CHECK ENCLOSED   ❏ VISA   ❏ MASTERCARD   ❏ AMEX

CREDIT CARD #   EXP. DATE

COMPANY PURCHASE ORDER #

Tell Us What You Think

PLEASE TELL US WHAT YOU THOUGHT OF THIS BOOK: TITLE:

WHAT OTHER BOOKS WOULD YOU LIKE US TO PUBLISH?

MAC   **PEACHPIT PRESS** • **2414 Sixth Street** • **Berkeley, CA 94710**